T. W. Schultz
1/21/80

Consensus and Conflict
in
U.S. Agriculture

Consensus and Conflict

in

U.S. Agriculture

PERSPECTIVES FROM THE
NATIONAL FARM SUMMIT

Edited by

BRUCE L. GARDNER *and* JAMES W. RICHARDSON

PUBLISHED FOR

Texas Agricultural Experiment Station

AND

Agriculture Council of America

BY

Texas A&M University Press
College Station

Copyright © 1979 by the Agriculture Council of America and
the Texas Agricultural Experiment Station

Library of Congress Cataloging in Publication Data

National Farm Summit, Texas A & M University, 1978. Consensus and conflict in U.S. agriculture.

    1. Agriculture—Economic aspects—United States—
Congresses. 2. Agriculture and state—United States—
Congresses. I. Gardner, Bruce L. II. Richardson, James,
1949– III. Texas. A & M University, College Station.
IV. Texas. Agricultural Experiment Station, College Station.
V. Agriculture Council of America. VI. Title
HD1755.N37 1978   338.1'0973   79-7412
ISBN 0-89096-084-4
ISBN 0-89096-085-2 pbk.

FIRST EDITION

Manufactured in the United States of America

Contents

Preface

THE very idea of a Farm Summit would seem pretentious were it not for a broadly shared sense of concern about agriculture's role in a rapidly changing society. That concern stems from such obvious manifestations of political change as the loss of the rural dominance in Congress, the increased power of the Congress over the Executive as well as the diffusion of power in the House of Representatives, and the explosive growth and power of federal regulatory activity. But it stems also from the recognition that U.S. agriculture has now entered a period of greatly magnified uncertainty.

Clearly the times require a fresh look. The nature and causes of problems and new insight regarding solutions for agriculture's problems must be found.

Given these concerns, Texas A&M University and the Agriculture Council of America (ACA) saw a need for a forum in which the issues could be clarified and the alternatives for dealing with them discussed by a diverse group interested and knowledgeable about agriculture. Thus the Summit.

It seemed extremely important to make the Summit as broad–based as possible. ACA and A&M consulted with producers and economists in preliminary planning sessions early in 1978. We are most grateful to those individuals who helped to shape the Summit concept and to develop the structure for examining issues. In particular, we were honored to have T. W. Schultz, recipient of the 1979 Nobel Prize for economics, participate in the planning and execution of the National Farm Summit. As a result of these planning sessions Task Forces were established in five subject matter areas, with membership of farmers, ranchers, government and academic economists, and representatives of commodity groups, agribusiness firms, farm organizations, and, where appropriate, labor and consumer groups. A prominent leader in each field was chosen to chair each Task Force and to be responsible for writing a report based on the Task Force's deliberations.

The reports form the core of this book. While the Task Force chairmen were responsible for preparing the reports, in many cases they were assisted in the writing by Task Force members. Each report is in the last analysis, however, the product of the chairman. In cases where a Task Force member had substantive disagreement with points in a report, the member was given the opportunity to prepare a dissenting statement or to provide footnotes to particular points of disagreement.

The Task Force reports were presented at the Summit meeting at Texas A&M University, December 4–6, 1978. Over 700 farmers, ranchers, economists, government and agribusiness officials, and others attended, including a large contingent from the American Agriculture Movement. Each session was marked by animated discussion and audience participation. Many points were raised in the discussion which are presented in this volume following the reports. In addition, members of the American Agriculture Movement prepared a statement in response to particular issues (Chapter 7).

At the beginning of the project, a separate committee was established for the purpose of reviewing the work of the Task Forces. This Review Committee was responsible for preparing a summary paper (Chapter 6) tying together the findings of the Task Forces, identifying broad areas of consensus and the potential for resolving disagreements.

We believe that through this project significant progress was made in bringing many different interests within the agricultural community together in such a way as to promote mutual understanding. In this light we offer this book containing the Task Force reports and Summit discussion not as an artifact of a historical event, but as a basis from which, we hope, further progress can be made.

Neville P. Clarke, Director
Texas Agricultural Experiment
Station

M. Allen Paul III, President
Agriculture Council of America

Acknowledgments

THE Agriculture Council of America and Texas A&M University wish to thank all those who volunteered their time, experience and ideas as members of the Farm Summit Task Forces and as Task Force Chairmen. In addition, we would like to thank those individuals, noted in the discussion section of each chapter, who provided reaction to the presentations made at the Farm Summit Conference and the many people who participated in the discussions at the Conference.

There are also a number of individuals on the staffs of both the Agriculture Council of America and Texas A&M University who devoted a great deal of time to the coordination of both the Conference and this book. In particular, we would like to acknowledge the contributions of Cecilia Kirby, Research Director of the Agriculture Council of America, who provided invaluable assistance in all phases of the Farm Summit Project. We also thank Dr. Peter Emerson of the Congressional Budget Office for his valuable suggestions on the manuscript.

A word of special appreciation is due to the generous and far–sighted companies and organizations whose financial assistance helped substantially to make the project possible. And, finally, we would like to acknowledge special contributions by the Farm Foundation, the Houston Livestock Show & Rodeo, and the Perry Foundation toward the project and the publication of this book.

Emery N. Castle*

CHAPTER I

Resource Allocation and Production Costs

Nature of the Problem

ALMOST every citizen recognizes that all is not well with U.S. agriculture. Farm groups lobbying for higher prices, stories of the demise of the family farm, and inflated farmland prices are all reasons for concern. Agriculture's problems seem to be even broader. There is recurring news of increased soil erosion, environmental damage from modern farming practices, drought and unfavorable weather as well as problems covered by other Task Forces.

Nevertheless, the signals are not all bad. Despite increased prices at the grocery stores, food remains relatively inexpensive. If nutrition is a problem, it has not yet been reflected in the life span of the populace. And, if productivity is declining, why is it that surpluses and depressed prices still result? This conflicting evidence presents a confusing picture. It is not surprising that there is controversy about what steps might be taken to address these ills.

There are many ways of looking at agriculture and evaluating its performance and problems. Farmers, themselves a very diverse group,

*It is only because of the arrangements made for the preparation of this report that I am shown as the sole author. When this work was commissioned the understanding was that the Chairman of the Task Force would be responsible for the preparation of the report and I accepted that responsibility. Because of the broad and complex nature of the subject "Resource Allocation and Production Costs," I was provided the special assistance of three highly qualified and able people: Chester Baker, Gerald Carlson, and Wallace Huffman. I have attempted to identify their specific contributions in various places in the Report although they assisted a great deal in the entire effort. The other members of the Task Force contributed greatly by their comments at two full–day meetings and by their written comments on earlier drafts. A list of Task Force members and their affiliations follows the report.

have a viewpoint which is often distinctly different from that of consumers, representatives of agribusiness, government officials, and others who also have legitimate interests in agriculture.

How are the conflicting interests of these groups to be reconciled? Can the issues and problems of agriculture be defined or described in any way other than in terms of the interests of particular groups? Fortunately it is possible to adopt a more comprehensive viewpoint. Questions such as the following can be raised: Are the total costs borne by society to produce and market its food and fiber greater than they need be to bring forth this production? Are the people engaged in these occupations suffering social and economic costs greater than is necessary to provide just compensation for the resources and effort they contribute? Are there social ills associated with the business and occupation of farming and rural living that are not found to the same extent elsewhere in society?

The upshot of examining U.S. agriculture from these different points of view is that it is probably not possible to say what *the* farm problem is. Rather, there are numerous problems that stem from different interests. The key to a unified approach is identifying fundamental forces underlying these problems. We advance the following diagnosis—a major resource allocation problem is our inability to distinguish between those forces resulting in fundamental (or permanent) changes in the socio–economic environment and those forces resulting in temporary (or transitory) changes.

If farmers could distinguish between the permanent and the transitory they would know whether to invest for long–run shifts in supply and demand, or whether to deploy their resources to take advantage of temporary changes over a one– two– or three–year time period. Consumers and society generally would be better served because fewer errors in resource allocation mean that food and fiber would be produced at a lower cost. Changes from farm to nonfarm occupations, and vice versa, would be more in response to long–run social needs and less in response to illusory price and income signals. And, farm families would be more inclined to base consumption decisions on permanent income rather than on temporary changes in income.

Of equal or perhaps greater importance would be the prospects for more intelligent group response, including government action. The history of U.S. agriculture is replete with examples of the government responding to short–run, transitory phenomena in such a way as to make long–run adjustment more difficult. Disastrously low prices, for example, may result in heavily subsidized and abundant government credit to assist farmers in meeting their immediate needs. But the long–run consequence is to put more resources into agriculture than can be maintained over time and to damage established credit channels that are needed for sustained performance.

Public sector decisions of both our own government and of foreign governments have been sources of short–run instability. While individual mistakes tend to be offset by other individuals acting in a different way, errors in collective action often have no countervailing reaction. Technical change is another source of instability; as in the case of a pesticide which has to be withdrawn because of adverse environmental effects after initial success in increasing production.

Variation in the forces of nature—climate, pests, and disease—also must be reckoned with. Changes in natural factors have both direct and indirect effects on producers. A drought in one part of the world adversely affects producers in that region but they will recognize that such conditions are transitory. Farmers in other parts of the world who are producing the same, or a substitute commodity, may benefit from the drought because of a temporary increase in demand for their crops. But, they may have difficulty in understanding that the increase in demand stems from drought in another part of the world and is not of a permanent nature.

This statement of the problem permits us to say something about a rational response by individual farmers as well as by groups. If farmers will seek information which will permit them to distinguish between the long–run tendencies and shorter–run variations, they can develop more rational strategies. For example, a farm couple who expect to continue farming over a lifetime may conclude that long–run trends are such that if the farm is to be their primary source of income, they must steadily enlarge their farming operation or they must diversify their sources of income. If they choose the latter route one or both may decide to pursue an off–farm occupation. In either case, considerable flexibility may be built into the farm operation to permit rapid adjustment to take advantage of unusually favorable years or for protection in unusually poor years. There is considerable evidence that millions of U.S. farm families have made this kind of adjustment. Unfortunately, there also is evidence that many have mistaken the unusually favorable years at the beginning of this decade as evidence of long–run permanent trends and did not provide sufficient flexibility to cushion the shock in case they were wrong. Yet, it should not be implied that the distinction between the permanent and the transitory forces can be made easily. Economists and others who devote their professional careers to the study of agriculture often fail to distinguish between long–run trends and short–run fluctuations.

Group response to these trends and uncertainties is subject to the same fundamental errors in perception. For example, a program may be proposed or designed to deal with an unfavorable event such as a drought or very low prices. Such a program provides a constant invitation to broaden its scope so that it applies to many situations in addition to the very unfavorable cases for which it was originally intended. The result of this change in coverage may be to attract and hold more resources in agriculture than is warranted by long–run supply and demand conditions. This, of course, may greatly increase the public cost of the program.

Beyond our difficulties in distinguishing between fundamental and transitory forces, there is a problem of inconsistency between the best individual and the best group action. Each farmer, acting in his own best interest, may currently choose a strategy of expansion. However, if all farmers view the situation in the same way and elect the same or a comparable strategy, the total response may be self–defeating, in this case resulting in overproduction, low incomes, and financial stress for farmers.

U.S. Agriculture: Its Social and Economic Environment

Agriculture is a major industry that depends upon the performance of numerous biological processes. It is not surprising that farming is sometimes regarded as synonymous with these biological processes, although as long as farmers have engaged in exchange, either by barter or the use of money, an understanding of the social environment has been important to success in farming. It may appear something of a paradox that as more and more progress has been made in understanding and controlling the biological processes of agriculture, its welfare has been more and more determined by the general social environment. But, what appears to be a puzzle may be simply another way of describing economic and social development. In this section we consider some specific features of the social and economic environment that affect farmers.

Farmers range from very large commercial operators to small, part–time producers. Some own their land and all or most of their capital. Others rent land and may be heavily in debt. Young farmers have a different set of problems than those faced by farmers approaching retirement. Not only is there a great deal of variation within the farming community at any particular time, but in addition U.S. agriculture is dynamic and much change occurs over time. Thus it is not very useful to speak of "the farmer."

Yet there are some indicators of performance that can be used to describe U.S. farmers as a group. Such an indicator is the return to resources used for food and fiber production comparable to what those resources would earn if used outside of agriculture. A persistent low income problem does exist in rural areas although both farm and nonfarm families are affected. Further, there are relatively fewer farm people in the upper income levels than exist outside of agriculture.

Income in an average year is not the only important factor. The instability of income has long been a major problem in U.S. agriculture. The individual farm family is aware of the "boom or bust" nature of farming. The variability of income is illustrated by the data presented in Table 1. The farm manager must plan under conditions of considerable risk and uncertainty, and the farm family must gear its consumption patterns and its way of living to highly variable income.

Despite the fact that the period reported in Table 1 includes some of the most profitable years experienced by American farmers, the number of farms declined throughout the period. In 1973 per capita nonfarm income as a percent of per capita farm income fell below 100. By 1976 it stood at 125 although that was less than it was in the late 1960's.

Nonfarm income is becoming increasingly important to the farm population. If an exception is made for the extremely profitable years of the early 1970's, the trend is clearly upward with more than half of per capita farm income coming from nonfarm sources. Thus the farmer and the farm family must view their occupational calling as one with an uncertain present and an uncertain future. Some farmers accumulate

TABLE 1.
Income and Related Statistics for Farm and Nonfarm Population, 1967–1977

Year	No. of farms	Realized net farm income per farm[a]	Realized net farm income per farm adjusted for inflation	Percentage of per capita farm income from nonfarm sources	Disposable personal income of farm population from all sources adjusted for inflation	Disposable personal income of nonfarm population from all sources adjusted for inflation
	(millions)	(dollars)	(dollars, 1967 = 100)	(%)	(dollars, 1967 = 100)	(dollars, 1967 = 100)
1967	3.16	3,695	3,695	51.3	1,925	2,788
1968	3.07	3,972	3,812	53.2	2,014	2,856
1969	3.00	4,733	4,311	51.8	2,124	2,871
1970	2.95	4,788	4,117	52.7	2,167	2,914
1971	2.91	4,550	3,751	53.2	2,522	2,992
1972	2.87	6,204	4,951	51.3	2,589	3,085
1973	2.84	10,529	7,911	40.2	3,531	3,205
1974	2.83	9,801	6,642	48.3	2,949	3,155
1975	2.81	7,410	4,597	50.8	2,804	3,172
1976	2.78	7,885	4,625	59.1	2,596	3,254
1977	2.75	7,413	4,084	57.4	2,720	3,327

SOURCE: U.S. Department of Agriculture (1977; 1978, July); U.S. Department of Commerce (1977).

[a]"Farm Income" is total income from farm and nonfarm sources.

great wealth in a lifetime and their families enjoy a superior standard of living. Yet there are others who are not nearly so fortunate and even those who are not confident of the final outcome on a year–to–year basis. The following discussion concentrates on major problems affecting farmers in general.

CHRONIC INFLATION

Inflation is one of the most difficult problems with which industrial societies must contend. This is not the place to discuss the causes and cures of inflation. We limit ourselves to two general observations. First, economists do not agree on the relationship of changes in the price level to certain other policy objectives, such as the level of employment. As a consequence they cannot agree on recommendations to achieve particular policy goals. Even if a nation is willing to exercise economic self–discipline, it may be uncertain as to just what policies it should adopt.

The second general observation is that chronic inflation obviously has many effects on agriculture. An industry, such as farming, that depends increasingly on purchased inputs faces the prospect of constantly escalating production costs during inflationary periods. On the other hand, the burden of debt repayment decreases over time with inflation so long as interest rates paid do not fully reflect the rate of increase in the price level. Dollars borrowed in one time period are repaid with dollars of less value in succeeding time periods. However, during periods of inflation all prices, costs, and values are not affected equally. Relative price changes tend to distort resource allocation over time.

PRICE FORMATION IN U.S. AGRICULTURE

From 1959 through 1977 prices paid by farmers increased every year save one when there was no change. In 9 of those 18 years the U.S. Department of Agriculture's (USDA) prices paid index increased by 5 percent or more. In two years, the index increased by 15 percent or more.

The USDA's index of prices received behaved quite differently. It decreased five times during the 18 year period, once by 6 percent and once by 4 percent. It increased by 5 percent or more five times, and from 1972 to 1973 the index increased by more than 43 percent. In general, the behavior of prices for the commodities that farmers sell is significantly different from the behavior of prices for the goods and services that farmers buy. This fact has a profound effect on resource allocation and production costs in U.S. agriculture. We believe it is a fundamental part of the social environment of U.S. agriculture. In an inflationary economy farmers can plan on steadily increasing costs, with the principal uncertainty relating to the amount of the increase. No such certainty exists on the revenue side where decreases as well as increases are possible.

FINANCIAL RESOURCES

One of the more significant developments in farm management during the past decade is the extent to which financial management has come to dominate other management problems. Agriculture has become more capital intensive and the acquisition and management of capital has often determined whether a farm could grow and survive. The financial resources on which the farmer can draw constitute an important part of his social environment. A number of factors combine to form this environment.

The way a farm family decides to value present consumption relative to future consumption will have an important effect on the amount of capital available for operation and growth of the farm. If all of the income generated by the farm is consumed, growth of the farm business will be made more difficult. Yet it often happens that the years when the consumption needs of the farm family are the greatest coincide with the years when the returns to capital invested in the farm business are the highest.

The financial resources available to a farmer are influenced by many institutions related to agriculture. Capital and credit are provided to agriculture through numerous commercial channels such as banks, insurance companies, firms that purchase agricultural products, and firms that sell to farmers. Commercial channels of credit are supplemented by public and semi–public sources. Recent legislation has provided additional capital for disaster and emergency situations. The Emergency Agricultural Credit Adjustment Act of 1978 (U.S. Congress 1978) provides an example. The impact of these programs on established credit channels is unknown but may be important.

The financial resources of agriculture also are affected by inflation, the amount of equity in assets, and the level of interest rates and taxes. The farmer has little control over such items but they may have a profound effect on the way he allocates his resources. Increasing costs under chronic inflation provide an incentive to acquire debt. Even though asset values increase because of inflation, the benefits to farmers may be realized only upon retirement unless refinancing occurs frequently. As the farmer's equity increases, his risk of insolvency is lessened. However, the smaller his equity, the better the hedge against inflation. Monetary policy has been relied upon increasingly in recent years as a means of combating inflation resulting in periodic credit "crunches." Although interest rates also have increased over time, generally they have not risen as rapidly as the price of land, making debt more attractive.

THE TAX ENVIRONMENT[1]

Federal Income Tax Structure. Federal income tax laws have historically granted preferred treatment, not only to those directly engaged in agricultural production, but to all individuals with agricultural incomes. One of the major benefits, the privilege of using the so–called "cash accounting method," allows farmers to accelerate or delay certain income and expense items. This departure from basic accounting procedures was first justified, and is still defended, on the basis of providing a simplified method of accounting to farmers who were (and presumably are) unable to cope with the more sophisticated accrual method and, further, who were believed unable to have access to competent accounting assistance. This development, combined with regulations and specific legislation permitting the current deduction of developmental expenses, allows deduction of costs before the income derived from the expenditures is realized.

These tax preferences, plus the availability of capital gains treatment for sales of livestock held for draft, breeding, dairy, or sporting purposes, create a strong incentive for the entry of capital from outside agriculture. The incentive to individuals with large nonfarm incomes who seek farm investments to reduce their effective tax rates and delay payment of taxes has been widely publicized. Such tax shelters have

---

[1]This section is taken from a paper by Fred Woods.

contributed to the rising demand for farmland and create a decided advantage in the access to capital for tax–shelter investors over those individuals who depend on farm income for a major portion of their livelihood.

What is not generally considered, however, are the inequities in the access to capital among those who depend on farm income for their livelihood. Even though most farmers do not base their decisions to increase the size of a farm operation solely on tax considerations, they are an important factor in their access to capital. Although special tax provisions are available to virtually all farmers, the ability to benefit is directly related to the farmer's marginal tax rate.

Tax provisions such as investment tax credit and accelerated depreciation encourage the shift to mechanization in farming and to increasingly larger sizes of machines by effectively shifting a portion of the machinery cost to fellow taxpayers. What better access to capital than to have the public at large share a portion of your investment cost? This subsidy encourages substitution of capital for labor and is most readily available to large–scale farmers who use expensive equipment.

The Revenue Act of 1978. When farm income becomes high enough, a farmer also may realize an additional tax saving by incorporating and gaining access to subsidized capital through retained earnings. Through this process, current income can be transferred into additional real property and land ownership tends to become more and more concentrated. The most recent federal tax legislation may be expected to accelerate the trend toward corporate farming. The Revenue Act of 1978 provides, for the first time, a graduated corporate income tax rate. The first $25,000 of corporate income will now be subject to a tax rate of 17 percent. The next $25,000 of income will be taxed at a 20 percent rate; the third $25,000 increment will be subject to a 30 percent rate; and the fourth increment to a 40 percent tax rate. Taxable income over $100,000 will be subject to a 46 percent tax rate. The change to a graduated tax rate is expected to provide a considerable incentive for smaller and medium size farms to incorporate.

Not only is there the positive incentive, but under the corporation there is a disincentive to use farm income for consumption purposes. Under the regular corporate income tax provisions, income paid out as dividends is subject to both corporate and personal income taxation.

Other provisions of the Revenue Act also affect farmers' access to capital. The 10 percent investment tax credit is made permanent and is extended to structures or enclosures used for single–purpose food or plant production. This includes structures used for poultry, eggs, hogs, other livestock, or plants. This provision effectively reduces the price that farmers pay for machinery and other eligible equipment. When combined with the accelerated depreciation deductions and additional first–year depreciation, tax savings of up to 50 percent of the purchase price can be realized in the first year of purchase.

The treatment of capital gains was further liberalized under the new law. Individual taxpayers may exclude 60 percent of net capital gains from gross income and include the remaining 40 percent in ordinary income. Under the old law, the individual taxpayer could deduct from gross income 50 percent of any net capital gain for the year with the remainder included in income and taxed at ordinary tax rates. The intent of the liberalization is to speed up the rate of economic growth by making more funds available for investment. But what is the effect of this provision on U.S. agriculture? There appears to be no general shortage of investment capital in American agriculture, and since the major capital asset in agriculture—farmland—exists in limited supply and is already under considerable inflationary pressure, the inevitable result of increasing its attractiveness as an investment will be further upward pressures on farmland prices.

The Tax Reform Act of 1976. Three provisions included in the Tax Reform Act of 1976 could have considerable impact on access to capital and changing farm structure. These are the special use valuation for farmland, the carryover basis provision, and the liberalized extended payment of federal estate tax liability.

The use–value assessment feature, even though it cannot reduce a gross estate by more than $500,000, benefits all qualifying farm estates. Thus, the real size of this apparent half million dollar benefit is directly proportionate to the marginal tax bracket of the estate. The use–value assessment feature may be expected to reduce farmland valuation for estate tax purposes from 35 to 50 percent on the average. However, this apparent advantage in financing will be quickly capitalized into increased land values, thus adding further upward pressures on farmland prices.

The primary beneficiaries of this tax shelter will be existing farmers who have family heirs who wish to continue farming. One effect
may be to encourage older farmers to shift capital investment into land
and away from other assets. It is difficult to predict the extent to which
wealthy non–farmers will enter agriculture to take advantage of this tax
shelter but there is a definite incentive for movement in this
direction—making it all the more difficult for the young, beginning
farmer to become established unless he is fortunate enough to be born
or marry into a landowning family.

The real financial boon from the Tax Reform Act comes from the
liberalized deferred payment of the estate tax liability. Under the new
law heirs can pay the federal estate tax (less the allowable credit) over a
15–year period. Four percent interest is charged on the unpaid tax up
to the $345,800 maximum which can be deferred. The economic bene-
fits arise from the excess of returns earned on the deferred taxes over
the 4 percent interest paid. At a 5 percent net rate of return (yielding a
1 percent excess over the 4 percent interest paid), compounded earnings reach 14.4 percent of the tax bill over the payment period. Assuming a 10 percent net rate of return, the compounded earnings pay all of
the tax and more than 80 percent of the interest. With such benefits
flowing from the deferred payment provision, substantial incentives
are generated to qualify property for the new provision. Since disposition of more than one–third of the estate's assets will trigger termination of the tax deferral, there is a disincentive for disposition of the
property prior to expiration of the installment payment period,
thereby encouraging continuation of farmland ownership in the same
family.

The carryover basis provision in the Tax Reform Act also will affect
agriculture. The former "stepped up" basis at death tended to lock
appreciated assets into estates by discouraging the sale of these assets
by retired farmers since the heirs would receive a tax–free, stepped–
up basis for their own estates. The carryover basis provision ends this
lock–in and, in the short run, may be expected to reduce substantially
the incentive for retired farmers to become nonoperator landlords by
holding appreciated assets. However, if farmland continues to appreciate as it has over the last decade, a different kind of lock–in may
well be created: a permanent disincentive for heirs to sell appreciated
assets, particularly land. But we may never realize the impact of this

revision, since the Revenue Act of 1978 postpones the effective date of the carryover basis until January 1, 1980. We may expect a strong effort to rescind carryover basis permanently sometime between now and 1980.

THE RURAL COMMUNITY.

It is not within the scope of this chapter to provide a complete or exhaustive treatment of the rural community. But, many rural communities are changing rapidly and these changes often influence resource allocation in agriculture. Therefore, it is appropriate that mention be made of some of the significant trends and developments.

Because of their population base relative to the remainder of the country, rural communities frequently experience significant in- or out-migration. In recent years many rural communities have lost population because of increased mechanization and reduced farm employment. Other communities have experienced in-migration because of urbanization or because of population movements to rural areas.

Agriculture is strongly influenced by such spatial adjustments. If population is lost, the financial burden of supporting existing social services may fall increasingly on agriculture. The cost of social services often has a large fixed cost component which cannot be altered in direct proportion to the services performed.

Yet rapid population increases pose problems for rural communities as well. Not only are additional social services required, but additional social constraints frequently result from greater population density. Land use control is one form of this greater regulation and often has a direct impact on agriculture, typically increasing the cost of agricultural production. Of course, certain farmers may benefit if their land becomes more valuable in non-agricultural uses. While many farmers favor measures which will minimize the interferences of nonfarm population with farm production, few wish to have a land use system established which will prevent them from selling their land for nonfarm uses if such a profitable opportunity materializes.

Human Resources[2]

Great skill is required to survive and prosper in a dynamic economic environment. The ability to acquire, interpret, and act efficiently on information is a valuable skill. A real test of this ability occurred during the early 1970's, when farm output prices increased temporarily. Many young farmers did not have the prior experience to evaluate the temporary situation and did not have adequate net worth to cushion the effects of a wrong decision.

THE FARM FAMILY

The trend toward decreasing numbers of farmers has long been apparent (Table 1). Many parents who have continued farming have recognized agriculture would not provide opportunities for all of their children and wanted to help their children adjust to the opportunities of an urban society. The public schools have been a great social vehicle for helping with this adjustment.

How effective is the U.S. educational system in assisting farm families at the present time? We do not pretend to have enough information to offer a complete answer but certain questions can be raised and tentative answers given.

Rural school districts have been consolidated to permit educational efficiencies. One effect has been to make rural schools much more like their urban counterparts. The agricultural colleges have become universities with a broad range of educational offerings. Even agricultural curricula in the schools and colleges of agriculture have a broader educational base than is commonly believed to be the case. The typical curriculum provides for biological, social and physical science courses with varying amounts of the humanities. Depth in these fields is sometimes sacrificed, however, because of the extensive coverage and because of emphasis on the applied rather than the fundamental.

While the educational system obviously needs to prepare farm people for multiple occupations, it is not clear just what the most desirable education is for the person who will work essentially full time in farming. Nor is it clear that extension education has adjusted fully to accommodate the continuing education needs of these people.

[2]Wallace Huffman provided help in preparing this section.

Entrepreneurship of a high order is required as well as access to technical information.

Just as the urban economy is the source of many of the shocks suffered by the agricultural sector, that economy also serves as a balance wheel for those resources which are permanently or temporarily in excess in agriculture. Two of three farm families receive more than half of their income from nonfarm sources. Furthermore, this practice is not confined to the small–scale or part–time farms. On larger farms, it is common for either the farmer or the farm wife to have off–farm employment. It is a logical and effective means of stabilizing family income.

FARM LABOR

The USDA index of wage rates for hired farm labor increased by 25 percent between 1950 and 1960, doubled between 1960 and 1972 and has continued to rise since that time. In addition, the relative price of farm labor has shown a strong upward trend historically. Between 1950 and 1970, the index of wage rates for hired labor divided by the index of prices paid by farmers doubled, after which the trend in the ratio leveled out. Undoubtedly this has hastened the substitution of capital services for labor services in agriculture.

Although annual worker–hours of hired farm labor have declined, the change in average worker–hours of hired farm labor per farm is less certain. Estimates of annual worker–hours of hired labor calculated from data in the Census of Agriculture show a dramatic decline in average worker–hours between 1969 and 1974 (see Table 2). However, estimates in Smith and Rowe show an increase since 1974.

Some of the socio–economic characteristics of hired farm workers are shown in Tables 3 and 4. The share of the farm hired workers who are less than 24 years of age has increased from 45 percent in 1961 to 54 percent in 1972. There also has been an increase from 54 to 60 percent in the share of the farm hired workers who work less than 25 days per year. Between 1961 and 1976 there was an increase in median years of schooling completed by hired workers 25 years of age and older (Table 3).

Farm and nonfarm labor markets have become increasingly integrated over the past 25 years. This change is the result of (1) competition of agriculture with the nonfarm sector for labor, (2) new govern-

Table 2.

Average Worker–Hours of Hired Farm Labor per Farm for Census Divisions
in Selected Years

Regions	Average manhours of hired labor per farm[a]			
	1950	1959	1969	1974
Census divisions				
New England	2,893	3,257	3,673	2,279
Middle Atlantic	2,147	2,494	2,657	1,187
East North Central	998	1,069	1,162	482
West North Central	786	776	852	429
South Atlantic	1,453	2,105	2,263	1,058
East South Central	1,034	1,263	1,065	458
West South Central	2,302	2,318	1,813	795
Mountain	2,625	2,978	3,139	1,647
Pacific	3,795	4,871	5,410	3,856
U.S.	1,621	1,805	1,778	878

SOURCE: U.S. Department of Commerce (1977); U.S. Department of Agriculture (1978, August).

[a]Worker–hours of hired labor calculated as annual expenditures on hired farm labor divided by the average farm wage rate, composite rate per hour.

Table 3.

Schooling Completed by Hired Farm Workers 25 Years of Age and
Older, 1961 and 1976

Year	Number of workers	Years of schooling completed				Median years completed
		0-4	5-8	9-11	12 or more	
	(1,000's)	(percent)				(years)
1961	1,832	28.6	44.1	13.0	14.3	6.9
1976, all	1,130	16	29	15	40	10.1
White	723	6	25	15	54	12.1
Hispanics	176	46	36	9	9	5.4
Blacks and others	231	22	40	19	19	7.9

SOURCES: Cowhig; Smith and Rowe.

TABLE 4.
Age Distribution of Hired Farm Labor, 1961 and 1972

Age	All workers			Days of farm wage work per year					
				25 days or more			Less than 25 days		
	Total	Male	Female	Total	Male	Female	Total	Male	Female
1961–Total (1,000's)	3,488 [100.0]a	2,445 [70.1]	1,043 [29.9]	1,889 [54.2]	1,468	421	1,600 [45.8]	978	622
				(percent)					
14–17 years	25	25	24	18	17	20	23	37	26
18–24 years	20	23	15	22	24	14	19	19	17
25–34 years	15	13	20	15	13	21	15	12	19
35–44 years	14	12	18	15	14	22	12	11	15
45–54 years	12	13	10	16	17	12	8	8	9
55–64 years	9	9	11	10	10	10	8	7	11
65 years and over	5	5	2	4	5	1	5	6	3
1972–Total (1,000's)	2,809 [100.0]	2,169 [77.2]	641 [32.8]	1,679 [59.8]	1,387	292	1,130 [40.2]	782	349
				(percent)					
14–17 years	30	30	26	22	22	20	40	44	31
18–24 years	24	25	23	24	25	25	24	26	20
25–34 years	15	15	17	17	17	17	13	11	17
35–44 years	10	9	16	12	10	18	8	6	14
45–54 years	9	9	9	12	12	10	6	4	9
55–64 years	7	7	7	9	9	8	4	3	6
65 years and over	5	5	2	4	5	2	5	6	3

SOURCES: Baum, Friend and Stansberry; McElroy.
aValues within brackets are percentages of total workers.

ment legislation covering working conditions and employe benefits, and (3) improved transportation and communication between rural and urban areas, making it possible for people to live a greater distance from their jobs.

The wage policy and associated benefits for hired farm workers have a history of being different from that for nonfarm workers (Huffman 1977). Part of this difference occurs because much farm work is short term or seasonal while permanent employment predominates in the nonfarm sector. In addition, agricultural work generally does not have provisions for overtime pay differentials to the same extent as does urban work.

For full–time workers in the nonfarm sector, the value of fringe benefits has become a significant (in excess of 35 percent in manufacturing) and increasing share of total employee compensation. Such benefits include provisions for paid vacations, paid sick leave, retirement plan, some health and life insurance coverage, and severance pay conditions. In addition, these workers are generally covered under government unemployment and workmen's compensation programs, as well as minimum wage legislation.

For full–time agricultural workers, fringe benefits continue to be mainly food and housing and paid vacations, with informal understandings on illness, injury, and retirement provisions. Most agricultural workers are covered under social security and Occupational Safety and Health Administration (OSHA) provisions and some are covered under government unemployment and minimum wage provisions.

The agricultural sector has adjusted to rising real wages in the nonfarm sector by paying higher real wages and substituting new forms of capital for labor services. There are individuals, however, who have a preference for the rural life style and for farm work over other types of work and are willing to accept lower wage rates for the non–money benefits they receive from farm work. But, rising real wage rates in the nonfarm sector increase the opportunity cost to these workers of staying in agriculture, so wage rates need to rise to keep even those individuals who prefer farm work in the farm sector.

There are many people in Mexico who are willing to cross the border illegally to work as farm workers in the United States. Wage rate differences between Mexico and the United States are large and the unemployment rate is high in Mexico. These workers can accept a lower wage in the United States than other workers and still be better off than by remaining in Mexico. Penalties for illegal entry or for hiring illegal immigrants have been small, so both the illegal immigrants and the farmers who hire them are better off. Thus, as long as the wage differential between the United States and Mexico remains large and penalties for illegal entry are small, the number of illegal immigrants is unlikely to decrease. (Good estimates of the number of manhours worked by illegal aliens are nearly impossible to obtain.) If wage differentials increase between the two countries, as seems likely, the number of illegal immigrants will most likely increase.

Unionization of farm workers seems unlikely to be a factor in employe–employer relations in most sections of U.S. agriculture. Union activity can be expected only when a sizeable group of people work for an employer for some reasonable length of time. In general, there are few farms or farming enterprises that employ 3 or more full–time hired workers who are not involved in the ownership of the business. Casual farm workers (say, with fewer than 25 days of work per year) do not have a financial interest in organizing. Initiation fees and membership dues for them would provide a low return. However, in large fruit, vegetable, and nut growing regions, farms often employ sizeable numbers of seasonal hired workers. These workers may work for one employer for 3 or so months doing preharvest, harvest, and post–harvest work. In California, the longer–term seasonal adult workers in fruit, vegetable, and nut growing areas have had some success in unionizing and in bargaining.

Martin and Rochin describe the farm labor situation as follows:

Labor relations in agriculture have been characterized by the absence of formal agreements negotiated between employer and labor representatives. Historically, labor law has assured agriculture a 'special and exempt' status, a condition obviating any legal responsibility for employers to respond to employee demands, making organizing efforts more difficult—agricultural labor relations within a defined legal framework are a product of the mid–1970's.[3] The passage of the Agricultural Labor

---

[3]Hawaii's labor relations statutes have covered agricultural labor since 1945, and Wisconsin's labor legislation was constructed to include agricultural laborers in 1967–1968. Four states, Idaho (1972), Arizona (1972), Kansas (1972), and California (1975) currently have agricultural labor relations statutes. For a comprehensive analysis, see Koziara (cited in Martin and Rochin).

Relations Act (ALRA) in California, the state with the largest hired work force, marks a new era in agricultural labor relations.

Martin and Rochin go on to say that immediate problems in the formulation of specific labor policies include the definition of bargaining units, the determination of voter eligibility, the timing of elections, the rights of union organizers, and the timely resolution of objectives. They believe much litigation will be associated with the resolution of these difficulties.

From this discussion we advance the following generalizations. First, we expect considerable uncertainty in agricultural labor relations in the period immediately ahead. Second, we believe that there is a probable trend toward extending the same benefits to farm workers that prevail in the economy generally. Third, farm workers probably will not be able to increase benefits as rapidly during the next decade as during the past two or three. The slowing in the rate of increase in labor productivity will undoubtedly establish a limit to the increased benefits that can be achieved by labor. Fourth, the push for mechanization will accelerate. While agricultural labor benefits are lagging behind nonfarm labor benefits, the latter are now increasing at a decelerating pace.

The Unique Resource and Production Problems of Smaller Farms

Since the time of Jefferson there has been concern about small farms. Numerous policies have been instituted with the explicit objective of aiding smaller farms although it is questionable whether these policies have always had this effect.

There is a growing concern with the current trend toward bigness in many areas of endeavor. Few would deny that there are certain desirable characteristics of smaller units in some circumstances. For example, consider the problems of fixing of responsibility and accountability in small or medium size versus very large units. Yet when there are powerful economic forces that make large units more profitable, it is questionable whether public policies in opposition to such trends are likely to be effective.

There is a wide range of farm sizes in the United States. Recent federal legislation has authorized funds for small farm research, but no funds have actually been appropriated to date. Under this legislation, small farms are defined as those farms with annual gross sales of less than $20,000. Using this definition, 65.5 percent of the farms in 1974 were small (Table 5). Forty–nine percent of the small farms were in the South, and more than 75 percent of all farms in each census division of the South were small.

There are several problems with this definition of small farms, besides the obvious problem of using nominal prices to determine the value of sales. First, returns to family labor and management seldom exceed 15 percent of gross sales, and for different farm types it may be much lower. Thus with $20,000 of annual gross sales, the expected return to family labor and management would be about $3000. If a family is dependent on farming for its income, and sales are less than $20,000, then there is likely to be a serious poverty problem. Alternatively, if a family on a small farm were to have an income equal to the median family income of all U.S. households, adjusted for cost of living differences, then as much as $9,000 of nonfarm income or returns from

TABLE 5.
Total Number of Farms and Share of Farms With Farm Sales less than
$20,000, 1974

Regions	Total number of farms	Percent of farms in region with sales less than $20,000	Percent of all farms in U.S. with sales less than $20,000
Census division			
New England	23,269	57.2	0.9
Middle Atlantic	104,262	60.9	4.2
East North Central	444,695	60.9	17.9
West North Central	572,672	50.6	19.2
South Atlantic	296,103	75.0	14.7
East South Central	306,010	85.6	17.3
West South Central	327,986	76.5	16.6
Mountain	111,868	57.1	4.2
Pacific	123,837	61.8	5.1
U.S.	2,310,702	65.5	100.0

SOURCE: U.S. Department of Commerce (1977).

farmland ownership may be required. Thus, a majority of the household's income would be from nonfarm sources.

Second, there is a life cycle pattern to farm sales for single–operator farms. Sales (in constant dollars) peak between 35 and 44 years of age, and are lower on average for younger and older farm operators. In particular, a relatively large share of farms with sales less than $20,000 have operators approaching retirement. These farmers face different problems from young farmers who are trying to get started in farming.

Third, a sizeable share of the households with farms falling in the definition of small are households that have nonfarm income that exceeds the median family income of all U.S. households. Society probably is not interested in providing special government assistance to them.

Fourth, an unresolved issue associated with the concern for small farms is whether a small farm size should be a permanent alternative to becoming larger or going out of business. The answer probably depends on off–farm work opportunities, availability of farmland for renting, the level of farm management skills of household members, and production cost differences between small and larger farms. As indicated in Table 6, there is a substantial difference in age distribution of farm operators by region.

The key to the future of small farms is likely to be found in the operation of the rental market for farmland and in the market for labor, both skilled and unskilled, and professional services in rural areas. There is no evidence to suggest that small farms are unduly handicapped in the capital and credit markets. While large amounts of credit may be arranged at favorable interest rates, this may be offset by the difficulty of arranging for very large amounts of credit in some rural areas. Agricultural technology, including machinery, is available for a very wide range of farm sizes.

Small farms probably are at a relative disadvantage in dealing with bureaucracy. As we note elsewhere, this is especially serious with respect to farm labor and environmental regulations, although it is not confined to these areas. Public programs, including extension education, that would help smaller farms cope with such matters should command the attention of those who are concerned with small farms.

With increased land values, it is difficult for farms of all sizes to

TABLE 6.
Geographical Distribution of Farm Operators less than 25 Years
of Age, for Selected Years

Census division	1950	1959	1969	1975
	(percent)			
New England	1	1	1	1
Middle Atlantic	3	2	4	3
East North Central	12	19	23	23
West North Central	19	30	30	35
South Atlantic	19	15	9	9
East South Central	25	14	12	11
West South Central	16	10	13	11
Mountain	3	4	4	4
Pacific	2	2	3	3
U.S.	100.0	100.0	100.0	100.0
(Number of farm operators less than 25 years of age)	(163,726)	(45,352)	(52,905)	(52,391)
[Farm operators less than 25 yrs. of age as share of all farm operators, percent]	[3.0]	[1.2]	[1.9]	[2.3]

SOURCE: U.S. Department of Commerce (1977).

purchase all of the land they need for an economic unit. It may be that
the ownership of farmland by those not actively engaged in farming
will increase. If it does, the amount of land available for renting will
also increase. But can the small–scale farmer compete for this land, or
will the large farm operators be able to outbid them? The size and the
location of the parcels to be rented will do much to determine the size
of farm for which it is best suited. The bulk of this land probably will go
to the large farms but some may be available for units of a smaller size.

What do census data show about the order of magnitude and
trends in rented land as opposed to ownership of farmland? For the
period 1950 to 1969, about 36 percent of the land in farms was rented
with a slight trend upward, but there are large regional differences. In
New England, less than 14 percent of the land in farms is rented, while

in the West North Central and West South Central divisions, rented
land amounts to more than 40 percent. The pattern across divisions
does parallel closely the share of cropland in all farmland. Over the
1950–1969 period, the Pacific and Mountain divisions show a strong
upward trend in farmland that is rented, but the East South Central
division shows a strong downward trend. Some of the movement in the
share rented in the South is undoubtedly due to economic forces causing the dramatic fall in sharecropping in cotton and tobacco producing
areas. Unfortunately, data are not available on the amount of land
rented by small–scale or young farm operators.

Families living on smaller farms obtain a higher percentage of
their income from off–farm work than do the families on larger farms.
This is true even though the absolute amount of income earned off the
farm tends to increase with size of farm. If the rural labor market
provides an opportunity for members of the farm family to market their
services, it will tend to increase the viability of farms of various sizes.

Natural Resources

SPECIAL PROBLEMS ASSOCIATED WITH LAND[4]

Land plays more than one role in U.S. agriculture. The most
obvious is its importance in agricultural production. Even though it is
still required for all significant food and fiber production, it is increasingly being supplemented by other inputs. Schultz (p. 29) was one of
the first to call attention to this in a systematic way. In 1960, he said
"the income attributable to farm real estate, divided by an index of the
quantity of farmland, and with farm structures removed, declined 29
percent in relation to farm product prices, between 1910–14 and
1956—." Yet, in recent years the nominal price of farmland has risen
so much that it is not clear that the trend identified by Schultz still
holds.

Earnings on farm real estate are related to the price of those
assets. However, as Figure 1 indicates, price appreciation since 1970
cannot be explained solely on the basis of the agricultural earnings of
land. Land has not always been a highly effective hedge against inflation. During the past 59 years, 18 years were found when the Con-

[4]Chester Baker provided help in preparing this section.

FIGURE 1:
Residual Return to Production Assets With and Without Adjustment for Price
Appreciation of Real Estate

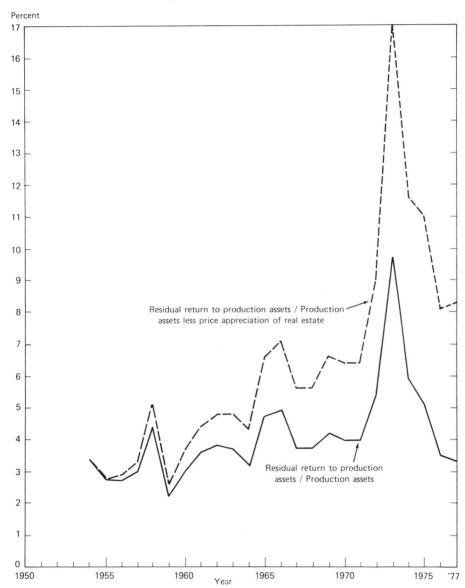

SOURCE: Melichar 1978, March and April.

sumer Price Index (CPI) rose by more than 3 percent. In these years of inflation the CPI increased at an average compound rate of 8.36 percent per year, while the Standard and Poor's Index of 500 common stock prices (S&P) rose by an average compound rate of 10.49 percent and farmland values by 9.22 percent. Adjusted for inflation, the S&P Index rose in real terms at an average compound rate of 1.97 percent, while farmland values rose by 0.79 percent. Thus on average, common stocks rose more than farmland (Reilly, *et al.*).

Comparisons of land prices, common stock prices, and the CPI are summarized in Table 7. Over the 59–year period, 1919–1978, U.S. farmland prices rose by more than the CPI but less than the S&P Index. However, farmland prices have risen by more than the S&P Index over the post–war period, 1946–1978, despite the 15–year period, 1952–1967, in which the S&P Index rose at more than twice the growth rate in farmland prices, both measured in real terms (i.e., "corrected" for inflation). The most dramatic difference is in the current period of inflation, 1967–1978, when in real terms farmland prices have risen at an annual compound rate of nearly four percent while the S&P Index has *declined* by more than six percent (Table 7).

The period 1952–1967 was characterized by stability in the CPI. Throughout this period, the CPI changed by less than two points per year. It was a period of steady and substantial growth in the S&P Index,

TABLE 7.

Compound Rates of Growth or Decline (–), in Consumer Price Index (CPI), in U.S. Farmland Prices and in Standard and Poor's Index of 500 Common Stocks (S&P) for Selected Time Periods

Item	1919–1978	1946–1978	1952–1967	1967–1978
		(percent)		
CPI	2.24	3.87	1.54	6.48
U.S. Farmland Prices	3.62	7.20	4.90	10.22
S&P	4.01	5.43	9.22	0.07
Farmland Prices–CPI	1.38	3.33	3.36	3.74
S&P–CPI	1.77	1.56	7.68	−6.41

SOURCE: Baker.

while the price of U.S. farmland grew far more modestly. However, the reverse has been true since 1967. In this period the CPI has risen by four or more points each year. Meanwhile, as the S&P Index fluctuated erratically about a compound rate of growth near zero, U.S. farmland prices grew at a compound rate nearly 50 percent higher than the CPI. These results are shown graphically in Figure 2.

Land prices, like other prices, are affected by demand and supply factors. The supply of land for sale is generated by people who perceive other investments to be more favorable than land, taking into account the managerial requirements and costs that are associated with land ownership. Among those were many who left farming for retirement or in response to off–farm employment opportunities. Through the 1950's and 1960's one farm in three disappeared from U.S. agriculture, the result of off–farm migration and consolidation of farms (U.S. Department of Agriculture 1977, July). The demand for land is generated by those who perceive land investment to be more favorable than other investments. Less than 5 percent of U.S. farmland is transferred each year, but this fraction is the principal source of estimates for the value of all U.S. farmland.

The overwhelming majority of buyers of farmland are farm operators who buy land to expand units they already operate. Expansion with rented land also occurs, especially among cash crop farms where land ownership tends to be retained more frequently by those who leave farming. The retention of land by departing operators inevitably reduces the market supply of farmland for sale. The increase in land values since 1970 would have been even greater had there not been a steady flow of land into the farm real estate market, and, in areas of especially high land prices, options of renting to expand the size of operating units (Reiss).

Forty percent of current farm operators have no debt outstanding. Most of these operators are near retirement (Penson). Not all of these are landowners, and those who are may not be large landowners. Nonetheless, the decisions of retirees and their heirs will influence the supply of land for sale and rental. Also, their departure through retirement provides the basis for significant changes in the debt structure of agriculture.

Debt financing already has increased substantially in farmland transfers. In 1945, 44 percent of all transfers involved debt financing

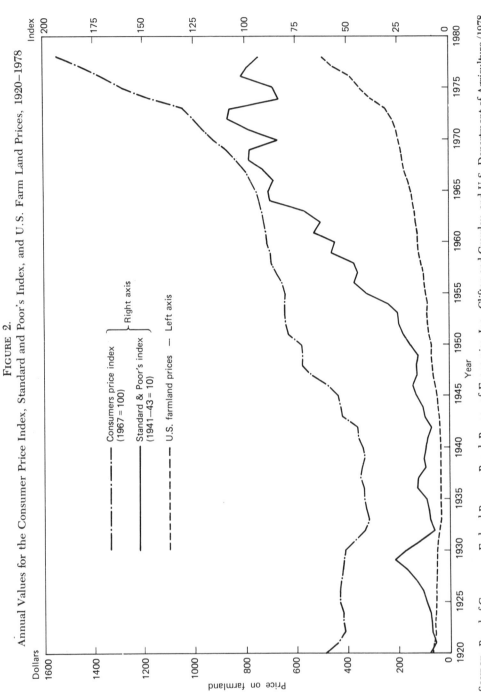

FIGURE 2.

Annual Values for the Consumer Price Index, Standard and Poor's Index, and U.S. Farm Land Prices, 1920–1978

Consumers price index (1967 = 100) ⎤ Right axis
Standard & Poor's index (1941–43 = 10) ⎦
U.S. farmland prices — Left axis

SOURCE: Board of Governors, Federal Reserve Board; Bureau of Economics, Inc.; Clifton and Crowley; and U.S. Department of Agriculture (1978,

(Penson). The amount of debt averaged 57 percent of the purchase price. By 1965 the percentage of transfers financed had risen to 73 and the amount of debt to 72 percent of purchase price; by 1975, these values had risen to 88 and 76 percent respectively.

The increase in land values since 1970 appears to reflect the increased importance of two factors. The first is a perception that the world's increasing population will inevitably generate increases in prices of farm commodities relative to prices of other commodities, and that such increases will force up the price of land. The second factor is a perception of land as a relatively favorable "store of value" in the presence of inflation. Holding money and near–money substitutes is costly during inflationary periods. Debt instruments often bear negative real rates of return. The perception of land as a favorable hedge may be a relatively recent phenomenon, but it may be the more important factor for the near future, while world food demand may be more important in the long run.

Higher land prices require a diversion of funds into land use and control that might otherwise be allocated to consumption and to the acquisition of other production inputs. Land price increases that exceed net cash flows may reduce efficiency in farm production. The effects are moderated as increased equity in farmland generates added borrowing capacity that can be drawn upon for the acquisition of non–land production inputs if net cash flows also rise to provide borrowers with sufficient means to meet their increased debt service requirements. The cost–price squeeze since 1975 has endangered those who have recently financed large land purchases at inflated prices. Increasing numbers of farmers are refinancing non–real estate debt with farm mortgages to restore operating liquidity, only to find the increased amortization commitments are difficult to meet.

Some of the consequences are reflected in federal disaster loans which totaled $3 billion in 1977. Heavy concentrations were in drought areas of Georgia and Iowa, along with, to a lesser extent, Minnesota, Indiana, and the eight Great Plains states. Refinancing real estate debt with farm mortgage loans in 1977 increased markedly in those states: from 150 percent more than 1976 in the case of Indiana and Oklahoma to a full 200 percent or more in the case of North Dakota and Georgia. In many of these states, applications for non–real estate loans were rejected at sharply higher rates (Miller and Millar).

The 1950's and 1960's witnessed an unprecedented increase in acreage per farm in the United States. The rate at which farms disappeared as operating units reached historic heights. Much of the land held by the departing operators was made available to remaining operators on a leased basis. Part–owned, part–leased farms grew more rapidly than did either fully owned or fully leased farms. Most of the land sold by departing operators was bought by remaining operators. Most of the financial stress caused by financing farm expansions was relieved by the flood of liquidity generated by the high prices of farm commodities in 1973–1975. However, these prices in turn led to still further expansions and to leveraged positions that are now the source of growing financial stress among farm operators.

The problems created by these events tend to be more episodic than new. They fall heavily on new farmers, especially where land accounts for a high percentage of asset values. It is difficult to say that consumers are hurt, except that remedies are sought in public programs that raise prices of farm commodities, taxes, or both. The agribusiness community is faced with a volatile demand for those farm inputs whose purchases can be delayed: such durables as machinery, equipment, buildings, and land improvements. The financial community, especially that part in direct contact with affected farmers, faces increasing lender risks and costs. But the principal cost is borne by those farmers in impacted farming areas who are left with high levels of debt service commitments.

It is difficult today to conceive of a passive public sector. Adjustments of individuals take place in the presence of and in anticipation of further government action such as commodity price supports, acreage set–asides, disaster payments, and emergency loans. Indeed, the expectation of public assistance to dampen the consequences of downside risks seems certain to have been anticipated in bids for land. Are such programs thus self–defeating?

To the extent that farm programs increase land prices they simply enrich land owners while increasing the cost to other farmers for all inputs associated with land—including land itself for the tenant operator and for operators of newly–purchased farms. Even those operators who buy land to add to that already owned are forced to divert a part of the cash flow that might otherwise be used to improve their standard of living. Yet many are persuaded by past history that to stand aside would reduce their welfare still more. The "remedies" that come to mind are unlikely to be popular in the farm sector: remove preferential treatment for land in inheritance taxes and in capital gains taxation generally, and redirect lending programs to improve farm viability rather than merely increase land values.

WATER AND AGRICULTURE

Water resource use and development is back on center stage for U.S. agriculture. In many areas, irrigation is an integral part of the resource allocation process in farming. Yet there is no single theme to all of the problems of water allocation. Here we mention but four current problems.

In the arid West, the development of water has been necessary for an intensive agriculture. Throughout this century the U.S. government has played a major role in promoting the development of water for agriculture. However, not all of the water development projects in the West have been accomplished with financial assistance from the government. There is more individual and group development of irrigated acreage in the West than U.S. government–developed acreage. When the government has developed the acreage, however, water is generally available at a lower price to farmers than it would have been in the absence of government assistance. The result is that water has been over used because it has not been costly. But agriculture is not alone in its profligate use of water. Municipal water use is notoriously wasteful because of ineffective pricing policies.

Increased agricultural water use is typically associated with off–farm economic development. Urbanization and industrialization create a need for a clean, reliable supply of water. Water districts or other water supply units, perhaps originally created to serve an agricultural clientele, may find they now have multiple user groups. As long as additional water can be developed at low cost, the institutional structure can usually accommodate additional demand. But when water is available only at considerably higher cost, stress is placed on the system. Under such circumstances, it makes economic sense to transfer water from agriculture to other uses if the economic value of water is greater in other uses. The transfer of water out of agriculture can be accommodated in varying degrees by the water laws of the West.

Energy development in the West has brought this problem to the fore. Some of the development proposals, such as coal slurry pipelines, would require substantial quantities of water. In many cases, the lowest cost source of water would be agriculture. Yet if such transfers were to occur, substantial adjustment would be required by farmers and those who serve them and process their farm output. It is doubtful that the total amount of water required for energy development would affect total U.S. agricultural output in any significant way but this argument is of little comfort to communities heavily dependent on agriculture. Yet in principle the process is no different than agriculture losing people and land to non–agricultural pursuits and this has been occurring for decades. Even so, there are some principles that can appropriately be observed as transfer is considered.

1. Water should be transferred out of agriculture only if it goes to a more socially valuable use and only if a lower–cost source for the nonagricultural use is not available. Communities which wish to retain water in agriculture should have a means of matching the economic incentive to transfer water out of agriculture. Alternative sources of water should be explored for energy uses outside of agriculture.

2. There is much low–value water use throughout the West; agriculture is not the only place water can be obtained. Nevertheless agriculture will not be well served in the long run by creating or supporting obstacles to water transfer when it can be put to a higher–valued use outside agriculture.

At the same time water is being transferred out of agriculture in some areas, more is being brought into agriculture in others. Irrigation is being used increasingly to enhance and stabilize agricultural production even though recent high prices may have induced over–investment in irrigation systems in some areas. Most of this development is by private individuals and groups, and government activity is not involved except through the establishment of property rights in water. And it is here that a problem may exist.

Water rights should possess two characteristics. First, they should have sufficient *certainty* and *stability* so that farmers will have confidence to make appropriate investments. Second, water rights should provide *flexibility*. Flexibility allows water rights to be transferred to another use or uses if conditions warrant. Permits for 5 or 10 years (say) have flexibility but they may not provide the necessary security for appropriate development. As long as a market for water rights exists it can provide for both flexibility and stability. If public use requires additional water, say for wildlife or recreation, government funds can be used to purchase private water rights. This entire area cries out for immediate attention in those regions where irrigation and other water uses are growing rapidly.

Except for projects designed to serve urban areas, numerous large–scale, federally financed water projects do not appear to be politically, economically and, in some instances, environmentally acceptable in the future. Agriculture's principal means of bringing additional water into farming will probably be for smaller projects and private developments. This may constitute a significant problem for certain areas, such as the High Plains where declining ground water levels and increased pumping costs threaten the continuation of an irrigated agriculture.

In an earlier era, water importation would have been an obvious solution. But competition for public funds and increased costs of such operations have diminished significantly the prospects for this solution. Yet significant adjustments are occurring. Farmers are adopting new practices and changing their choice of crops. Nonfarm interests in these areas, both groups and individuals, need to be equally imaginative in their responses.

ENERGY AND AGRICULTURE

Changes in the costs and availability of energy have triggered adjustments on U.S. farms. Some of these adjustments are known but there are many that are not. Such adjustments will continue to be made just as they are when the price of any input changes. The prospect of still higher prices or even temporary shortages may encourage certain farmers to invest to help them better meet such possibilities. For example, such prospects may suggest greater financial liquidity to meet unanticipated costs. The net result will be to increase production costs in U.S. agriculture. There are those who argue that higher energy prices may create a market for agricultural commodities. There is, of course, considerable appeal in the notion that renewable resources might be used as a source of energy. This would have the dual advantage of increasing the market for agricultural products as well as making the nation more self–sufficient in energy.

The potential for aiding the agricultural and energy sectors simultaneously by producing energy from farm products is currently a subject of intensive research. It is expected that our knowledge of the possibilities in this area will be greatly improved in the near future. As an example of existing studies, Tyner has surveyed some of these possibilities in Indiana. He concludes that grain fermentation for industrial alcohol is much closer to being economically feasible than either "gasohol" based on the fermentation of grain or alcohol resulting from the fermentation of cellulose by–products in farming. Tyner believes that a major factor inhibiting investments in the corn fermentation process is swings in the price of corn. He suggests the government might guarantee a stable corn price to ethanol producers to create an incentive for the use of corn for ethanol. Yet if stable prices are desired by such plants they can be achieved by forward contracting. This occurs elsewhere in agriculture. A contracted price for part of a corn crop would be welcomed by many farmers.

Tyner also reports that if the corn fermentation process could capture the entire synthetic alcohol market, about 100 million bushels of corn would be needed each year to produce the 300 million gallons of ethanol currently used. This would amount to about one and one–half percent of the 1976 corn crop.

Environmental Impacts, Technical Change and Investment in Research[5]

ENVIRONMENTAL IMPACT

The environmental movement in the U.S. which developed in the sixties and continued to grow in the seventies did not bypass U.S. agriculture. Modern farming methods, like nonfarm industrial production, affect the environment. Fertilizers, various kinds of pesticides, and soil often escape from the farm and enter the public waterways or the atmosphere where they may affect wildlife and influence human activity and welfare. In other instances, the quality of farm products which enters into commerce also may be affected. These problems have become a concern of public policy and programs have been developed to regulate farming practices.

Many farmers are resentful of environmental regulations. Some

[5]Gerald Carlson and Wallace Huffman provided help in preparing this section.

farmers believe, correctly, that they knew a great deal about "ecology" before it was "discovered" by the general public in the 1960's. Historically, much farm conservation has been based on voluntary activity stimulated by government incentives. The imposition of external regulation was destined to be viewed with disfavor.

The Environmental Protection Agency (EPA) has imposed restraints on the use of pesticides in U.S. agriculture. Some argue that these regulations threaten the efficiency of U.S. agriculture. Yet EPA estimates that the cost of these constraints amounts to only about $.54 per capita annually (Aspelin). Most of these costs will be passed on to the consumer, although some will be borne by producers because of consumer response to higher food prices. Even though there is substantial room for controversy, there are also some facts which can be agreed to. Soil loss is serious in some of the marginal areas where land has been brought into farming. Not only do these losses raise questions as to whether agricultural productivity can be sustained in such areas, but they impose costs elsewhere in society because of siltation and other detrimental effects. Pesticides can have toxic effects. Furthermore, some insect and weed species have developed a genetic immunity to pesticides.

Farmers can expect environmental regulation to continue. Nevertheless, there is substantial room for improvement in the way environmental regulations are applied in farming. It is hoped that EPA will balance the benefits against the costs of future regulations. If this happens, uniform standards throughout agriculture will not be rigidly enforced. EPA is showing greater concern about understanding the benefits and costs of certain regulations, and it can be expected that benefits will increasingly be matched against their costs.

Environmental regulation adds to the cost of food and fiber production. If the benefit of a regulation exceeds its cost, most economists would argue that it is appropriate that the consumers of food and fiber products pay the increased production cost. If, however, social benefits do not exceed social costs, the consumers of food and fiber products are subsidizing those who benefit from improved environmental quality.

LAND USE CONTROL

Land use control is being employed increasingly to provide environmental regulation, to control economic growth, and for other purposes. Urban and rural land use are so closely related that agricultural land is inevitably affected. The net result of these many controls is to affect property rights in real property in a fundamental way. Private rights in real property are being modified and are becoming public rights.

There is need for a substantial educational effort on this problem. Citizen groups need to discuss the objectives of land use control and whether other means can be utilized to accomplish these objectives. The cumulative effects of land use control measures need to be pondered as well as the incremental effects.

Agricultural use of land needs to be considered when rural and urban zoning occurs. Yet as a general rule no good empirical basis exists for preventing the conversion of agricultural land to non–agricultural uses. There are, of course, areas where urban development can occur at the same or lower cost on other than prime agricultural land. When this is the case, the better agricultural land should be used for agriculture.

The United States is currently running a substantial trade deficit. Under these circumstances, investment in U.S. assets will be attractive to foreign investors who have U.S. dollars. It has been argued that investment by foreign interests in U.S. agricultural land should be prohibited. There is little evidence that increases in U.S. agricultural land prices have been stimulated to any significant degree by foreign demand. If one area of investment such as land is prohibited, the demand for other areas of investment such as financial institutions or hotels will be increased. Under these circumstances there seems to be little justification for special legislation to prohibit foreign investment in agricultural land. Nevertheless, the current action of the Congress and USDA to obtain better information on what is occurring in this area is applauded.

TECHNICAL CHANGE AND INVESTMENT IN RESEARCH

U.S. agriculture has often been used as an example of rapid technical change stimulated by publicly supported research. Concern has recently been expressed, however, on two counts. First there is the belief by some that the rate of increase in agricultural productivity has slowed. Second, there are those who argue that the agricultural research establishment has not always emphasized the most desirable activities and, as a result, is not having the impact it had in an earlier period.

Scholars who have studied productivity change for U.S. agriculture do not agree on productivity trends. Weather, changes in the quality of land that is used at different times, and technology all have to be taken into account, as well as farmer motivation. The issue is an important one. Not only will the price of food and fiber be affected but the return going to the different factors of production in agriculture will be influenced by changes in productivity. The ability to acquire information about new farming opportunities and to manage new technology in imaginative ways has been the source of financial reward in farming in recent years. If production should become more standardized, returns would be shifted toward other factors of production, such as the control of land and natural resources. Yet public policy relative to publicly supported research can have a great deal to do with the amount and the effect of agricultural research.

The major data series on productivity of U.S. agriculture is published annually by the USDA in *Changes in Farm Production and Efficiency* (1977, November). The index is published for the United States and for 10 production regions. Over the period 1940 to 1970 the trend in the productivity index was upward at an annual rate of 1.9 percent. The trend in productivity seemed to level off in the 1960's and productivity was relatively unchanged from 1968 to 1970. The index rose 8 percent between 1970 and 1971, remained essentially unchanged for 1971, 1972, and 1973, followed by a 6 percent decline in 1974 and a recovery of 10 percent in 1975. The productivity index was unchanged in 1976.

Investigation of expenditures on agricultural research and the effect of this research on agricultural productivity has provided considerable knowledge about the productivity of research. Evensen, and Huffman and Miranowski have shown that extension activity, applied research, graduate education, and basic research are highly complementary. Basic research probably has been neglected in recent years, but it would be a mistake if basic research were to be stimulated in the absence of the opportunity for application. Size of research undertaking is less important than the quality of the research activity. The opportunities for increasing agricultural research expenditures are the greatest in agricultural states with considerable state revenue. The more agriculturally diversified states have a greater tendency to support research than do the more specialized states.

Considerable concern has been expressed recently that agricultural land is losing productivity as a result of erosion and intensive farming practices. The problem is a complex one because the effects of weather, changing technology, and the quality of land as it moves in and out of agricultural production must all be taken into account. Despite intensive study of this problem, definitive answers are not available at this time.

Crosson and Brubaker have been unable to explain recent yield shortfalls by adjusting for weather, land quality, and technology. Carlson has called attention, however, to the fact that much new technology may be adopted for the purpose of stabilizing rather than increasing yields. He has shown that cotton, tobacco and peanut yields have become more stable in the last decade. Under these circumstances even though a yield index may not increase or perhaps even decline, yield variability has stabilized and both farmers and consumers may be better off.

It is our belief that U.S. agriculture is capable of achieving and sustaining increased agricultural production. However, this will require increased public support for research and education, including basic research. It also will require that attention be paid to the development of new means of controlling pests as resistant strains of insects and weeds develop, and to ways of conserving soil in environmentally fragile areas.

Solutions

ON THE NATURE OF A SOLUTION

After a social problem has been stated and its causes analyzed the reader has every right to expect some solutions to be advanced. But what is a solution? Does a solution exist if one problem is solved even though another, possibly worse, problem is created? Can it be said that a problem is solved if one group is made better off at the expense of another group in society? How does one decide if solutions should be sought through individual actions or by group (possibly governmental) response?

In the solutions advanced in this section, information has been presented to permit the reader to tell what position the Task Force has taken on such questions. In each case we have tried to state the general problem area, the nature of the problem, the seriousness of the problem and the proposed remedy. We hope this will make it easier for the reader to decide whether he or she agrees or disagrees.

Generally the solutions advanced recognize the relation between the social environment (established by government) and individual response. Thus many of our recommendations are designed to provide an incentive that will encourage individual responses that will work for the common good. Seriousness of the problems is described as unknown, moderate, serious and very serious. The reader is encouraged to read the text for more information concerning each of the problem areas.

PROBLEM #1–CHRONIC INFLATION

Chronic inflation tends to result in rapid increases in costs incurred by farmers without necessarily resulting in corresponding increases in prices received and is indeed a serious problem for American agriculture. Inflation has rewarded the ownership of land relative to the ownership of other resources used in farming. It also rewards debtors rather than creditors, thus encouraging increasing financial leverage which leads to higher financial risks, a major problem for many farmers.

The U.S. government should show greater fiscal restraint and work to remove constraints on productivity throughout the economy, with special attention given to the effects of regulations on agriculture. Easier credit, emergency credit, or more credit often are suggested to reduce financial stress for farmers. The financial stress caused by farmer response to easy credit, during periods of chronic inflation, is likely to become worse, rather than better as a result of such remedies. The remedy to chronic inflation lies outside agriculture rather than within.

PROBLEM #2–PRICE FORMATION IN U.S. AGRICULTURE

Not all markets affecting U.S. agriculture are equally perfect, even though long–run forces tend to eliminate short–run distortions. This results in hardships being suffered by many farmers who are too small to influence markets for those commodities they produce.

A general policy should be developed to make all markets more responsive rather than constraining markets further. The Task Force recommends the development of new information for input markets, such as forward contracts, land and machinery leases, tailored weather information, and pest infestation information. We also recommend the development and distribution of information permitting better choices to be made by consumers. Additional research is needed to bring about a greater understanding of food price determination and the risks associated with different marketing strategies, such as hedging and forward contracts.

PROBLEM #3–FINANCIAL RESOURCES AND SPECIAL CREDIT PROGRAMS

Special credit programs instituted by the federal government may tend to impair the operation of established credit channels. The seriousness of this problem is unknown presently since we do not know how special credit programs affect established credit institutions. The Task Force recommends that the situation be monitored in the future to determine the effects of special credit programs on existing agricultural lenders.

PROBLEM #4–TAX POLICY

Income tax policies in this country tend to dictate resource allocation in agriculture. As a result resource allocation may be adversely affected by tax policies. The problem is serious for agriculture. Solutions to this problem should be based on careful study beyond the scope of this report. However, it should be pointed out that preferential taxation for agriculture is a double edged sword. Preferential taxation tends to attract resources into agriculture and these resources compete with those already committed to the industry.

PROBLEM #5–EDUCATION FOR THE FARM FAMILY

Public education serves U.S. agriculture in many ways. It provides an opportunity for farm people to learn employable, nonfarm skills, which will enable them to leave agriculture if they must. These same skills may be used to supplement farm income. The educational system, including extension education, also provides technical information and management training for those who remain on the farm.

Generally the public education system has served U.S. agriculture well and the problem is only of moderate seriousness. Nevertheless, sight should not be lost of the special educational needs of rural residents. Extension programs should give special attention to the educational needs of farm managers with an emphasis on the information needs of modern farming and small–scale farmers. The Task Force also recommends that the education system continue to be supported by local investment and to be controlled largely at the local level.

PROBLEM #6–FARM LABOR

There are several problems related to agricultural labor; some are managerial and some are social. These problems are of moderate seriousness.

While questions may be raised about the wisdom of some general labor policies, it is not wise to attempt to isolate labor relations in agriculture. Agriculture has been a residual claimant for labor in the past and has provided an opportunity for many who could not otherwise work for wages. This opportunity will be diminished with the imposition of a minimum wage for agriculture. The social costs from a minimum wage in agriculture will be a burden to all taxpayers.

PROBLEM #7–SMALL FARMS

The trend toward bigness has not by–passed agriculture because farms are continuing to grow. There is considerable concern over this trend. The trend tends to lessen the opportunities for the young or beginning farmer. The problem is of moderate seriousness.

It is *not* recommended that any legal constraints be placed on size of farm, but it is appropriate that the special needs of small–scale and beginning farmers be recognized by public programs. Information on the rental markets for land and machinery, as well as opportunities for employment off the farm are examples of informational needs of small–scale farmers. Because small–scale farmers may be at a relative disadvantage in dealing with the bureaucracy, special programs that would assist them in coping with such problems are appropriate.

All farm programs and policies should be reviewed to determine if they are biased in favor of large–scale farmers. If such bias exists, it should be removed. The economies of size are such that constant costs prevail over a wide range of output; the advantage of large relative to small farms lies more in finance and marketing rather than production. There is little social justification for subsidy or favoritism based on size alone.

PROBLEM #8–THE SPECIAL PROBLEMS OF LAND

Farmland prices have increased beyond the level that can be sustained by the contribution of land to farm income. This is a very serious problem for those drawn into a highly leveraged financial position in order to own land.

Record farm income in the early part of this decade, continued inflation which makes the holding of debt desirable, the availability of credit, and increased nonfarm use of land have all contributed to the increase in land prices. Given the reasons for the increase in land prices, it is *not* recommended that there be any intervention in the operation of the market for land. Stabilizing farm income and controlling inflation would undoubtedly slow the rise in land prices. Operation of the credit markets to permit the refinancing of land so that the higher land prices can be transferred to other uses, is noted with approval.

PROBLEM #9–WATER RIGHTS AND AGRICULTURE

Water is being transferred out of agriculture in certain regions even though irrigation is being increased in other areas. This is a very serious problem in some communities, but it does not exist for much of American agriculture.

It is *not* recommended that water be permanently fixed in agricultural uses by political means. Water rights should be defined in such a way as to permit a market for water rights to develop or work more efficiently where such markets already exist. These markets would provide both security and flexibility and would permit farmers to be compensated for the loss of an asset if water is transferred out of agriculture. It would also permit communities to bid against nonagricultural water users if the community wishes to retain irrigated agriculture.

PROBLEM #10–THE 160 ACRE LIMITATION

The 160 acre limitation was originally established in the Reclamation Act of 1902 to provide greater opportunity in agriculture. It has not been enforced historically although recent announcements suggest that this will change. If the limitation were strictly enforced, there would be substantial impacts in many irrigated areas of the West.

Any restriction on farm size is certain to reduce efficiency and unlikely to create additional farming opportunities. The 160 acre limitation should be lifted. If there is a public desire to encourage small farms on federally supported irrigation projects, this probably can be accomplished more efficiently by water pricing. For example, water subsidies could be removed for larger farms using such water.

PROBLEM #11–ENVIRONMENTAL REGULATION OF FARMING

Many farmers believe they are being harassed and made inefficient by environmental regulations. Modern farming practices result in some negative environmental effects off the farm. This is a serious problem because neither the means of control nor the ultimate consequences of the environmental effects are well understood.

Farmers cannot escape environmental regulations. The benefits of such regulations should be weighed against their costs. The Agricultural Extension Service should accept the responsibility for bringing about a greater understanding of agriculture by those who impose environmental regulations, as well as assisting farmers to understand the environmental damage associated with various farming practices. Alternative ways of reducing or eliminating such damages should be investigated.

PROBLEM #12–LAND USE CONTROL

Land use is being subjected to greater control by local, state and national governments. Some of this control is exemplified by land use legislation in states such as Vermont, Hawaii, California and Oregon. But some restrictions come packaged in different ways, such as strip–mining legislation and environmental regulation. Land use control is a crude device for many purposes, but it is being used increasingly. This is an important and serious problem.

There is a need for intensive educational programs on land use. A consensus needs to be reached on the goals and purposes of land use control and inconsistent goals and purposes need to be identified. In addition, alternative means of achieving different objectives of land use control need to be identified and evaluated.

PROBLEM #13–SUSTAINING AGRICULTURAL PRODUCTIVITY

It is not clear whether agricultural productivity is declining or not. Even so, the problem is potentially serious.

Increased agricultural research is recommended. Such research should totally encompass commercial agriculture, including managerial and marketing facets, as well as the less traditional areas, such as environmental impacts and human nutrition. The productivity of such research will be enhanced if it encompasses both basic as well as applied research.

PROBLEM #14–CONTROLLING COSTS OF PRODUCTION

Prices received by farmers have failed to keep pace with prices paid by farmers thus putting pressure on net farm income. This has become very serious for many farmers.

Some farmers can obtain relief by improving their internal management, but for others help can come only from outside agriculture. Government farm programs may provide assistance for some farmers but others may find it necessary to supplement farm income with income from nonfarm sources or leave the farm entirely.

References

Aspelin, A. L. 1978. "Briefing on Economic Impact Analysis as an Input to Risk/Benefit Decision Making on RPAR Pesticides ." EPA–Office of Pesticide Programs, March.

Baker, C. 1978. Personal communication with the author. Department of Agricultural Economics, University of Illinois.

Baum, S., R. E. Friend and R. R. Stansberry. 1963. "The Hired Farm Working Force of 1961." USDA–ERS–ESAD, Agr. Econ. Rep. 36.

Board of Governors, Federal Reserve System, 1978. *Federal Reserve Bulletin.* Various issues.

Bureau of Economics, Inc. 1978. *The Handbook of Basic Economic Statistics.* Washington: Gov't. Stat. Bur. 32: 101–02.

Carlson, G. A. "The Role of Pesticides in Stabilizing Agricultural Production." in *Pesticides: Their Contemporary Roles in Agriculture, Energy, Wealth and the Environment.* Edited by J. Sheets and D. Pimentel. Clifton, N.J.: Humana Press, in press.

Clifton, I. D. and W. D. Crowley, Jr. 1973. *Farm Real Estate Historical Series Data: 1850–1970.* USDA–ERS, Agr. Econ. Rep. 520.

Cowhig, J. D. 1961. "Education, Skill Level and Earnings of the Hired Farm Working Force of 1961." USDA–ERS–ESAD, Agr. Econ. Rep. 266.

Crosson, P. and S. Brubaker. 1978. "Resource and Environmental Issues of Agriculture in the United States: A Report on Research in Progress." Resources for the Future, Washington, D.C., mimeo.

Evenson, R. E. 1978. "A Century of Agricultural Research and Productivity Changes in U.S. Agriculture: An Historical Decomposition Analysis." Paper presented at a Symposium on Agricultural Research and Extension Evaluation, Moscow, Idaho.

Goldsmith, R. W. 1956. *A Study of Savings in the U.S.* Princeton: Princeton University Press.

Huffman, W. E. 1977. "Interaction Between Farm and Non-farm Labor Markets." *Amer. J. Agr. Econ.* 59: 1054–61.

Huffman, W. E. and J. A. Miranowski. 1978. "An Economic Analysis of State Expenditures on Experiment Station Research." Iowa State University, Department of Economics, mimeo.

Martin, P. L., and R. Rochin. 1977. "Emerging Issues of Agricultural Labor Relations." *Amer. J. Agr. Econ.* 59: 1045–53.

McElroy, R. C. 1973. "The Hired Farm Working Force of 1972." USDA–ERS, Agr. Econ. Rep. 239.

Melichar, E. March 1978. "The Relationship Between Farm Income and Asset Values, 1950–1977." Paper presented at a Seminar on Capital, Financial and Credit Needs, Spring Hill Center, University of Minnesota.

Melichar, E. 1978. "Rural Banking and Farm Credit Conditions: Agricultural Finance Commentary." Federal Reserve System, Washington, D.C., mimeo.

Miller, T. A., and R. H. Millar. 1977. "A Stochastic Model of Disaster Payments Under the 1973 Farm Credit Act." *Agr. Econ. Res.* 29: 63–9.

Penson, J. B., Jr. 1977. "External Finance: A Necessary Component in Growth Projections for Southern Agriculture." *S. J. Agr. Econ.* 9: 25–34.

Reilly, F. K. *et al.* 1975. *Real Estate As An Inflation Hedge.* University of Illinois, College of Commerce and Business Administration, Faculty Workshop Paper.

Reiss, F. J. 1978. *Landlord and Tenant Shares: 1977.* University of Illinois, Agr. Econ. Res. Rep. 157.

Schultz, T. W. 1960. "Land in Economic Growth." in *Modern Land Policy.* Edited by H. G. Halcrow *et al.* Urbana: University of Illinois Press.

Smith, L. W. and G. Rowe. 1978. *The Hired Farm Working Force of 1976.* USDA–ESCS, Agr. Econ. Rep. 405.

Tyner, W. E. 1978. "Agriculture as a Source of Fluid Energy: Gasahol *et al.*" Paper presented at the Amer. Agr. Econ. Assoc. meetings, Blacksburg, Virginia.

U.S. Congress, House of Representatives. 1978. *Agricultural Credit Act of 1978.* House Bill 11504, 95th Cong., 2nd. sess.

U.S. Congress, Senate. 1971. *Farm Credit Act of 1971.* PL 92–181, Senate Bill 1438, 92nd Cong., 1st. sess.

U.S. Department of Agriculture. 1977. *Agricultural Statistics, 1977.* Washington: U.S. Gov't. Printing Office.

U.S. Department of Agriculture. October 1977. *Balance Sheet of the Farming Sector, 1977.* ERS, Agr. Info. Bul. 411. October and earlier issues.

U. S. Department of Agriculture. November 1977. *Changes in Farm Production and Efficiency, 1977.* ERS, Stat. Bul. 581.

U. S. Department of Agriculture. July 1977. *Farm Real Estate Market Developments.* ERS, CD–82.

U. S. Department of Agriculture. May 1978. *Farm Credit Survey, March 1978.* ESCS–17.

U. S. Department of Agriculture. July 1978. *Farm Income Statistics.* ESCS, Stat. Bul. 609.

U. S. Department of Agriculture. August 1978. *Farm Labor.* ESCS–CRB, La 1.

U. S. Department of Agriculture. July 1978. *Farm Real Estate Market Developments.* ERS, CD–83.

U. S. Department of Commerce. 1977. *Census of Agriculture, 1974.* Bur. of the Census, Washington: U.S. Government Printing Office.

U. S. Department of Commerce. 1978. *Business Statistics, 1977.* BEA, 21st Biennial Edition.

Woods, W. F. 1978. "Access to Capital in Agriculture: The Federal Tax Issue." Paper presented at a Seminar on Agricultural Marketing and Policy, University of Missouri.

List of Task Force Members

RESOURCE ALLOCATION AND PRODUCTION COSTS

Emery N. Castle (Chairman)
President
Resources for the Future
Washington, D.C.

C. B. Baker
Department of Agricultural
 Economics
University of Illinois
Urbana, Illinois

Paul Brower
Agricultural Division
Olin Corporation
Little Rock, Arkansas

Gerald Carlson
Department of Economics and
 Business
North Carolina State University
Raleigh, North Carolina

L. S. Fife
International Harvester
Chicago, Illinois

Michael Fitch
Wells Fargo Bank
San Francisco, California

Forrest Goetsch
Doane's Agricultural Services
St. Louis, Missouri

Lawerance Gray
L.V. Gray Farms
Nampa, Idaho

Wallace Huffman
Department of Economics
Iowa State University
Ames, Iowa

Emanuel Melichar
Federal Reserve Board
Washington, D.C.

Bob Meyer
Bob Meyer Farms
Brawley, California

Ron Michieli
National Cattlemen's Association
Washington, D.C.

Bruce H. Millien
Department of Labor
Washington, D.C.

Wally Rustad
National Rural Electric
 Cooperative Association
Washington, D.C.

Herman Schmitz
Farmer
Williston, North Dakota

Nick Theos
Public Lands Council
(Past President)
Meeker, Colorado

Fred Woods
Science and Education
 Administration–Extension
U.S. Dept. of Agriculture
Washington, D.C.

DISCUSSION

The formal discussants were: Gene Swackhamer, President, Farm Credit Banks of Baltimore; John Kautz, farmer and former President, Tri–Valley Growers, California; Luther T. Wallace, University of California; and Arnold Aspelin, U.S. Environmental Protection Agency. The main points made by the discussants were as follows.

Swackhamer said that while the Task Force partially addressed the impacts of inflation, more could have been said on the effects of inflation on financing agriculture, particularly the impact on the cost and productivity of money. He also emphasized the effects of inflation on the demand for land, particularly by nonfarm people, as very important. He forecast that considerations of social costs and social benefits, as opposed to private costs and benefits, would continue to increase in importance as an issue in resource and production policy. Swackhamer questioned the long–run versus short–run distinction that was emphasized in the report. He emphasized the increasingly bimodal distribution of types of farms—small, noncommercial farms whose families rely on off–farm income as opposed to large commercial farms which may not. This and other elements of heterogeneity create considerable complications for policy determination and for conferences such as this one, because different people come with such different perspectives and see different things as being problems.

Kautz agreed with the Task Force that the primary problem faced by farmers today is inflation, and said that the only way for producers to survive is to become more productive and to substitute capital for other inputs wherever possible. Two problems for California agriculture, not fully considered by the Task Force, are tax–loss farmers and farm labor. Tax–loss farmers tend to influence the supply of commodities in response to tax laws rather than prices. Kautz proposed regulation that would prevent outsiders from coming into agriculture solely to benefit from tax laws. The main farm labor problem in California is the threat posed by harvest–time strikes. Binding arbitration was suggested as a means of settling strikes. Kautz disagreed with the panel's recommendation on the subject of land use planning and instead recommended tax incentives to encourage development of cities in nonagricultural areas.

Wallace addressed realities that agriculture faces, such as (1) farmers deal in three markets (inputs, product and land) not just one, and any could make or break the farm business, (2) production of raw materials is only the first step in the food chain, the others being input suppliers, food processors, distributors and retailers, (3) the U.S. Treasury is the key to imports and exports yet few farmers know about it, (4) the U.S. State Department, not the USDA, controls food aid for distribution abroad, (5) farmers need to consider coalitions in obtaining what they want from legislators; they need issue–by–issue help and therefore must come to grips with what they are willing to trade off in order to get the necessary votes, and (6) once and for all solutions to farm problems do not exist; the same type of problems persists—only the answers change. In the face of these realities farmers need to determine what they want and what they are willing to give up to get it in the political bargaining process.

Aspelin talked about how farmers can best work with regulatory agencies such as EPA in the establishment of regulations. Farmers could help in establishing regulations by (1) ensuring that the agency has a clear and acceptable mandate, (2) making sure that the agency has qualified teams of people with backgrounds in agriculture and the sciences, (3) demanding that agency decisions be open and candid and involve the public, and (4) determining whether the agencies have state level organizations that can be helpful in developing regulations as well as enforcing them.

Comments and Questions From the Floor

Several comments expressed concern about foreign investment in U.S. farmland. Some Task Force members responded that land price increases have been mainly attributable to internal U.S. demand rather than from foreign investors entering the land market. It was suggested that tax considerations favoring foreign investors be abolished. A comment was made from the floor that the Missouri legislature recently passed a bill prohibiting foreign ownership of more than 5 acres, and limiting the number of years that a foreign investor can own Missouri land. Similar legislation is in effect or being considered in other states.

The problem of the 160 acre limitation being imposed on farmers receiving water from federally–funded irrigation projects was raised. A questioner wished to know the panel's reaction to a graduated water pricing plan, in lieu of acreage limitations. The response was that a strict acreage limitation was unworkable, and that a change in the water pricing system that graduated the price according to the number of acres owned would probably be better than an acreage restriction.

On the question of the impacts of higher energy costs on agriculture and what might be done about it, the response was that higher energy costs are inevitable, and that farmers individually and agriculture as a whole would in the end simply have to adjust to the situation.

The following suggestion for changing the tax system was presented from the floor and debated by the panel members: allow farmers to place periodic profits in tax–free accounts to be drawn on in years of low income. It was pointed out that difficulties would arise in identifying farmers who were really qualified, and that such a plan could be another incentive for nonagricultural interests to invest in agriculture. Moreover, it was suggested that creditors could indirectly aid farmers in smoothing out their incomes by reducing credit for expansion during periods of high prices and expanding credit during periods of low prices.

An American Agriculture Movement (AAM) member saw problems arising from creditors' discretionary power. He said that several lending institutions in his area have made it more difficult for AAM members to get credit. In several cases, he said, farmers had been approved for credit but when they became active in AAM they were reclassified as not credit–worthy.

The panel members were asked whether or not a parity pricing system for grains would improve relations between grain producers and cattle feeders. In response it was indicated that this pricing system might indeed help; but, that such a pricing system has almost no chance of being approved by Congress because it would increase food costs and generally be inflationary.

A final comment was made on the subject of stocks of agricultural commodities. It was said that when private industry has an increase in inventories it is called a reserve, while a similar situation for agriculture is called a surplus. New terminology was proposed, calling a 1–year supply a normal carryover, a 2–year supply an inventory, and any amount over a 2–year supply a reserve.

LUTHER TWEETEN*

CHAPTER 2

Farm Commodity Prices and Income

HALF–truths and myths abound in discussion of the economics of
agriculture. This is not a new phenomenon, but some relatively new
myths and half–truths are circulating today. Examples are that farming
efficiency should be measured by output per unit of nonrenewable
energy, that farming should be energy self–sustaining, that small farms
are more efficient than large farms, that the marketing system is highly
inefficient and exploits farmers and consumers, that benefits of public
research and extension accrue to large farms and not to consumers, that
economic vitality of the nation requires pricing of raw materials at 100
percent of "parity," that some conspiracy forces farmers to over–invest
in machinery and nonrenewable energy inputs, that organic farming is
more efficient than conventional farming, that the commercial farming
industry receives low rates of return on resources, that nations and
regions should be self–sufficient in food production, that food produced by conventional farming systems is unwholesome and that substitution of capital for labor on farms is undesirable. The list could go on
but seems sufficient to highlight the point: an acute need exists for
factual information on the economic realities of food and agriculture.

The objective of this report is to provide basic information needed
to improve equity and efficiency in farm commodity policy. As background, the report addresses some, but not all, of the currently popular assertions. The first section focuses on the economic structure of
agriculture and the economy as it relates to farm price and income
problems and policy; the second section examines current legislation
and suggests changes consistent with greater economic efficiency and
equity. Perceptions of the Task Force regarding price and income

*Shortcomings of the report are solely the responsibility of the author. A list of
Task Force members and their affiliations follows the report.

policy are then reviewed. A concluding section summarizes highlights of the report.

The Setting: Economic Structure and Problems of the Farming Industry

SYMPTOMS OF FARM PROBLEMS

Economic ills, like human ailments, have symptoms, causes and cures. Before turning to possible policy cures, it is important to review briefly symptoms and causes of economic ills of the farming industry. Symptoms include levels of income and wealth and rates of return to resources in farming.

Balance Sheet Data. Assets of the farming sector increased more than 12–fold from 1940 to 1977 when they totaled $671 billion (Table 1).[1] But growth in farm assets in real terms was modest, less than 1 percent per year, from 1940 to 1977. The small increase in real capital of the farming industry belies large changes taking place in the farm firm. A full–time family farm, providing labor–management returns equal to national median family income, now entails assets of approximately $1 million and sales of $100,000 (see U.S. Department of Agriculture, forthcoming).

Liabilities increased 10–fold, during this same period, reducing the debt–asset ratio from 18.9 percent in 1940 to 15.2 percent in 1977. U.S. nonfinancial corporations' assets increased 17–fold during the same period and their debt–asset ratio was 61 percent in 1977 (Council of Economic Advisers, p. 358). The reported debt–asset ratio of corporations is overstated relative to the farming sector, because corporate assets are reported at "book value" below current prices whereas farming sector assets are valued at current prices. The debt–asset ratio of U.S. nonfinancial corporations was 31 percent in 1977 based on a rather crude adjustment of corporate assets to current value using the Wholesale Price Index. Hence, the financial health of the farming sector appears favorable both in absolute terms and in relation to that of other industries. Proprietors' equities of $569 billion in 1977 aver-

[1]See Evans *et al.* for the balance sheet by economic sales class of farms. See U.S. Department of Agriculture (forthcoming) for comparisons of the concentration of wealth versus income by economic class of farms.

TABLE 1.

Balance Sheet of the Farming Sector, January 1 in Selected Years

Item	1940	1950	1960	1970	1975	1976	1977
				(billion dollars)			
Physical assets:							
Real estate	33.6	77.6	137.2	215.9	378.7	429.1	497.1
Non-real estate:							
Livestock and poultry	5.1	12.9	15.2	23.5	24.6	29.5	29.1
Machinery and motor vehicles	3.0	12.2	22.7	32.3	55.7	65.0	72.3
Crops stored on and off farms	2.7	7.6	7.7	10.9	23.3	21.3	21.9
Household equipment and furnishings	4.2	8.6	9.6	9.7	15.3	16.2	17.4
Financial assets:							
Deposits and currency	3.2	9.1	9.2	11.9	15.1	15.6	15.9
U.S. savings bonds	.2	4.7	4.7	3.7	4.3	4.4	4.4
Investments in cooperatives	.8	2.0	4.2	7.2	10.5	11.7	12.8
Total	53.0	134.7	210.6	315.2	527.5	592.8	670.9
Liabilities:							
Real estate debt	6.6	5.6	12.1	29.2	46.3	51.1	56.4
Non-real estate debt to:							
CCC	.4	1.7	1.2	2.7	.3	.3	1.0
Other reporting institutions	1.5	2.8	6.7	15.8	29.2	33.0	37.8
Nonreporting creditors	1.5	2.3	4.9	5.3	6.0	6.3	6.9
Total liabilities	10.0	12.5	24.8	53.0	81.8	90.8	102.1
Proprietors' equities	42.9	122.3	185.8	252.1	445.6	502.0	568.8
Total	53.0	134.7	210.6	315.2	527.5	592.8	670.9
				(percent)			
Debt to asset ratio	18.8	9.2	11.8	16.8	15.5	15.3	15.2

SOURCE: Evans *et al.* (p. 2). See source for footnotes.

aged about $210,000 per farm. These data veil the facts that many large farms have substantially greater wealth than the average, that many family size farms with high debt face severe cash flow problems, and that many small farmers have inadequate resources.

The share of farm receipts required to cover the carrying cost of farm real estate (estimated at 4 percent of the current asset value) increased from 14 percent in 1960 and 15 percent in 1970 to 19 percent in 1977. This rising factor share may represent growing scarcity of land, capitalization of government commodity program benefits into land prices and speculative landholding. Whatever the source, the 1970–1977 trend in land prices relative to receipts cannot continue indefinitely or, ultimately, all receipts in agriculture would be used to pay land costs.

Income. Income and wealth data by economic sales class of farms for 1970 and 1977 in Table 2 provide further insight into the economic position of farm operators and their families. The parity ratio, or ratio of prices received to prices paid by farmers adjusted to include direct payments from government, averaged 77 percent of the 1910–1914 average in 1970 and only 67 percent in 1977. The table shows that:

(1) Farm output as measured by receipts is heavily concentrated on large farms. In 1977, only 6 percent of all farms accounted for 52.6 percent of output; at the other extreme 46.5 percent of all farms accounted for only 5.3 percent of output. Even after correcting for product price inflation, concentration of production on large farms is increasing.

(2) Farmers receive the majority of their net income, 61 percent in 1977, from off–farm sources. That proportion is growing—off–farm income accounted for 68 percent of the growth in total net income of farmers between 1970 and 1977. This finding highlights the importance of overall rural job development to the economic well–being of farmers.

(3) Capital gains, an average of $8,265 per farm in 1977, contribute substantially to the economic position of farm people. The 8.8 percent rate of increase in land prices in 1977 was reasonably typical of annual gains since 1960. Most farm capital gains are from real estate and most accrue to farm operators. Capital gains are not realized until assets are sold, hence are a less accessible source of economic livelihood than

TABLE 2.
Farm Numbers, Receipts, Income and Capital Gains by Economic Class, 1970 and 1977, United States

Item		IA $100,000 and over	IB $40,000 to 99,999	II $20,000 to 39,999	III $10,000 to 19,999	IV $5,000 to 9,999	V $2,500 to 4,999	VI Less than $2,500	All Farms
					Economic class, by farm sales				
No. of farms (1,000)	1970	57	178	326	390	402	423	1,173	2,949
	1977	162	348	321	311	302	304	958	2,706
(Percent of all farms)	1970	(1.9)	(6.1)	(11.1)	(13.2)	(13.6)	(14.3)	(39.8)	(100.0)
	1977	(6.0)	(12.9)	(11.9)	(11.5)	(11.2)	(11.2)	(35.3)	(100.0)
					(dollars per farm)				
Cash receipts from farming[a]	1970	320,877	68,179	32,813	17,341	8,854	4,367	1,285	18,582
	1977	322,371	73,186	34,545	17,392	8,931	4,443	1,264	36,752
(Percent of all receipts)	1970	(33.4)	(22.1)	(19.5)	(12.3)	(6.5)	(3.4)	(2.8)	(100.0)
	1977	(52.6)	(25.6)	(11.1)	(5.4)	(2.7)	(1.4)	(1.2)	(100.0)
Realized net farm income	1970	40,543	17,319	10,405	5,856	3,235	1,696	902	4,797
	1977	38,310	18,502	9,993	4,987	2,696	1,508	1,518	7,439
Off-farm income	1970	7,614	3,949	3,359	4,190	5,450	6,184	7,437	5,899
	1977	9,636	6,011	6,956	9,466	12,179	14,559	15,077	11,596
Total net income[b]	1970	48,157	21,268	13,764	10,046	8,685	7,880	8,339	10,696
	1977	47,946	24,513	16,949	14,453	14,875	16,067	16,595	19,035

TABLE 2. Continued

Farm operators' capital gains[c]	1970	19,458	7,775	4,784	3,300	2,358	1,846	1,183	2,866
	1977	54,154	19,655	12,139	8,667	6,429	5,084	3,280	8,265
Total net income plus capital gains	1970	67,615	29,043	18,548	13,346	11,043	9,726	9,522	13,562
	1977	102,100	44,168	29,088	23,120	21,304	21,151	19,875	27,300

SOURCE: U.S. Department of Agriculture (1978 July).

[a]Includes "other income" from machine hire, custom work and recreation; also includes direct government payments.

[b]Includes realized net farm income and off-farm income plus the value of food grown and consumed on farm, rent on farm dwelling and government payments.

[c]Estimates for 1970 from Evans et al. Capital gains for 1977 based on 1976 data from Evans et al. adjusted by author to 8.8 percent gain in farm real estate price per acre in 1977. Capital gains are accrued, not realized.

current income. But capital gains are taxed at lower rates than ordinary income, provide security for obtaining credit and assist in building a retirement fund.

(4) Each economic class of farm receives more than adequate net income plus capital gains to remove it from a category of need for federal assistance on welfare grounds. Net income from farm sources alone is very low on farms with sales under $10,000 per year, but these farms receive several times as much income from off–farm as from farm sources. Many of their operators could be classified more realistically as doctors, mechanics, machinists, or in other occupations from which they make most of their living.

Per capita disposable income of farm people was 32.8 percent of the corresponding figure for nonfarm people in 1934 (U.S. Department of Agriculture 1978, July). Since then, progress in reducing the disparity in income has been substantial though erratic. Farm income as a percentage of nonfarm income reached a peak of 110.2 in 1973, declining to 81.8 in 1977. If differences in living costs and capital gains between sectors are considered, it seems safe to conclude that per capita income plus capital gains of *commercial* farms (class II and larger) are at least as high on the average as those of the nonfarm population.

Although each economic class of farms in Table 2 received income well above the poverty threshold *on the average*, income varies greatly among farms within classes. Analysis of federal income tax returns indicates that many adequate–sized farms have low or negative net income even in years when average farm income is considerable (Reinsel). Sixteen percent of all farm families were in poverty in 1975, down from 51 percent in 1960 (Edwards and Coffman). The nonfarm family poverty incidence fell from 22 percent in 1960 to 12 percent in 1975. Thus the incidence of farm poverty dropped more sharply but was still higher than the incidence of nonfarm poverty in 1975. Most families on small farms are not poor but most of the farm poor, particularly the chronically poor, are on small farms. The incidence of farm poverty is especially high in the South and among minorities.

Rates of Return on Farm Resources. Net farm income and wealth gains on farm assets are a return to operator–family labor and to equity capital. Because equity capital investment per worker in farming is high, commercial farmers could be receiving a low rate of return on owned resources even with high income and wealth gains. Low rates of return not only would suggest economic inefficiency but also could justify farmers' complaints that they are unfairly rewarded for their efforts.

Data in Table 3 show that total rates of return on farming resources have not been low for some time. From 1960 to 1976, current earnings averaged 4.0 percent of farm equity capital. Adding capital gains averaging 8.3 percent of equity for the same period brings overall returns to 12.3 percent. Problems arise in computing returns to equity because net income (defined as gross income less production expenses) is a return to equity capital and operator–family labor. This labor is imputed a return equal to the hired farm labor force wage rate, which underestimates its opportunity cost (value in other employment). However, a management opportunity cost of 5 percent of receipts is added to wages, bringing the total labor–management charge to a more reasonable figure. If equity capital is charged an opportunity cost rate, and remaining net returns are imputed to labor, returns to farm operators for their labor are high relative to alternatives.

The rate of return on farm equity capital from 1960 to 1976 was more than double the rate of return on common stocks including dividends and capital gains (see footnote a, Table 3). Farm mortgage loans, another alternative to investment of farm equity capital, returned an interest rate of 6.9 percent on the average for the same period.

Higher rates of return could be required in farming than elsewhere if risks were greater. Rates of return on investment in the stock market not only are lower but also are much more variable from year to year. The average returns in Table 3 mask considerable variation in returns among farms and among common stocks. Over time, capital gains have occurred with greater consistency in farm real estate than in common stocks. Thus returns are not necessarily more variable among farms than among common stocks.

One measure of risk in farming is the foreclosure rate, which was 0.9 per 1,000 farms in 1974; 1.4 in 1975, 1976 and 1977; and 2.0 in 1978. The nonfarm business failure rate was 3.8 per 1,000 businesses in 1974, 4.3 in 1975 and 3.5 in 1976. In short, economic risk does not necessarily justify higher rates of return on equity in farming than in other sectors.

TABLE 3.

Rates of Return on Farm Equity, Common Stock and Interest on Federal Land Bank Loans, 1960–1976[a]

Year	Rates of return on farm equity[b]			Rates of return on common stock[c]			Interest rates on new loans, Federal Land Banks[d]
	Earnings	Capital gains	Total	Dividends	Capital gains	Total	
				(percent)			
1960	2.6	1.3	3.9	3.5	-2.7	.8	6.0
1961	3.2	4.5	7.7	3.0	15.7	18.7	5.6
1962	3.4	4.2	7.6	3.4	-6.2	-2.8	5.6
1963	3.2	4.1	7.3	3.2	10.7	13.9	5.6
1964	2.6	4.8	7.4	3.0	14.1	17.1	5.6
1965	4.4	7.9	12.3	3.0	7.7	10.6	5.6
1966	4.6	6.5	11.1	3.4	-3.4	0.0	5.8
1967	3.1	5.4	8.5	3.2	7.3	10.5	6.0
1968	3.1	5.8	8.9	3.1	6.9	10.0	6.8
1969	3.6	4.9	8.5	3.2	-.9	2.3	7.8
1970	3.3	4.5	7.8	3.8	-17.6	-13.8	8.7
1971	3.3	8.8	12.1	3.1	15.3	18.4	7.9
1972	5.0	15.3	20.3	2.8	10.0	12.8	7.4
1973	10.2	24.7	24.9	3.1	-1.7	1.4	7.5
1974	5.5	9.5	15.0	4.5	-29.7	-25.2	8.1
1975	4.4	13.5	17.9	4.3	3.8	8.1	8.7
1976	2.4	15.4	17.8	3.8	15.5	19.3	8.7
Average	4.0	8.3	12.3	3.4	2.6	6.0	6.9

[a] The comparisons show broad alternatives for individual investors and are not relevant for comparing rates of return among industries in gauging economic performance. The ratio of profits after income taxes to stockholders' equity in all manufacturing corporations averaged 11.4 percent from 1960 to 1976 (Council of Economic Advisers, p. 355). However attractive, such profit rates are not accessible to the individual investor.

[b] Computed from Evans et al.

[c] Based on Standard and Poor's 500 stock composite index (Council of Economic Advisers, p. 360).

On the other hand, returns to operator and family labor, as a residual after paying other costs, are highly variable—much more variable than nonfarm labor income. Thus the issue of whether risk is greater in farming than in other sectors depends in part on whether farmers are classified as laborers or businessmen.

The individual farm operator faces substantial economic risk due to weather, pests, markets and other uncertainties. Returns compensating for risk on the average are of little consolation to the farmer struggling to make ends meet in the current year. Risk is a source of economic inefficiency as farmers sacrifice net income to diversify, hold liquid assets to meet contingencies and sacrifice economies of specialization. Government commodity programs have in the past played, and can in the future play a major role in reducing market uncertainties.

Systematic patterns in rates of return appear among farms classified by annual gross sales (Table 4). Large farms as measured by sales tend to have high rates of return on equity capital; small farms have low returns. The pattern is consistent among regions. The heterogeneous nature of the farming economy apparent in Table 4 highlights a fundamental problem in programs which support commodity prices: a given level of price support may provide windfall profits to some farmers, while others are unable to cover all of their costs. In 1970, the parity ratio required to cover all costs of production (including equity capital and operator–family labor cost) by economic class of farms varied from 73 percent (1910–1914 = 100) for farms with sales of over $100,000 to 172 percent for farms with sales of less than $2,500 per year (Table 5). The 4 percent return to equity used to compute the required parity ratio appears adequate for landowners because capital gains (not included in Table 5) compensate for inflation. Nonetheless, the percentage of parity required to provide higher rates of return are shown in Table 5.

Cash Flow. We have identified poverty and low rates of return to equity, characteristics identified mainly with small farms, as farm problem symptoms. The economic vital signs (net worth, net income and rates of return on equity) of commercial agriculture indicate economic health. To be sure, instability poses difficulties for commercial farmers, but this is not a new problem and has been alleviated to a degree by government programs. Then why do commercial farmers complain

TABLE 4.

Rate of Return to Farm Equity Capital by Economic Class of Farms,
U.S. and Ten Regions, 1970

	Economic class, by farm sales[a]						
	IA	IB	II	III	IV	V	VI
	(percent)						
Net returns to equity[b]							
U.S.	6.9	5.9	4.4	2.9	−.1	−6.5	−6.1
Capital gains	3.9	3.7	3.5	3.4	3.3	3.2	3.3
Total	10.8	9.6	7.9	6.3	3.2	−3.3	−3.2
Region							
Northeast	7.6	6.4	4.5	.9	−2.3	−14.7	−10.8
Lake States	9.1	8.4	8.1	5.7	−2.6	−11.2	−13.3
Corn Belt	6.3	6.1	4.8	3.0	−.2	−3.9	−10.0
Northern Plains	5.6	5.1	3.9	2.4	1.9	−7.3	−7.0
Appalachian	8.0	6.4	3.6	2.5	−2.0	−5.3	−2.0
Southeast	10.7	7.1	2.1	−.3	−1.2	−9.4	−4.8
Delta States	11.9	9.7	5.7	2.3	1.5	−3.3	−2.7
Southern Plains	6.2	5.4	4.1	3.7	1.6	−4.8	−4.4
Mountain	8.6	5.4	4.2	3.3	1.9	−3.9	−5.1
Pacific	4.2	2.0	1.2	.2	−1.7	−10.9	−5.5

SOURCE: Hottel and Reinsel.

[a] See Table 2 for sales in dollars.

[b] Does not include capital gains.

that they are "hurting"? The difficulty is mainly cash flow, a comparatively new ailment. Examples of the cash flow squeeze on typical farms are presented by Strickland and Fawcett. Documentation of the scope of the problem is not available, but the symptoms are apparent— heavily indebted young and expanding family farmers having difficulty servicing debt and frequently being forced to refinance.

SOME CAUSES OF FARM PROBLEMS

Instability, cash flow and poverty are manifestations or symptoms of more basic problems of economic inefficiency and inequity. Causes of instability include unpredictable weather, pests and market structure. Farmers cannot change production quickly in response to price

TABLE 5.
Parity Ratio Required to Cover All Costs of Production, by
Economic Class of Farms, 1970

	Economic class, by farm sales[a]						
	IA	IB	II	III	IV	V	VI
	(percent, 1910–1914 = 100)						
Return to equity[b]							
4 percent	73	73	76	81	96	143	172
7 percent	77	79	85	92	109	162	209
10 percent	81	86	94	103	123	181	229

SOURCE: Compiled using basic data from Hottel and Reinsel.

[a]See Table 2 for dollar classes. The actual adjusted parity ratio in 1970 was 77.

[b]Does not include capital gains.

(low short–run supply elasticity) and small changes in output cause large changes in price (low short–run demand elasticity). Because of the atomistic competitive structure of the farming industry, farmers are price takers, not price makers. The imperfectly competitive structure of many other industries is characterized by administered or negotiated prices. Delays between initiation and completion of production due to biological processes coupled with uncertain price expectations give rise to instability in the form of cycles especially apparent in cattle and hog production

Inflation. Perhaps the most serious economic problem confronting the farm sector is national inflation. "National inflation" here refers to increases in the general price level that result from demand–pull and cost–push sources validated by growth of the money supply. Such inflation is rather quickly apparent in prices paid by farmers but not in prices received by farmers. Inflation associated with short supplies of food and feed such as occurred in the 1972–1975 period has a very different impact.[2] Unlike less competitive sectors, the farm sector has no immediate means to pass on steadily rising input costs. Farmers

[2]For a more technical and detailed discussion of the effects of inflation on the parity ratio and the economic health of the farming industry, see Tweeten, Quance and Yeh.

eventually pass on costs by restraining input use and output, but experience a cost–price squeeze while making adjustments. A sharply lower parity ratio has been averted in recent years only because of strong demand for exports, slower productivity growth, and government commodity programs.

The cash flow problem is not averted, however. The entry–level farm owner–operator is particularly hard hit. In the absence of inflation, he might receive approximately a 4 percent return on land investment and pay 3 percent rate of interest on his real estate mortgage. With inflation of 6 percent, he will receive approximately 4 percent initial return on land but will pay 3 percent real rate of interest plus an inflation premium of 6 percent for a total of 9 percent nominal interest on his mortgage. Thus there is a net negative cash flow generated of 5 percent of the loan value plus principal repayment. If land returns and prices increase at the rate of inflation, by the thirtieth year of farming he will be receiving a return of 24 percent of his initial investment and will average a real rate of return of 4 percent plus an inflation premium of 6 percent for a total of 10 percent over the life of the investment.

One of the insidious aspects of inflation is that, like a drug habit, it creates dependency and withdrawal symptoms. Borrowers who are locked into long–term loans at high interest rates find the only thing worse than continued inflation is deflation. Their high debt service costs and cash flow problems continue until debts are repaid if inflationary expectations built into interest rates are not realized in rising returns on land investment over time. Two alternatives to deal with this difficult problem are (1) indexing of interest rates to inflation, and (2) not allowing inflation to become permanent and hence be built into long–term interest rates.

Table 6 illustrates the inflation–generated cash flow problem for a newly established mid–size farm with sales of $40,000 to $99,999 in 1976. Physical assets for the average farms in the class totaling $452,085 could be purchased with principal and interest payments of $44,007 per year for 30 years with 9 percent interest and of $23,065 with 3 percent interest. The annual means to service the debt include assets earning 4 percent of current value, labor–management earnings and off–farm income totaling $34,183 in 1976. With inflation, applying the entire means to service the debt leaves a $9,824 cash flow deficit in 1976. Without inflation, debt would be serviced with $18,083 of asset

TABLE 6.

Illustration of Cash Flow With and Without Inflation Using Data for
Class IB Farms With Sales of $40,000 to $99,999 in 1976

Item	With 6 percent inflation (year)		Without inflation (year)	
	1976	2007	1976	2007
	(dollars per farm)			
Requirements				
Physical assets	425,085	2,904,075	452,085	452,085
Annual payment to retire mortgage in 30 years	44,007	0	23,065	0
Means				
Asset earnings	18,083	116,163	18,083	18,083
Labor-management earnings	10,400	66,807	10,400	10,400
Off-farm income	5,700	36,615	5,700	5,700
	34,183	219,585	34,183	34,183
Cash flow surplus (deficit)[a]	(9,824)	219,585	11,118	34,183

SOURCE: Basic data compiled from Evans, *et al.*; Hottel and Reinsel; and U.S.
Department of Agriculture (1978, July).

[a]The cash flow surplus is considered to be consumed, left idle or placed in another
investment for which returns are not considered in the illustration.

earnings plus $4,982 or 31 percent of labor–management and off–farm
income—a feasible savings rate.

Applying the same savings rate, with inflation the operator can
support a mortgage of $86,891 to own 19 percent of assets and rent the
remaining 81 percent. The mortgage payments of $8,458 per year are
serviced with a 4 percent return on $86,891 or $3,476 plus $4,982 of
other earnings as above. A second alternative is to "marry" or inherit
$215,122 of equity (48 percent of assets), leaving a mortgage of
$236,963 with annual payments of $23,065 to be serviced by $18,083 of
assets earnings plus $4,982 of labor–management and off–farm earn-
ings. The impact of inflation is either to forego full ownership by
renting four–fifths of farm assets or somehow secure equity in half the
assets to become established in farming.

With inflation, the operator who is somehow able to meet mortgage payments for the farm in Table 6 is in excellent financial shape in
later years. In the year 2006, the thirtieth year, even after making
mortgage payments of $44,007 the cash flow surplus is $162,403. This
commanding financial position is enhanced in 2007, when the owner
need no longer service the mortgage payment and the cash flow
surplus is $219,585.

With 6 percent inflation in land earnings and prices, 14 years are
required for land earnings to equal interest payments on a perpetual
mortgage—until that time a renter will have a more favorable cash flow
than the owner. A more complete accounting for capital other than real
estate and for uncertainty in Table 6 would make the cash flow problem
for the entry–level owner–operator appear more rather than less severe with inflation.

In short, after surviving the initial cash flow crisis, the owner–
operator is in a position to use his equity base to outbid competitors for
land. The problem for the entry–level owner–operator is to survive the
liquidity crisis in the early years. The two major means to cope have
been part–ownership (renting some land in early years of farming to
combine with owned land in forming an economic size unit) and off–
farm employment to supplement farm earnings. Each of these alternatives compromises the traditional concept of a family farm.

Inflation is not the only source of cash flow problems that threaten
the long–term existence of the family farm structure. Farmers have
substituted machinery and other capital for labor at a rapid rate. In
earlier times, farmers could "tighten their belts" and apply much of
their labor–management returns to service debts. Now, with massive
capital requirements per operator and narrow labor–management
margins, that opportunity is eroding. Mechanization is the major
source of the problem but another is federal income tax incentives for
farmers to substitute capital for labor.

Decreasing Costs. Increasing returns to size and decreasing costs
shown in Figure 1 help to explain a chronic tendency for low returns in
farming. Figure 1 is a long–run marginal cost curve computed by
dividing *all* costs of production (including operator–family labor and
management plus a 7 percent current return to equity capital) by gross
farm income on each economic class of farms. In 1970 on the average it

FIGURE 1.
Long–Run Marginal Cost of Farm Production, by Economic Class of Farms in 1970

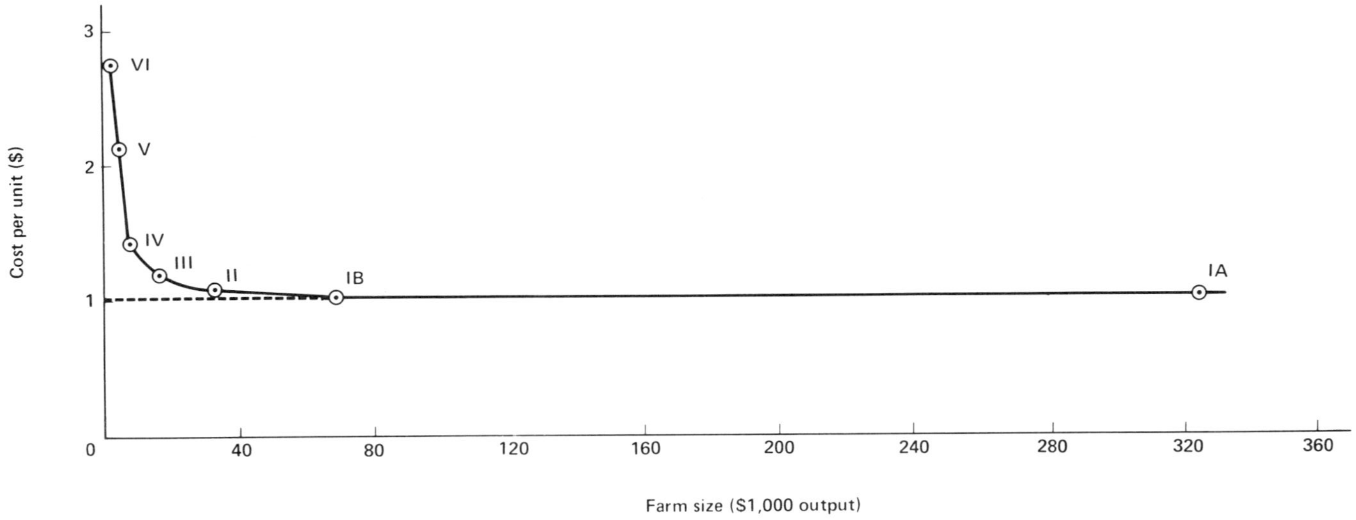

Cost per unit ($)

Farm size ($1,000 output)

SOURCE: Compiled using basic data from Hottel and Reinsel.

cost $1.00 to produce $1.00 of output on farms with sales of $100,000 or more. In the same year, it cost $2.72 to produce $1.00 of output on farms with sales of $2,500 or less. Efficient operators of adequate size farms tend to bid the price of land to a level which brings a return comparable to that on alternative investments. This market price applies to all farms, large and small, efficient and inefficient. When the returns of farmers who are just breaking even are averaged with the returns of the majority of farmers who are not covering all costs, *rates of return averaged over all farmers will be low, whatever the parity price ratio, given that land prices have time to adjust.*[3]

Given the structure of the farming industry, it is surprising that the return on farm equity capital has not been lower. The ratio of cash rent to land value was 5.4 percent in 1977 for 22 states reported (U.S. Department of Agriculture 1977, July, p. 53). Subtracting real estate taxes leaves a return of 4.4 percent plus capital gains to landowners. The cash rental rate of return on land has trended downward for several years and has led to charges that farmland is currently overpriced (Gardner and Pope; Raup). If cash rent is an adequate measure of current returns to land ownership, then a more realistic conclusion is that land was *underpriced* in earlier years rather than *overpriced* currently. If farm equity capital provides a current return of 4 percent plus capital gains equal to the rate of inflation, then equity investment in farming is as attractive as alternative investments in, for example, the stock market. Efficiently operated, adequate–sized farms seem to be doing better than this—perhaps this is the reason land prices continue to climb in the face of a declining parity ratio. Land prices may continue to rise until the current rate of return is only 2 percent, averaged over efficient and inefficient farms based on the decreasing cost theory (see footnote 3).

Even higher support prices might be regarded as desirable, even necessary, by the smaller, less efficient producers. But the price

[3]To restate this proposition in technical economic terms, average cost of production exceeds marginal cost which equals marginal revenue and average revenue. It follows that total costs exceed total revenue. Price supports set to equal average long–run cost of production will provide windfall gains to efficient producers which will again raise costs. If farms with sales of $100,000 per year and over drive up land prices so they earn a 5 percent current rate of return on equity (which provides an 11 percent total return if land values increase at 6 percent annually), then the current rate of return on equity averaged over all farms will only be about 2 percent.

mechanism is attended by an insidious spoiler—economic rent in the form of land prices inflated by producers with costs below the support level.

Technology. In the 1950's the "treadmill" theory became popular. The theory holds that rates of return on farming resources were low because supply, expanded by technology, increased at a faster rate than demand for farm products. The theory made sense for the 1950's when productivity (measured by output per unit of conventional resources) increased over 2 percent annually, a considerably faster pace than demand. Unfortunately, the theory is still used to explain tendencies for low rates of return although demand has been expanding faster than supply of farm output for many years.

Demand growth can be divided into three components: domestic population, income, and exports. From 1960 to 1977, domestic population increased 1.1 percent per year, domestic per capita real disposable personal income 2.8 percent per year, and exports 6.4 percent per year. With an income elasticity of demand of 0.15 and exports 20 percent of demand, total demand for farm products grew at the rate of $0.80[1.1 + 0.15(2.8)] + 0.20[6.4] = 2.6$ percent per year.

In contrast, the nominal supply curve shifted backwards due to inflation at a rate equal to input–price inflation times the elasticity of supply or 1 percent in the short run and 5 percent in the long run. Adding the increase in supply due to productivity (1.6 percent per year) gives a total increase in the supply curve of $1.6 - 1.0 = 0.6$ percent in the short run and $1.6 - 5.0 = -3.4$ percent in the long run.[4] The rate of increase in demand exceeded the increase in productivity

---

[4]The technical background for this statement is as follows. Based on a short–run elasticity of 0.2, productivity increasing by 1.6 percent per year and input prices by 5.0 percent per year from 1960 to 1977, the resulting short–run supply function for farm output is:
$$Q_t = \alpha \, (P_t/P_0 e^{.05t})^{.2} e^{.016t}$$
where Q is output, α is a constant, P_t is prices received by farmers, P_0 is initial prices paid by farmers, e is the base of the natural logarithms and t is time. Inflation–induced increases in prices paid by farmers are not offset by inflation–induced increases in prices received by farmers (Tweeten and Griffin), hence the rate of increase in the supply curve in the short run was 0.6 percent per year according to the above equation.

Based on a long–run supply elasticity of 1.0, the long–run supply function for the 1960–1977 period can be represented by
$$Q_t = \beta(P_t/P_0 e^{.05t})e^{.016t}$$
where β is constant. The equation indicates a decrease in the supply curve of 3.4 percent per year.

and greatly exceeded the increase in the total supply curve, the latter shifting upward and to the left for the 1960–1977 period as a whole.

The inability of the treadmill theory to explain farm problems and the declining amount of unneeded labor in farming should not blind us to the fact that labor–saving technology continues to be adopted at rapid rates by farmers. The great rural–urban exodus is over, but many farm people continue to be released from farm employment as four–wheel–drive tractors, mechanical harvesters for tobacco, fruits and vegetables, and other labor–saving technologies are adopted by farmers. Public policy should continue to be concerned with general education and vocational–technical training and nonfarm job development to ease adjustments of the workers and their families displaced from farming.

ECONOMIC ISSUES BY SIZE OF FARM

Economic problems and appropriate public policy to deal with them differ by class of farms. Because large farms tend to be economically viable without public programs and small farms receive few benefits from them, the moderate–size family farm has the greatest stake in commodity programs. Entry–level and expanding family farms especially need economic security to cope with cash flow problems. Care must be taken in provision of benefits, however, to avoid giving large farms an unfair competitive advantage.

The Small Farm. Figure 1 raises the uneasy question of why anyone would operate a small farm costing over two dollars to produce one dollar of output. An explanation may be found in the characteristics of people living on these farms. They include: (1) full–time operators locked into small farms by lack of education, disability or old age, (2) operators who are primarily nonfarm workers residing on a farm, and (3) a residual of able–bodied, bona–fide operators who rely on farm earnings for their livelihood. Each category tends to earn low absolute income from farming alone and tends to be inefficient because of inability to buy at discounts, sell at premiums and use labor–saving machinery which reduces cost per unit of output.

Farms in the first category are declining in numbers; their operators accept low incomes and low returns for lack of alternatives. For this category, the opportunity cost of owned resources is likely to be overestimated in Figure 1. "Farmers" in the second category for the most part are *not* poor. They earn substantial off–farm income, are increasing in numbers and accept low rates of return because farm residence is a consumption good for which they are willing to pay.

The makeup of small farms bears on appropriate policy prescriptions. Aged and disabled farmers will benefit from improved welfare programs but will not benefit much from production–marketing research and extension services. City workers residing in the country can benefit from increased research and extension activities from land grant universities, but these people do not have low incomes and may not have the time to respond markedly to research–extension activities. With limited research and extension resources, the efficiency payoff is greater from focusing on family size farms, which account for the majority of farm output. On the other hand, it may be argued on equity grounds that, because private agribusiness firms now provide substantial research and outreach to large commercial farms, public research and extension services can focus to a greater extent on conservation, low income and underemployment problems in rural areas.

The third category (able–bodied, non–aged, bona–fide small–farm operators who depend on the farm for their livelihood) can benefit from credit assistance to help expand operations, rural development to offer nonfarm jobs and, finally, research–extension services to improve efficiency even while remaining small. But the 1974 Census of Agriculture suggests this third category contains few operators.

The agricultural agenda in Washington now gives high priority to small farms, emphasizing a policy of research–extension services so they can improve their economic well–being without growing larger, securing off–farm employment or depending on public assistance. That priority which properly recognizes past unmet needs of small farmers in public research and extension could unduly redirect efforts away from improving total farming industry productivity which benefits consumers more than farmers. More importantly, the priority diverts attention from the rural development and welfare reform efforts that are necessary to deal with the most serious problems of small–farm residents and rural people—underemployment and low income.

The Large Farm. The portion of gross farm returns accruing to farm labor and management is now approximately 16 percent based on a large number of commodities and resource situations. Thus approximately $6 of output are required to generate $1 of labor–management income. A full–time crop farm operator household earning the national median family income requires annual farm sales of approximately $100,000 and assets of $1 million on the average. Such an economic farming unit can realize economies of size (most economies of size can be realized on a unit with $50,000 sales, with the operator devoting half his time to the farm) and few efficiency gains are obtained from larger farms except in selected enterprises such as fruits, vegetables and cattle feeding. Larger–than–family farms (defined as farms hiring more than half their labor, and nonfamily corporate farms and partnerships) account for 5 percent of all farms and 30 percent of farm output in 1976, and constitute a growing threat to family farms (U.S. Department of Agriculture forthcoming). Price supports designed to make small farms viable are likely to give large farms a competitive advantage and ultimately undermine the small farm when applied across the board. Whether federal income tax and other policies should be designed to discourage growth of large farms will be considered later in this report.

The Moderate–Size Farm. Many moderate–size farms, ranging from $20,000 to $100,000 in sales, experience severe economic pressures. Families on such farms tend to rely on farm income for their economic livelihood and may be more adversely affected by uncertainties of nature and the markets than families on large farms (who have the volume of production and resources to forward contract, hedge in the futures market, etc.) or families on small farms (who can cushion economic setbacks by relying on off–farm income). Moderate–size farms are in a less favorable position to bargain for input price discounts and output price premiums than large farms. Unlike large farms, which tend to have high net farm income, and small farms which have high off–farm income, many moderate–size farms do not have sufficient net income against which to take advantage of accelerated depreciation, investment tax credits and other federal income tax provisions. To the extent that large farms can reduce unit costs of environmental protection investments (spreading high fixed costs over a large number of units of output) and small farms are exempt from environmental regulations, the moderate–size farm is further threatened. The large farm proprietor with adequate income from farming and the small farm operator with income from off–farm sources are not under pressure to expand in the face of narrow profit margins and high land prices. But the moderate–size farm operator, who depends on farm income, feels the need to expand to achieve an economic size unit.

Data in Table 7 for three economic classes selected to represent small, moderate–size and large farms quantify several observations made above. Moderate–size farms have less equity than large farms and a less favorable debt–asset ratio than small farms. Based on debt–asset and debt–net income ratios, small farms are less vulnerable to economic setbacks than moderate–size or large farms. Ratios of debt to cash farm receipts are more favorable for large farms than for moderate–size farms. The moderate–size class shown is under pressure to expand in size, and total net income less an allowance for family living (arbitrarily set at two–thirds of national median family income) is available to finance expansion. The incremental cost of assets per dollar of investment income in 1976 ranged from $10.29 for small farms and $26.84 for large farms to $41.51 for moderate–size farms. The data not only reveal barriers to expansion of moderate–size farms because the incremental cost of assets is high relative to investment income, but also indicate a declining competitive position from 1965 to 1976. The ratio of farm capital to net income fell sharply for small farms and rose modestly for large farms during that period. The ratio for the moderate–size class not only was high in 1965 but increased considerably by 1976.

In summary, the major economic problems facing established commercial farmers are inflation (with its tendency to generate a cost–price squeeze) and instability. Entry level farmers and modest–size farms attempting to expand face the same problems, but asset–acquisition and cash flow problems caused by inflation are especially acute. Small farms, because they have low debt–equity ratios on the average and sizable off–farm income, are troubled less by instability but frequently have low returns on farming resources and many have low incomes.

Excessive profit rates of firms supplying farm inputs and marketing farm products, rapid adoption of output increasing technology, and excessive labor on farms are currently not major problems. While con-

TABLE 7.

Selected Measures of Economic Viability of Large, Moderate–Size and Small Farms, U.S., 1965 and 1976

Item	Large farms Sales of $100,000 and over		Moderate–size farms Sales of $20,000 to $39,999		Small farms Sales of less than $2,500	
	1965	1976	1965	1976	1965	1976
			(dollars per farm)			
Total net income	40,362	54,873	11,085	16,517	5,612	15,815
Potential investment income[a]	31,952	44,851	2,675	6,495	−2,798	5,793
Real estate assets	525,778	877,490	66,063	193,075	18,537	41,955
Other assets	245,472	326,465	31,125	76,561	8,405	17,673
Total assets	771,250	1,203,955	97,188	269,636	26,942	59,628
Liabilities	157,417	285,394	25,910	31,337	2,325	4,035
Proprietors' equities	613,833	918,651	131,076	238,299	24,617	55,593
Debt–asset ratio (%)	20.4	23.9	16.5	11.6	8.6	6.8
Debt–cash receipts ratio (%)	54.6	88.6	85.7	43.0	188.3	340.5
Debt–net income ratio (%)	390.0	520.1	233.7	189.7	41.4	25.5
Asset–investment income ratio	24.14	26.84	36.33	41.51	—	10.29

SOURCE: U.S. Department of Agriculture (1977; 1978, July).

[a]Investment income is defined here as total net farm income less family living expenses computed as two–thirds of national median family income, or $8,410 in 1965 and $10,022 in 1976.

[b]Farms move from one economic class to another, in part because of inflation, hence the same farms are not being compared even within a class in 1965 and 1976.

tinuing efforts are needed to improve productivity and competition in the marketing sector, success in such efforts is unlikely to alleviate farm problems. A large number of market conduct, structure and performance studies reveal no major opportunities to reduce marketing costs that would be passed to farmers. The rising share of the consumers' food dollar going to the marketing sector is largely accounted for by normal working of the market system. Income elasticities of demand indicate that as consumers' incomes rise, demand for food marketing services (including processing, storage, etc.) increases faster than demand for food raw materials from the farm. Thus with growth in income, the share of the consumers' food dollar going to farmers falls. The marketing sector share, often viewed as a cost, is value added for services that give raw materials place, form and time utility demanded by consumers. One study (Council on Wage and Price Stability) of margins found that marketing firms act as shock absorbers, not fully passing farm price gains or losses to consumers in the short run. After a few months, however, farm price losses and gains both tend to be fully passed to consumers.

Turning to the energy issue, no absolute shortages of energy are anticipated, but energy prices will rise. Without speculating about exact future price trends, it is of interest that the price paid by farmers for bulk gasoline was 26.2 cents per gallon in September 1956 and 26.7 cents in September 1978, the latter deflated by prices received by farmers (1956 = 100). In the 22 years, the price of gasoline and diesel fuel increased less than prices of other inputs purchased by farmers. Of course, natural gas prices increased sharply for some farmers, creating special hardships for irrigated farms.

Policy Legislation for the Farming Industry

Before addressing current and prospective farm policy, it is useful to review the objectives of farm price and income policy. Although not fully articulated in legislation, commodity legislation seeks to (1) provide comparable earning power for farm and nonfarm people, (2) hold reserve capacity to supply unforeseeable food and fiber needs which the private trade cannot be expected to supply because of high risk and capital requirements, (3) maintain economic vitality of the farming industry to provide adequate supplies of quality food and fiber at a reasonable cost for domestic and foreign needs, (4) preserve the environment, and (5) maintain the family farm structure. These objectives are interrelated. Holding reserve capacity in the form of commodity stocks, for example, not only contributes to price stability but also avoids environmental damage that results when erosion–prone soils in pasture are plowed to provide additional output as occurred in 1973–1974. The principal purpose of commodity programs is to eliminate excessive fluctuations in prices to farmers and consumers and maintain vitality of adequate–sized, well–managed farms. Temptations exist to use commodity programs to enhance returns to farm labor and management in the long run. This cannot be done for several reasons.

(1) Prices supported above equilibrium generate excessive output which, unless removed from the market at considerable cost, depresses market prices.

(2) The long–run demand for farm products is less inelastic than short–run demand, and may even be elastic when account is taken of export markets. Thus restrictions on output do not necessarily increase farming receipts over an extended period.

(3) Benefits of commodity programs are capitalized into land values. New owners paying inflated prices lose income benefits of programs. Renters and hired workers realize few of the dollar benefits of programs. Approximately one–third of farmland is owned by non-farmers and the percentage may be rising. Given the high returns to farmland investment, it is surprising that nonfarmers have not purchased more farm real estate.

Other considerations such as high Treasury costs, restrictions on production and marketing decisions, and excessive bureaucratic involvement in administering and policing programs also argue against extensive government involvement. Recommendations of the Task Force call for a continued role of government in farm price and income policy. But such policy should avoid undue capitalization of benefits, restrictions on freedom of decisions by farmers, inefficiency in allocating inputs and outputs to appropriate uses, and pricing farm commodities out of world markets. Because of these and other considerations, the appropriate public policy is to set price supports at a level no higher than costs of production on well–managed, adequately sized family farms in areas of comparative advantage.

FOOD AND AGRICULTURE ACT OF 1977

Deliberations on farm legislation in 1976 emphasized the need for revisions in the 1973 legislation (1) tying target prices to nonland costs of production, (2) establishing a farmer–held grain reserve with storage payments of 25 to 35 cents per bushel per annum with termination of payments when market prices reach 150 percent of the loan levels, and (3) updating bases and allotments to a more recent period to recognize cropping adjustments farmers had made to increased food demands in the early 1970's. The Food and Agriculture Act of 1977, when subsequently enacted, maintained the substance of 1973 legislation plus these revisions. With these changes, the 1977 Act has much to commend it and seems broadly consistent with farmers' preferences.

Opinion polls of farmers in Illinois, Indiana, Minnesota, Georgia, Alabama and Tennessee revealed that "The Food and Agriculture Act of 1977 appears to represent a reasonable compromise if we consider the views and preferences expressed by farmers to the six–state surveys" (Guither and Jones, p. 554). Major farm organizations, although somewhat flaccid in their support for the 1977 legislation, were at least not in opposition.

With farm people comprising only 3.6 percent of the population, it is notable that the ability of the farm bloc to deliver legislation favorable to farmers seemed undiminished—the Senate passed the 1977 bill by a 63 to 8 margin and the House by a 283 to 107 margin (Spitze). Later, as farm protest movements swept the nation, the Carter Administration increased the wheat target price and grain set–aside acreage and took other action that, according to Secretary of Agriculture Bergland, added from $3 to $4 billion to farm income.

The performance of commodity programs must be judged by the objectives listed earlier. Many of these objectives imply pursuit of economic efficiency and equity, which economists have tools to analyze. At issue is how well the 1977 legislation measures up to these standards.

ECONOMIC EFFICIENCY

Diversion of cropland causes inefficiency by idling land which has little value in alternative uses, generates an inappropriate input mix, and reduces output (raises food prices) to consumers. Tweeten (1977) estimated that short–run inefficiency, in reduced real value of goods and services produced, equaled approximately 2 percent of farm receipts in the 1960's. In the long run, inefficiency was even less, mainly because programs speeded outmovement of redundant farm labor which was more valuable in nonfarm employment. Yet, efficiency of programs can be improved.

The 1977 Act continues the tilt toward a market orientation which has prevailed since the turning back of an extensive system of mandatory controls proposed in the early 1960's. The tobacco program operated under "permanent legislation" is an exception, although the higher tobacco prices and smaller farms preserved by that program may not be at variance with social objectives. Some glaring inefficiencies in the sugar, rice, and peanut programs have been reduced. But several sources of inefficiency remain in programs operating under current legislation.

The programs perform better in responding to markets on the demand side than on the supply side. The Secretary of Agriculture has discretion to set loan rates at levels competitive in markets at home and abroad. By tying target prices and deficiency payments to actual production, however, the target price tends to become the supply price. Whereas the 1977 Act ended the practice (objected to by some) of allowing farmers to receive payments for crops they do not produce, it does so at the cost of making the target price rather than the loan rate the marginal minimum price. The 1978 target price for wheat, $3.40 per bushel, generates more supply quantity (in the absence of set aside) than is demanded at the loan rate. The result may be a chronic need for wheat set aside if the target price is maintained at this level in relation to the cost of production.

Allotments, based largely on cropping patterns in 1959–1960 or earlier years, were clearly antiquated. The shift to set aside based on planted acres did not do away with the concept of historic allotments—it only updated them to a 1977 cropping base and pooled them into a "normal crop acreage." One problem is that 1977 was not a representative cropping year for many farmers. And a farmer, who because of specialized skills, desires to conserve soil or for other reasons chose to produce hay and other crops not counted in program acreage on part of his tillable acreage is severely disadvantaged if he or a prospective buyer wishes to shift to program acreage crops. County

Agricultural Stabilization and Conservation Service (ASCS) committees have considerable discretion in correcting such injustice, particularly if national program acreage allotted to counties is well in excess of program acreage requested by farmers—a condition that occurs most frequently in marginal farming areas characterized by much off–farm employment.

A problem in leaving considerable discretion to ASCS committees is the opportunity for personal favoritism and program slippage. Tweeten (1977) concluded that, in part because of lax enforcement, each three acres of set aside removed only two acres harvested and that productivity (potential yield per acre) of set–aside acres averaged no more than three–fourths that of producing cropland. This combined acreage and yield slippage, implying that two acres needed to be set aside to reduce production equal to one acre of producing cropland, was again prominent in 1978. Provisions such as required rotation of set–aside land and use of sealed bids (to remove as much production as possible on set–aside acres per dollar of program funds) can be applied under the 1977 Act. Such cost–effectiveness does not appeal to local ASCS offices, which view (rationally enough) their role as providing as much payments as possible for as little set aside as possible. This tends to defeat the program's purpose because, with a limited federal budget, income of the farm sector is raised most by administering programs to remove as much production as possible per dollar of program funds. Set–aside programs have not been much more cost–effective in raising net farm income per dollar of program outlay than direct payments in the absence of production controls. Perhaps it is time to consider reliance on direct payments without production controls.

The extended loan program contributes to economic efficiency to the extent that the private trade alone would not, because of excessive risk and capital requirements, hold socially desired reserves. The extended loan program is a compromise giving farmers some control of stocks and a payment to compensate them for the lower farm prices that result from stabilizing prices with adequate reserves. Government–held or supported stocks tend to replace private stocks, shifting storage costs from consumers to taxpayers. Opportunities to release stocks only when price is over 140 percent of the loan rate is not the way of a perfect market. But the discontinuity inherent in this provision is offset by operations of the private trade, which is induced to hold working stocks that dampen and smooth price adjustments below extended–reserve trigger prices.

Restrictions on imports deny American consumers the opportunity to purchase lower–cost imported beef and dairy products. Import quotas provide a position from which to bargain for a reduction in trade barriers with other countries but conflict with our broad commitment to lessening of barriers to exports of our agricultural products. Studies (Salathe *et al.*; Novakovic and Thompson) indicate that the short–run impact on U.S. producers of milk for manufactured dairy products could be sizable from removing dairy product import restrictions.

Past beef import quotas were proportional to domestic production, allowing greater imports when prices are depressed from excessive domestic production. Failure of exporters to fill quotas when our beef supplies are large and periodic suspension of quotas when our beef supplies are short introduce countercyclical elements. But the chaotic current system is economically inefficient and politically factious. A useful middle ground between continuation and termination of beef import quotas is initiation of countercyclical quotas, allowing greater (perhaps unrestricted) imports of beef when domestic production is low and allowing fewer imports when domestic production is high. This would encourage producers of beef in nations exporting to the United States to develop beef cycles countercyclical to ours.

As a general rule, grazing and haying of set–aside acreage work against the intent of production controls. But herein lies an opportunity to extend the stabilization features that have worked for major crops to counter the cyclical swings in beef production. When beef production lags, there is reason to turn excess capacity in grains into expanded beef production by grazing and haying set–aside acres. The Secretary has such an option and exercised it in 1977. He may be unable to stop the practice when it is no longer desirable—as the high production point in the beef cycle approaches. What is needed is a federal policy specifying utilization of set aside for grazing and haying when beef supplies are short of a set level per capita and restricting such utilization when beef supplies exceed a set level per capita. Legislation could provide contracts to use set–aside cropland for haying and grazing a prescribed number of years when beef supplies are low. This would encourage permanent forage stands to be established and used for cow–calf operations to expand beef cattle numbers. The duration of such contracts would be tied to the cattle cycle. As beef supplies per capita decline, initial contracts might be up to five years. New contracts in subsequent years would be for shorter periods until use of set–aside acreage for forage is prohibited as beef supplies per capita reach the cutoff level.

Disaster payments constitute another source of economic inefficiency in commodity legislation. Such payments shift to taxpayers some of the private costs of production. When social costs exceed private costs, excess output is generated in uneconomic, high–cost locations. Furthermore, the burden of excess output produced in high–cost areas falls on other producers. "All–risk, all–commodity" insurance paid for mostly by producers but financed in part by taxpayers would be an improvement. Designation of disaster areas with attendant broad access to low–interest loans could be sharply curtailed under such a revised and expanded insurance program.

Control of land to reduce production forecloses the opportunity for farmers to use the least–cost combination of resources to produce commodities. Land control becomes a less effective means of production control as fertilizers, pesticides and other nonland inputs—some of which society would like to curtail in use to protect the environment—are substituted for land. Use of bushel or poundage quotas with allowances for farmers to store production in excess of quotas in years of excess output to be applied to fill quotas in years of short supply could reduce problems associated with uncontrollable influences on output. The peanut program which now utilizes a poundage quota system will provide experience applicable to use of bushel and poundage quotas to other commodities. In keeping with a policy of supporting commodity prices no higher than the average cost of production, new directions for the peanut, dairy and sugar programs are suggested below.

Peanut Program. The Food and Agriculture Act of 1977 contains the first significant change in the peanut program in over 20 years. The new program in part replaces acreage quotas with poundage quotas. Undermarketings from quotas in one year may be stored and used to fill quotas in subsequent years.

The 1977 legislation reduces federal costs, incentives to bid up land prices on land with peanut allotments, and tendencies to increase yields to circumvent allotments. Peanuts moving into low–value uses no longer receive high support prices. Additional changes to improve economic efficiency include.

(1) Gradually removing acreage allotments and support prices on nonquota peanuts while maintaining poundage quotas on peanuts used in the edible market. Support prices above production costs on the edible portion would provide income stability and protection against large losses attending decapitalization of allotments to producers while marginal production would be allowed to compete in the market. Absence of acreage quotas would allow peanut production to move to areas of comparative advantage—current legislation allows allotments to be transferred only within counties.

(2) Eventually, phase out the two–price plan, replacing high support prices on poundage quota peanuts with direct government payments. This would shift the cost of the peanut program from consumers to taxpayers and reduce erosion of peanut consumption in the edible market.

Dairy Program. Incomes of dairy farmers are maintained by federal milk marketing orders and price supports. The minimum support price for milk has been raised from 75 percent of 1910–1914 parity level in the basic law to 80 percent by Congress three times—1960, 1973, and 1977. In 1957, 1975, and 1976, legislation raising the minimum level of price support was passed but vetoed. With no production controls, high support levels have increased milk production to levels that could not be sustained by market demand. Commodity Credit Corporation (CCC) stocks have accumulated within one to two years after support prices have been set above 75 percent of parity. Based on 1953–1973 experience, the long–run supply–demand balance is maintained with milk prices about 75 percent of parity (Manchester).

The support price was set by the Secretary of Agriculture at 82.3 percent of parity on April 1, 1977. Although some months later supports were reduced to 80 percent of parity, surpluses accumulated. With the Commodity Credit Corporation removing approximately 5 percent of marketings in 1976–1978 at an average annual cost of nearly $600 million, the dairy program was one of the most costly to the federal government per dollar of farm receipts. These removals were typical of those in the 1964–1972 period. The Food and Agriculture Act of 1977 set a minimum price support level of 80 percent of parity through March 31, 1979, dropping to 75 percent thereafter. Outlets for disposal of dairy surpluses through domestic commodity distributions and foreign exports under Public Law 480 are no longer readily available. Little value is obtained from surplus milk.

The basic structure of federal dairy price policy has remained largely unchanged for more than 40 years despite major changes in the dairy industry. The federal milk marketing order system is unable to respond efficiently to changing local supply–demand conditions. Farm record data for Wisconsin and New York indicate that dairy farmers are receiving net income from farming (excluding capital gains and off–farm income) at least as high as that of nonfarmers (Manchester, p.30). The problem with the current program is not so much inadequate returns to producers as tendencies to encourage overproduction, inflated prices to consumers, and high costs to taxpayers for disposing of surplus production.

The milk program has considerable support and promotes economic stability of benefit to producers as well as consumers. But a number of changes could improve the program.

(1) Restraint must be exercised in raising support prices. The Secretary of Agriculture needs authority to set a support price that will bring forth an adequate but not excessive supply of milk to serve the needs of American consumers and preserve production capacity to meet anticipated future needs. Unfortunately, such authority has sometimes been preempted by Congress or been mismanaged by the Secretary of Agriculture, creating surpluses. By encouraging restraint in setting a support price above 75 percent of parity, the Secretary could make needed adjustment to avoid excessive accumulation of stocks while maintaining reasonable stability in the milk market through only periodic changes in the support prices.

(2) Producers of milk under marketing orders now receive a price that is a blend of an administered premium price for milk utilized in fresh fluid consumption and the market price for residual milk sold for manufactured product use. Milk for fluid consumption receives a premium price in part to reflect costs of maintaining sanitary and quality standards and in part to provide income security to farmers. Milk sold

in excess of that for fluid consumption would receive the market price rather than a blend price to discourage overproduction.

(3) A problem with the two–price plan (featuring a higher price in the fluid milk market and a lower price in other markets) is that it constitutes a milk "tax" which burdens consumers. It also erodes fluid milk sales by discouraging consumption and encouraging substitutes. For these reasons, the majority of the Task Force favored replacing the fluid consumption price premium with direct government payments. This change would substitute receipts from progressive taxes for a price premium paid by consumers. Payments would be made to producers when market prices fall below a stated target or support level. Payments could be made on quotas related to past production for fluid milk markets. Some Task Force members objected to direct payments because they could make milk producers dependent on capricious political factors involved in provision of payments. Other Task Force members felt that reliance on direct payments is no more precarious than reliance on price supports and suggested that price supports be terminated with initiation of direct payments.

(4) Use a cull–cow incentive payment program to reduce production in times of excess supply.

Sugar Program. Direct payments to producers are suggested for the sugar program as well as for the dairy and peanut programs. Recommended features include.

(1) Terminating import duties and fees and allowing sugar imports to enter at the price set by international sugar agreement or world price if higher. Quotas, except as established under an international sugar agreement, should not be used to hold the domestic price above the world price of sugar.

(2) Providing producers a direct payment per unit of production at a rate equal to some portion of the difference between the import price in (1) and production cost.

(3) Limiting payment bases to historic production with overall payments to each recipient gradually reduced to limitations specified for other supported commodities. Payments should not be scaled down abruptly but should be reduced over a period of years to avoid undue hardships and give time for adjustments. A sizable one–time adjustment payment could be made to sugar producers terminating produc-

tion to compensate for sunk costs and assist in redirecting resources to other uses.

Perhaps the most serious shortcoming of the 1977 legislation is failure to confront the issue of what some refer to as a "structure policy." Legislative deliberations have paid scant heed to the long–term consequences of short–term expedients. Of concern is the long–term impact of 1977 Act price supports, payment limitations and production controls on land prices and on the size and number of farms. Before turning to these issues, it is necessary to review the cost of production data used to set target prices.

Cost of Production. Much debate has focused on what is the cost of production. One problem is that there is no single national cost of production for setting target prices—costs vary greatly among farms. Some agreement prevails that costs should reflect resource costs (not cash outlays) of family–size commercial farms in areas of comparative advantage; much less agreement exists on how to handle specific components of costs. Target prices in the Food and Agriculture Act of 1977 were initially established for 1978 near a level equal to all costs of production in 1977 with land charged at the long–term interest rate times average acquisition value (Table 8). Inflation will increase 1978 costs (not yet available for this report), but higher yields in 1978 will lower the cost per unit of producing some crops.

In deliberations prior to passage of the 1977 Act, three principal approaches were considered to measure land's contribution to costs: (1) rental value, (2) average acquisition cost of land times current long–term mortgage interest rate, and (3) current land price times the current long–term interest rate. An overlooked but attractive alternative is to charge for land at its current price times the long–term real rate of return, approximately 4 percent. The real cost of owning land is the current interest rate times the price of land plus property tax minus capital gains. It follows that, based on experience of the past two decades, the cost of owning land has been *no more* than 4 percent of current land value. Alternatively, land can be costed at the real rate of interest plus a risk premium. With the real rate of interest approximately 3 percent, the greater risk in land investment would warrant a

TABLE 8.
Preliminary Estimates of 1977 Production Costs of
Selected Crops, and Support Rates

Item	Commodity			
	Corn	Wheat	Cotton	Soybeans
	($/bu.)	($/bu.)	($/lb. lint)	($/bu.)
Production cost				
Nonland				
Variable	.95	1.14	.290	1.51
Labor	.11	.26	.044	.34
Management	.12	.14	.041	.34
Machinery ownership	.31	.68	.122	.85
Overhead	.11	.21	.022	.22
Subtotal	1.60	2.43	.519	3.26
Byproducts	--	.06	.055	--
Subtotal	1.60	2.37	.464	3.26
Land (acq.)[a]	.52	.67	.073	1.52
Total	2.12	3.04	.537	4.78
Land (current)[b]	.64	.91	.068	1.81
Total	2.24	3.28	.532	5.07
(Percent of 1910–1914 parity)	(63)	(67)	(63)	(66)
Target price 1978	2.10	3.40[c]	.52	4.50[d]

SOURCE: Cost data from U.S. Department of Agriculture (1978, March).

[a] Acquisition price times current mortgage interest rate.

[b] Current price times 4 percent real rate of return, plus property tax. The resulting land cost overestimates production cost because the land price includes the value of the farm dwelling. Use of rent rather than current land price to determine land cost would give results similar to those shown. An advantage of using rental value is that it avoids inclusion of speculative land purchases in production costs.

[c] Initially set at $3.00.

[d] Loan rate; soybeans have no target price.

real return of perhaps 4 percent. If land earnings and prices keep pace with inflation as they have in the past, a current real return on land of 4 percent is equivalent to an average of a 10 percent nominal return over the life of the investment if the inflation rate is 6 percent. The nominal return will average 14 percent if the inflation rate is 10 percent.

If land values do not increase with inflation, then the appropriate land charge is the current land price times the current nominal interest rate, the latter reflecting the real interest rate plus expected national inflation. In addition, a risk premium of perhaps 1 percentage point could be added to the nominal interest rate, bringing the total to 10 percent.

The issue of whether to apply a 4 percent or 10 percent current charge to land resolves to whether land prices will keep pace with general inflation. The historic record and economic theory suggest land prices will keep pace with inflation in the long run. Indeed, it is difficult to conclude otherwise if target prices continue to keep pace with the cost of production. The current price support legislation almost assures a close relationship between national inflation and land prices. Target prices will be increased by non–land production cost gains which in turn will follow closely national inflation rates.

It is notable that current cash rents less property taxes average approximately 4 percent of current land values based on data from 22 states (U.S. Department of Agriculture 1977, July). Because valuing land at its historic actual average acquisition cost essentially takes the long–term rate of return into account, it is not surprising that quite similar conclusions are reached by costing land by that crude method compared to the two preferred methods: (1) rental value less real estate property tax, and (2) current land value times the real rate of return (approximately 4 percent).

Costing land at its current value times current rate of interest overestimates the resource cost of land if land prices continue to increase at the national rate of inflation. Supporting prices to cover all costs including land at current acquisition price times current interest rates would yield approximately a 9 percent current land return. Adding an inflation premium of 6 percent gives an expected overall return over the life of the investment of 15 percent. Such an expected rate of return is highly attractive to investors and unattainable given time for land prices to adjust. Investment will occur until land prices are driven up to a level that yields a current return of 4 percent, which in turn requires a higher price support.

In addition to the handling of land prices, issues concerning the

U.S. Department of Agriculture's (1978, March) cost of production estimates include the accuracy of the survey data, the appropriate measurement of labor and management costs, and what costs to include in computing support prices. Basic data on crop production technology and practices are only obtained periodically—about every four years, with the next survey for the major crops to be taken in March and April of 1979. The sample of 6,000 to 7,000 operators is designed to give each acre of a crop equal probability of being included. Some operators complete questionnaires for two crops, and the total number of questionnaires completed is approximately 9,000. The sample is stratified by type–of–production of each crop, with over– or undersampling adjustments made to bring sampling errors to acceptable levels in each type–of–production area with appropriate subsequent weighting of samples to restore representativeness of all acres planted of each crop. Annual yield, acreage and price data are obtained from Crop Reporting Board surveys separate from the production technology and practices survey. Thus production practices and technology are not changed every year, but the budgets are updated annually for prices, yields and abandoned acres. In addition, special surveys for fertilizers and pesticides supplement the data. Labor requirements and annualized costs for machinery use and ownership are from other sources. The use of the same production technology and practices data for four years is dictated by the high cost of surveys. The procedure overestimates costs to the extent farmers are continually improving production efficiency.

One concern is the extent to which survey responses are biased by operators' lapses of memory (for example, some operators fail to report that they replanted wheat or grazed it out) or attempts to influence results. Another concern is possible bias from combining crop production practices obtained from one survey of producers with prices, yields and acreage abandonment data obtained from surveys of other producers.

Past procedures include a management charge calculated as 7 percent of gross crop receipts. Revised procedures will calculate the charge as 10 percent of nonland costs of production. The past procedure was based on fees charged by farm management firms on the landlord's portion of receipts. This portion compensates for organizational management of the operator. By applying the same rate to all receipts, not just the landlord's portion, the added fee can be considered compensation for the operator's operational management.

The labor cost is all labor hours times the state hired labor wage rate including perquisites and employers' contribution to Social Security—5.85 percent of wages in 1977. A difficulty is that state average labor wages do not necessarily represent labor rates for each crop or area to which they are applied. The total labor rate averaged $3.04 per hour in 1977 for the United States. Additional study is needed of the appropriate opportunity cost of operator–family labor and management.

Target prices are adjusted by a moving average of costs of production. For example, the target price of a crop in 1979 is computed as the target price in 1978 plus the change in production cost (excluding land and management) between 1977–1978 (two year average) and 1976–1977 (two year average). This procedure at least to some extent averages out the effect of random variation in yields and input prices. The procedure makes land and management charges an issue in setting initial target prices but not an issue in annual adjustments.

The finding that total production costs for major crops are covered with prices at 63 to 67 percent of 1910–1914 parity (see Table 8) may appear incongruent. To explain this finding, total productivity of U.S. agriculture is used as an example because data on productivity of production resources for individual commodities are unavailable (yields do not measure productivity). In equilibrium in a competitive industry, total returns measured by prices received (P) times output (Q) are equal to total costs measured by prices paid (P_x) times input (X), or $PQ = P_x X$. Rearranging terms, it follows that $(Q/X) = P_x/P$. Hence productivity (Q/X) is equal to the ratio of prices paid to prices received by farmers (P_x/P), the inverse of the parity ratio. The index of productivity of U.S. agriculture increased from 100 in 1910–1914 to 233 in 1976, indicating that the parity ratio could decrease from an index of 100 in 1910–1914 to 43 in 1976 and cover all costs of production. A major reason the parity ratio did not in fact fall to this level is because farming was in disequilibrium in the 1910–1914 period, with farmers earning only 61 percent as much as nonfarmers on the average despite 1910–1914 being labeled a "golden age" for farmers. Much of the disequilibrium in earnings of farm and nonfarm people had dissipated by 1976 when per capita personal income of the farm population averaged 80 percent that of the nonfarm population, although 90 percent may be preferred. Adjusting for this latter factor leaves a required parity price ratio of 63 for 1976. Errors in construction of productivity and price indices preclude precise conclusions, but the equilibrium parity ratio now appears to be about 70 percent of the 1910–1914 average for all farm output based on current cost of production and other economic data. This estimate is an average for all farm output; the required parity ratio is higher for livestock and livestock products than for crops (Table 8) because livestock have not experienced as high productivity gains as crops.

In short, the above considerations suggest that current support rates are below total production costs per unit of output on an average, commercial farm. There is considerable variation in production costs among farms. The majority of farm output is produced below the computed cost and the majority of farm operators have costs above the computed cost. Knowledge of the extent to which differences in production costs are the result of fundamental differences in efficiency among farms rather than random, short–run differences (due to weather and other chance elements) would help to determine the contribution of current target prices to land price inflation and incentives for farm consolidation. Annual adjustments of target prices for changes in nonland costs of production will increase supports but avoid a spiral (accelerating) of support prices and land prices. Annual adjustments in support prices will tend to raise land prices in line with inflation rates over an extended period. Of course, periods of relative farm prosperity and depressed economic conditions will fluctuate around the long–term trend.

Setting target prices at the average cost on the average production unit virtually assures returns above costs for the average–cost producer over a period of years. In years of low market prices, returns will be equal to the target price; in years of high market prices, returns will be above target price. The average of these returns exceeds the cost of production, creating incentives to bid up the price of land even on farms with average costs of production. Because the Task Force did not favor use of commodity programs to support resource returns above the cost of production on adequately managed family–size farms, the issue is whether target prices provided in 1977 legislation are adequate in light of foregoing analysis. Sub–issues are the relationships (1) of the

U.S. Department of Agriculture's cost of production data to actual producers' costs, (2) of cost of production to target prices, and (3) of target prices to producers' returns.

Procedures for calculating the cost of production overestimate costs by omitting input price discounts and product price premiums, by failing to adjust annually for changes in farm production practices that are a response to changes in prices and new technology and by underestimating benefits from graze–out or cover cropping and from any questionnaire responses deliberately biased to give high costs. Failure to include the value of grain straw and the soil carryover of fertilizers, crop residues and weed control also tends to overestimate production costs. Current procedures underestimate costs from failure to record soil loss and all production practices and inputs. The net bias is unknown but estimates need to be continually refined.

The 1978 target prices were set slightly below total production costs for 1977 based on land costs estimated by rent or real cost of land at current prices shown in Table 8 and might fall even lower in relation to actual 1978 production costs. But because most production occurs at costs below those shown in Table 8 and because farm returns will average above target prices for reasons given above, the target price levels seem sufficiently high to provide farming returns covering production costs on adequately managed family farms over a period of years. To avoid providing windfall wealth to land owners, transfer of income from lower income consumers and taxpayers to higher income producers, inflation of land prices that would create even greater cash flow problems to new entrants or expanding family farms, and to allow resources and products to adjust to demand, the conclusion is that support prices above levels provided in current legislation seem justified neither on grounds of economic equity or efficiency.

Payment Limitations. The influence of consumers and taxpayers on the 1977 legislation was obscure. Such interests presumably got their foot in the door with largely symbolic payment limitations of $55,000 per major commodity in the Agriculture Act of 1970. The portents became more ominous in the Agriculture and Consumer Protection Act of 1973 which limited payments to $20,000 per recipient. Although inflation warranted an increase of $27,000 by 1977 to maintain the real level of limitations, the 1977 Act raised the maximum sum

of payments to any recipient to $40,000 in 1978, $45,000 in 1979 and
$50,000 in 1980 and 1981 for wheat, feed grain and upland cotton.

Payments for rice producers were limited to $52,500 in 1978 and
$50,000 in 1979, 1980 and 1981. Payments for disaster, public recrea-
tion access, receipts from Commodity Credit Corporation acquisitions,
and for extra–long staple cotton, sugar and wool programs were
exempted from limitations. Based on maximum deficiency payments
equal to the difference between the loan rate and target price in 1978
times representative yields, program acreage could be 1,159 acres of
wheat, 4,000 acres of corn and 2,000 acres of upland cotton before
payment limitations are imposed. With a market price during the first
five months of the marketing year above the loan rate and opportunities to subdivide ownership, payment limitations in the 1977 Act
are largely symbolic and will have an imperceptible impact on the
distribution of payments among farmers and on restraining growth of
large farms.

It may be argued that if production controls rather than direct
payments are relied upon to support farm income, stringent payment
limitations are inappropriate because production control would be concentrated on smaller farms, virtually putting them out of business
when considerable overcapacity exists. Since larger farms would be
setting aside land as a strategic reserve desired by society, they need to
be compensated for this service. On the other hand, if commodity
stocks provide sufficient reserves, then direct payments without production controls can provide economic security to family farms to
which they could be targeted.

Major commodity programs as operated in the past combined
direct payments (grants or transfers) with production diversion payments in a manner that achieved neither the potentially high cost
effectiveness of production control nor the potentially high target efficiency of direct payments.

Commodity Program Impact on Farm Structure. Government
program payments are considerably larger for big farms than small
farms. This fact does not in itself mean that commodity programs
encourage growth of large farms and consolidation of small farms. At
issue is how commodity programs influence economies of size, defined
as costs per unit of production. Calculations for 1970 (the last year for

which reliable data are available) reveal that direct payments decreased costs per unit of gross farm income by 3 percent on farms with sales of over $100,000 and by 13 percent on farms with sales of under $2,500, hence flattening the unit cost curve in Figure 1. Furthermore, commodity programs were a smaller proportion of receipts on large farms than on small farms. These direct effects alone do not create incentives for farm consolidation.

But indirect effects seem to outweigh the direct effects. The decreasing cost structure of the farming industry discussed earlier and illustrated in Figure 1 suggests caution in the use of price supports. Large farms on the average are more efficient than small farms. The unit cost curve indicates no major economies or diseconomies of size above approximately $50,000 of sales. While this finding indicates profit rates are not enhanced for larger farms on the average, as equity is leveraged to purchase an ever larger farming unit, a smaller and smaller drop in product prices can wipe out that equity. Commodity programs provided a price floor of economic security for large farms which enabled them to use their greater efficiency to outbid their smaller competitors for land. This consolidation was carried out, not so much by large corporate, partnership or vertically integrated farms, but by family–run farms. Commodity programs helped keep some farms in business. But the net effect of past commodity programs seemed to be to increase farm size and reduce the number of farms (Tyner and Tweeten; Ray and Heady; Nelson and Cochrane). This led Duncan to conclude that the greatest threat to the family farm comes from the adequate–sized, well–managed, adequately capitalized family farm bent on expansion. Commodity programs as now structured give impetus to this process. While the trend is not inconsistent with economic efficiency, it offers few efficiency gains and poses threats in the form of replacing the traditional family farm and reducing the number of farms to a point where bargaining power in the hands of producers can unduly raise food costs.

Public policy failing to recognize the diversity in farming depicted earlier in this report may accomplish the opposite of its intended purpose. A program to raise all farm prices to make small farms, entry–level farms with cash flow problems, drought–stricken farms or irrigated farms (troubled by rising energy costs and declining water tables) economically viable will improve the competitive position of large farm operators who then outbid others for land. The cost to taxpayers is large and new barriers to enter farming are posed by land prices inflated by across–the–board price and income supports. The protest movement of 1977–1978 highlights that a broad–based program cannot meet the very real needs of all farmers. Rather, these unique problems need to be dealt with by credit and adjustment programs tailored to individual needs. Similarly, federal income tax provisions to aid farmers with accelerated depreciation and investment tax credits encourage substitution of capital for farm labor and nonfarm investments in agriculture that can hasten the demise of family farms.

Task Force Perceptions

Eleven Task Force members (chairman abstaining) completed questionnaires eliciting their perceptions of government programs for agriculture. Task Force responses are not a random sample designed to represent views of all farmers or any other segment of agriculture. Task Force members are from farms, farm organizations, agricultural businesses and cooperatives, and from government. They were selected and are respected for their judgment and knowledge of the agricultural industry. Their concern was for the long–term as well as the short–term well being of farmers and society. Nonetheless, the group is a small and nonrandom sample, and it is not claimed that their views are necessarily representative of the agricultural community as a whole.

Responses were given on a scale ranging from strongly agree (SA), agree (A), undecided (U), disagree (D), to strongly disagree (SD). Responses were calculated for each category.

MAIN DIRECTIONS

Expert opinions solicited by Leo Mayer (Congressional Research Service) judged as unworkable a proposal for 100 percent of parity on all farm commodities. The Task Force response (1) in Table 9 was also unfavorable. The proposal was rejected because it would require massive bureaucracy and policing to administer and because it would provide an attractive environment for inroads into farming of corporate and other nonfarm investors. Raising farm household income well above incomes in the rest of society would regressively redistribute income, generate inflation, worsen our foreign trade balance and re-

TABLE 9.
Task Force Preferences for Major Directions for Farm Policy

	SA	A	U	D	SD
(1) Support prices of all farm commodities at 100 percent of parity.	1	0	0	0	10
(2) Move further toward a free–market orientation than provided in the Food and Agriculture Act of 1977 through an appropriate transition program.	2	3	0.5	4.5	1
(3) Require mandatory diversion of land after producers of (say) 60 percent of commodity agree to quotas in referendum.	1	1	0	6	3
(4) Continue the Food and Agriculture Act of 1977 (with minor modifications if necessary).	1	6	1	2	1
(5) Emphasize direct payments (without production controls) and commodity storage reserves to reduce economic fluctuations in farm (and food) prices to commercial farmers and provide nationwide income maintenance program for low income farmers.	1	5	0.5	0.5	4

tard economic growth. National output of goods and services would be
reduced because farm output would need to be sharply curtailed to
maintain commodity prices and because greater spending on food and
fiber would leave less income for nonfarmers to spend on consumption
or investment in growth industries.

Other alternatives offered were a move toward a free market
orientation (2), mandatory controls (3), continuation of current legislation (4), and direct payments with no controls (5). The Task Force
strongly opposed mandatory controls and was almost evenly divided in
supporting or opposing a move to a free market orientation. Some
government involvement to stabilize the farming economy was accepted, with the strongest support for continuing the 1977 Act with
modifications if necessary. A majority either strongly agreed or agreed
with direct payments without controls. Judging from only the alternatives listed above, farm policy is a choice among "least–bad"
programs—only continuation of the Food and Agriculture Act of 1977
received a generally positive (though low) response.

A DEFINITIVE PROGRAM

Because somewhat favorable responses came only to proposals for
direct payments with no production controls and for continuation of
the 1977 Act, reactions to these proposals are examined further, with
the former expanded into a comprehensive policy that recognizes the
need to integrate farm, rural development and welfare programs. The
preambles and responses of the Task Force to the comprehensive
policy with components for established commercial farms, entry–level
and expanding modest–size farms, and low–income farms were as
shown in Table 10.

The policy for commercial farms contained four programs (a) direct
payments without production controls to give economic vitality to
adequate–size, well–managed farms, (b) commodity stock management to reduce economic instability to farmers and consumers, (c)
"all–risk, all–commodity" insurance to replace disaster payments and
federal crop insurance, and (d) monetary–fiscal policy to restrain inflation. The Task Force reacted favorably to each of these programs.

Beginning and expanding modest–size family farmers experience
severe cash flow problems because of high capital requirements, especially for ownership, compounded by inflation. To deal with this situa-

TABLE 10.
Task Force Preferences for Program Provisions

	SA	A	U	D	SD
(1) Programs for *commercial farmers* would not support farm prices and income above a free market equilibrium for an extended period but rather would be designed only to preserve economic vitality of adequate–size, well–managed farms. Key features would include:					
(a) A support rate based on operating costs of production (perhaps including a return to labor but excluding land). Direct payments paid to farmers based on the shortfall of market prices below the support rate times (say) 80 percent of historic production. (This base would not be increased for higher yields or acreage over time.)	1	8	2	0	0
(b) Commodity reserve management with emphasis on farmer–owned reserves with a storage payment to farmers. Storage payments would cease and farmers could release stocks at (say) 150 percent of the support rate. Farmers would be encouraged to release stock to the market when market prices reach (say) 200 percent of the support rate. No additional stocks would be accepted for the storage program when total stocks reached a pre–set level and commodity prices would be allowed to fall to a level set by the market. The Secretary of Agriculture would have discretion in setting storage payment rates to acquire desired stocks.		·			
(c) An "all–risk, all–commodity" insurance program available in all counties would replace existing disaster payment and federal crop insurance programs.	1	9	0	1	0
(d) The government would move toward monetary–fiscal policy to bring national inflation to no more than (say) 3 percent annually. Elements of such an effort include a more nearly balanced federal budget and a wage or earnings supplement (or related income maintenance program) to encourage national growth and employment financed by termination of revenue sharing and savings in existing welfare and unemployment insurance programs.	3	6.5	1.5	0	0

TABLE 10. Continued

	SA	A	U	D	SD
(2) In addition to programs for commercial farmers, provide *entry–level farmers* some re-direction in programs of the Farmers Home Administration (FmHA):					
(a) Target more resources of the FmHA to entry-level farmers to reduce liquidity problems in early years as operators become established	3	7	0	1	0
(b) Target more FmHA rural development funds to expanding job opportunities. Provide incentives for private industry to develop jobs within reach of farm residents to assist especially the young farmers and their families overcome cash flow problems in early years of farming. FmHA could reduce emphasis on loans and grants funding rural services and rather would emphasize programs to expand the economic base in rural communities.	1	5	0	5	0
(3) Needs for *low–income* farmers are in some ways similar to those for entry–level farmers, but low–income farmers who are aged or otherwise boxed–in (by lack of general education, nonfarm work experience, etc.) may need other assistance:					
(a) Provide nationwide income maintenance program that would include the working poor and be funded by the federal government with nationwide eligibility and assistance standards (adjusted for cost of living).	0	6	1	3	1
(b) Provide more funds for work force programs to upgrade skills and secure employment in nonfarm jobs for persons in low income farm households.	0	9	0	1	1

tion, proposals are to target more funds of the Farmers Home Administration for (2a) assisting entry–level farmers to become established and (2b) rural job development. The Task Force strongly supported the former program; less support was given to federal efforts to expand job opportunities so that entry farmers or others in their family could supplement farm earnings with off–farm jobs in early years when farm liquidity problems are pressing.

Low–income farmers constitute a third category of critical concern. A bare majority of the Task Force supported a nationwide income maintenance program to be funded by the federal government with nationwide eligibility and assistance standards (3a). Strong support was apparent for work force programs to upgrade skills and secure employment in nonfarm jobs (3b).

MODIFICATIONS OF EXISTING LEGISLATION

As noted earlier, the Task Force was favorably disposed toward the 1977 commodity legislation. Responses of the Task Force to a number of proposals to modify commodity legislation are recorded in Table 11.

Considerable support was expressed for simplifying current legislation, reform in milk pricing to reduce incentives for excess milk production, use of sealed bids (provided for in current legislation) and other means to raise cost–effectiveness of land diversion programs, and more comprehensive discussion of carryover and other provisions prior to imposition of set–aside programs.

The Task Force did not favor making allotments or bases negotiable, establishing an Agricultural Board to administer commodity programs, proscribing transfer of allotments among two or more farming units under one owner, or imposition of more stringent payment limitations. Conservative price support levels were favored—the majority would set supports to cover only operating expenditures while others would vary support from higher levels when stocks are down to lower levels when stocks are up.

OTHER POLICY ISSUES

A number of proposals, not necessarily related to commodity programs, have been suggested to change, if not to improve, public policy

TABLE 11.
Response of Task Force Members to Modifications in Legislation

	SA	A	U	D	SD
(1) Make all allotments and bases negotiable with no restrictions on sale of allotments or bases.	1	2	2	5	1
(2) Shift to bushel or poundage quotas on all commodities, remove all acreage restrictions.	1	4	1	4	1
(3) Simplify administration of programs. The Food and Agriculture Act of 1977 is unduly complicated.	3	6	0	2	0
(4) Establish Agricultural Board to administer all commodity programs, comprised of appointees from farm, consumer and other groups somewhat insulated from narrow, short–run political pressures—patterned after Federal Reserve Board.	1	4	0	4	2
(5) Allow no shift of allotments over time among farms. Purpose is to discourage purchase and consolidation of farms just to get allotments or bases moved to better land.	1	1	3	5	1
(6) Pay milk producers actual market price on manufactured grade milk and end the current practice of paying a blend of fluid and manufactured grade milk price which encourages excess production. (Fluid grade milk base could be expanded to reduce inequities that would arise from the shift.)	2	7	1	1	0
(7) Use sealed bids, required rotation of bases and allotments among cropland acres and in other ways administer programs to remove as much production as possible per dollar of ASCS program funds.	1	7	1	0	1
(8) Impose more stringent payment limitations. Graduate payments with full direct payments to small producers and no payments of more than (say) $20,000 to any recipient.	1	2	1	5	2

TABLE 11. Continued

	SA	A	U	D	SD
(9) Government establish carryover targets for all grains and soybeans with guidelines tied to expected U.S. and world needs. The carryover targets would be announced publicly in advance of planting allowing scrutiny by farmers and others of the targets. Set–aside acreage level would be designed each year to result in desired carryover given normal yields.	1	9	0	1	0
(10) Farmers must accept government measures to hold down farm prices in times of "national emergency," if they accept supports to keep farm prices from falling to low levels.	0	8	0	2	0
(11) Government price supports should be (a) set to cover only operating expenses, (b) set equal to all costs of production including land charges, (c) varied with low supports in times of large stock reserves and high supports in times of low reserves, (d) set according to some proportion of parity, (e) eliminated.	(a) 6	(b) 1	(c) 4	(d) 0	(e) 0

relating to agriculture. Some of the proposals have sound economic credentials, others do not. Task Force responses are shown in Table 12.

The majority of the Task Force expressed concern over federal tax policies encouraging investment in a farming industry troubled by chronic excess capacity and encouraging substitution of capital for labor. The Task Force would like to see more funds made available to the Farmers Home Administration to help finance moderate–size family farms and showed some support for ending subsidies for rural services that encourage city people to acquire farms and reside in the country while holding jobs in town. Such assistance not only may transfer dollars from moderate income taxpayers to more wealthy taxpayers choosing to reside on a country estate, but also may use land inefficiently that otherwise might have been in family farms. In 1978, 10 percent of farm real estate transfers were intended for use as a rural residence. The 1974 Census of Agriculture provides clues that the number of small farms is increasing in some areas (Gardner and Pope, p. 247). Sprawl apparent in these figures interferes with efficiency in use of energy as well as farming resources.

The Task Force was skeptical about a significantly enlarged role of government in agriculture, especially one that would sacrifice efficiency to gain equity. This view was apparent in rejection of breakup of large farms upon death of owner for creation of family farms; government land purchase for resale to young, family farmers; placing restrictions on nonfarmer (particularly foreign) investment in farmland; and, in general, using government subsidies to preserve the family farm. Unwillingness of the Task Force to recommend specific restrictions on nonfarm ownership of farmland stems in part from the need for rented land—renting is a major strategy used by farm operators to reduce cash flow pressures. Skepticism was also apparent in disapproval of proposals employing bargaining power to raise returns. The majority rejected government legislation to enhance farm bargaining power (legislation requiring buyers to bargain in good faith, police power to enforce controls, etc.) and a proposal to form a wheat cartel. A middle ground consistent with other Task Force perceptions is apparent in rejection of dependence on the private trade alone for commodity stock operations.

TABLE 12.

Response of Task Force Members to Miscellaneous Farm Policy Issues

	SA	A	U	D	SD
(1) End or set tight limits on income tax provisions that encourage substitution of capital for labor in farming. Examples of such provisions include accelerated depreciation allowances, investment tax credits, cash accounting, interest deductions, special capital gains tax rates, writeoff of capital expenditures against ordinary income. Limits might be set only for those who make majority of income from off-farm sources.	3	5	0	2	1
(2) Change estate tax allowances. Lower estate tax exemptions to encourage breakup of large farms upon death of owner with attendant program to encourage takeover of farms by family sized operations.	0	3	2	1	4
(3) Government buy land as it becomes available and rent or sell it at concessional terms to young, family farmers.	1	1	0	3	5
(4) End subsidies for electrical, telephone, water and other services that encourage city people to acquire farms and reside in country while holding job in town.	1	4.5	1.5	2	2
(5) Government pass legislation that would make it easier for farmers to form collective bargaining groups and provide police powers to enforce production or marketing controls.	1	2.5	1.5	5	1
(6) Government form a wheat agreement with Canada, Australia and Argentina, specifying minimum wheat prices for export each year and allotting share of world wheat markets according to historic pattern.	1	1	4	3	2
(7) Government place explicit restrictions on nonfarmer (particularly foreign) investment in farmland.	1	1	1	5	3

TABLE 12. Continued

	SA	A	U	D	SD
(8) Government should take necessary measures to preserve the family farm structure and restrain growth of large farms, even if such measures entail subsidies and interference with the market.	1	2	1.5	4.5	2
(9) Commodity stock reserves should be solely left to the private trade (no government stocks or payments to farmers to store commodities).	0	1	1	7	2
(10) Government should make more funds available to the Farmers Home Administration to help finance family farms, with loan application processing expedited to reduce the time between application and decision regarding granting of the loan.	2	6	1	1	1

Several issues not included in the questionnaire were of concern to selected Task Force members and warrant attention.

(1) The government is subsidizing lending to large producers, many of them wealthy enough to weather the temporary set–backs occasioning disaster loans. The problem of overlapping federal programs and inappropriate lending policies to large farmers who can obtain credit from commercial or cooperative sources was noted with the entrance of the Small Business Administration into farm credit market. The need was emphasized to coordinate with programs of the Farmers Home Administration.

(2) Another concern was the lack of emphasis on soil conservation in current legislation. It seems incongruent that the emergence of the environmental movement has occurred at a time of diminished attention to soil conservation—given that soil erosion is viewed by experts as the number one environmental problem in farming. Tying set–aside payments more closely to soil conservation practices and provisions for longer–term land retirement may be appropriate responses.

(3) "Thinness" in commodity wholesale markets for meats and some dairy products has made price discovery difficult and has led to allegations that pricing is unrepresentative and subject to manipulation. A case in point is the wholesale meat market where an estimated 75 to 90 percent of meat sold annually is purchased under formulas. The formulas are tied to prices in the "Yellow Sheet" prepared by a few individuals sampling a small percent of the market using techniques about which little is known and without scrutiny from disinterested observers. "The Fair Meat Trading Act of 1978" was introduced for comment near the end of the 95th Congress by Congressman Neal Smith. The House Small Business Committee of which Smith is chairman recommended licensing of market news reporting services such as the Yellow Sheet, promoting formation of more than one market reporting service, establishing a Meat Industry Standards Board, making it a criminal violation to provide false information affecting meat prices and calling for the U.S. Department of Agriculture to study feasibility of a computer market system in the meat industry. The Task Force could not study the issues in sufficient depth to make specific recommendations, but feels that concerns over "thin" markets for farm products need to be resolved.

Summary and Conclusions

Public policy for the farm sector must recognize emerging economic realities. Farming is not uniformly a low–equity, low–income or low rate of return industry. It is heterogeneous—tailoring one program to suit all of farming would be a straightjacket. Major problems of commercial agriculture are inflation, which emerged in this decade, and instability, which has been around for a long time. The principal problems of beginning and expanding modest–size farms include those of established commercial farms, but inflation is particularly troublesome because it generates formidable barriers to entry and severe cash–flow problems. Small farms are less troubled by instability in farm prices and income because of low debt–asset ratios and substantial off–farm income, but many of them have low incomes and are impacted by old age and lack of general education and skills.

Productivity advancing faster than demand for farm output and a large reservoir of excess labor are no longer significant problems. However, labor–saving technology continues to displace people from farming, and policies to prepare people for the transition should not be overlooked.

For commercial farmers, the Task Force favored price supports no higher than the cost of production, "all–risk, all–commodity" insurance, commodity reserve management and more responsible monetary–fiscal policy to restrain inflation. The Task Force would target more funds of the Farmers Home Administration (FmHA) to help entry–level farmers meet credit needs and it mildly favored redirection of FmHA efforts from financing rural services to financing rural job–creation through incentives afforded private industry. The Task Force strongly favored more training and employment programs and mildly favored a nationwide income maintenance program to help low income farmers.

The Food and Agriculture Act of 1977 seems to be on the right track based on opinion surveys of farmers and of this Task Force on farm prices and incomes. The Act provides considerable market orientation, flexibility and tools to stabilize prices to farmers and consumers. Some modifications are called for. Farm output demand prices are related to loan rates which seem sufficiently flexible to keep our farm products competitive in markets at home and abroad. Farm output supply price has become tied to target price, creating tendencies for overproduction and chronic need for set aside for some commodities. Policies could be devised to reduce the amplitude of the cattle cycle. Suggested changes include allowances for grazing and haying of set aside and increasing import quotas when beef supplies are low and curtailing these allowances when beef supplies are high. More stringent payment limitations to restrain growth of large farms and reduce shrinkage in number of farms received little support from the Task Force but need further analysis. The Task Force was critical of the provisions in federal income tax policies which shelter nonfarm income, encourage substitution of capital for farm labor and speed out-movement of farm people.

New directions in policy include moving toward direct payments without government production controls. Set–aside of land is an increasingly obsolete and cost–ineffective method of controlling production, requiring a substantial administrative bureaucracy and arbitrary judgments. Two–price plans maintaining prices above production costs undermine sales in the long run and create a burden, especially for consumers with low incomes. Opportunities to restrain food price increases and to target program benefits to family farms would be enhanced with direct payments.

Temptations exist to treat problem symptoms such as the cash flow squeeze on beginning and expanding owner–operators with high, rigid price supports. Such "medicine" will help existing farmers facing a liquidity crisis but will make the farming sector "patient" worse by creating windfall benefits to established commercial farms and provide an environment favoring entry of nonfarm corporations or other legal devices to funnel capital into farming. The result will be farm consolidation and fewer family farmers. The cause of the cash flow problem is the combination of national inflation and the high capital–labor ratios in agriculture. The problem can be treated by improved monetary–fiscal policy, and by appropriate changes in lending, insurance and tax policies. The rate of substitution of capital for labor could be abated by payment limitations or a graduated excise tax on new farm machinery. The Task Force considered some of these medications to be too strong.

The Secretary of Agriculture needs to be allowed the flexibility to adjust milk price supports to levels that will not induce excessive surpluses and high government costs. Phasing out of the two–price milk system in favor of direct payment programs can maintain farm income while retarding incentives for consumers to reduce milk consumption.

Other modifications in current policies suggested by the Task Force include replacing the existing federal crop insurance program and disaster payments with an "all–risk, all–commodity" insurance program, and coordination of Farmers Home Administration and Small Business Administration lending activities in targeting federal credit programs to moderate–size, entry–level and low–income farmers.

The Task Force expressed support for simplifying current legislation and administering set aside for greater cost effectiveness (removing more production per program dollar). Little or no support was expressed for making allotments or bases negotiable, establishing an Agricultural Board to administer food and farm programs, proscribing transfer of allotments, bases or established program acreage among farms under the same owner, or shifting to bushel or poundage quotas.

References

Congressional Research Service, The Library of Congress. 1978. "Evaluation of Proposals Guaranteeing Full Parity for Farmers in the Marketplace." Committee on Agriculture, U.S. House of Representatives, 95th Cong., 2nd. sess. Washington: U.S. Gov't. Printing Office.

Council of Economic Advisers. 1978. *Economic Report of the President.* Washington: U.S. Gov't. Printing Office.

Council on Wage and Price Stability. 1976. "Responsiveness of Wholesale and Retail Food Prices to Changes in the Cost of Food Production and Distribution." Staff Report. Washington: Executive Office of the President.

Duncan, M. 1977. "Farm Real Estate: Who Buys and How?" *Monthly Rev.* Kansas City: Federal Reserve Bank, June.

Edwards, R. and G. Coffman. 1977. "Farm Poverty: A Current Assessment and Research Focus." USDA–ESCS–NEAD, Working Paper.

Evans, C., P. Allen, R. Simunek, L. Walker and B. Hottel. 1977. "Balance Sheet of the Farming Sector, 1977." USDA–ERS, Agr. Info. Bul. No. 411.

Gardner, D. and R. Pope. 1978. "How is Scale and Structure Determined in Agriculture." *Amer. J. Agr. Econ.* 60: 295–302.

Guither, H. and B. Jones. 1978. "How Farmers Viewed Farm and Food Policy Issues Compared with Selected Provisions of the 1977 Agricultural Act." *Amer. J. Agr. Econ.* 60: 550–54.

Hottel, B. and R. Reinsel. 1976. "Returns to Equity Capital by Economic Class of Farm." USDA–ERS, Agr. Econ. Rep. No. 347.

Manchester, A. 1978. "Dairy Price Policy: Setting, Problems, Alternatives." USDA–ESCS, Agr. Econ. Rep. No. 402.

Nelson, F. and W. Cochrane. 1976. "Economic Consequences of Federal Farm Commodity Programs, 1953–72." *Agr. Econ. Res.* 28: 52–64.

Novakovic, A. and R. Thompson. 1977. "The Impact of Imports of Manufactured Milk Products on the U.S. Dairy Industry." *Amer. J. Agr. Econ.* 59: 507–19.

Raup, P. 1978. "Some Questions of Value and Scale in American Agriculture." *Amer. J. Agr. Econ.* 60: 303–08.

Ray, D. and E. Heady. 1974. "Simulated Effects of Alternative Policy and Economic Environments on U.S. Agriculture." Center for Agricultural and Rural Development, Iowa State University, CARD Rep. 46.

Reinsel, E. 1968. "Farm and Off–farm Income Reported on Federal Income Tax Returns." USDA–ERS, Agr. Econ. Rep. No. 385.

Salathe, L., W. Dobson and G. Peterson. 1977. "Analysis of the Impact of Alternative U.S. Dairy Import Policies." *Amer. J. Agr. Econ.* 59: 496–506.

Spitze, R. G. F. 1978. "The Food and Agriculture Act of 1977: Issues and Decisions." *Amer. J. Agr. Econ.* 60: 225–35.

Strickland, P. L. and D. Fawcett. "Selected Typical Farming Operations in the United States, 1976." USDA–ESCS, Agr. Econ. Rep., forthcoming.

Tweeten, L. 1977. "Agricultural Policy: A Review of Legislation, Programs and Policy." *Food and Agricultural Policy.* Washington: American Enterprise Institute for Public Policy Research.

Tweeten, L. and S. Griffin. 1976. "General Inflation and the Farming Economy." Okla. Agr. Exp. Sta. Res. Rep. P–732.

Tweeten, L., L. Quance and C. Yeh. 1978. "U.S. Production Capacity: Reply." *Amer. J. Agr. Econ.* 60: 706–08.

Tyner, F. and L. Tweeten. 1968. "Simulation as a Method of Appraising Farm Programs." *Amer. J. Agr. Econ.* 50: 66–81.

U.S. Department of Agriculture. March 1978. "Costs of Producing Selected Crops in the United States—1976, 1977 and Projections for 1978." (Prepared by ESCS for the Committee on Agriculture, Nutrition and Forestry, 95th Cong., 2nd sess., U.S. Senate.) Washington: U.S. Gov't. Printing Office.

U.S. Department of Agriculture. 1977. *Agricultural Statistics, 1977.* Washington: U.S. Gov't. Printing Office.

U.S. Department of Agriculture. "Structural Characteristics of the U.S. Farm Sector." USDA–ESCS, forthcoming.

U.S. Department of Agriculture. July 1978. "Farm Income Statistics." USDA–ESCS, Stat. Bul. No. 609.

U.S. Department of Agriculture. July 1977. "Farm Real Estate Market Developments." USDA–ESCS–CS–82.

U.S. Department of Commerce. 1977. *Census of Agriculture, 1974.* Bur. of the Census, Washington: U.S. Gov't. Printing Office.

List of Task Force Members

FARM COMMODITY PRICES AND INCOME

Luther Tweeten (Chairman)
Dept. of Agricultural Economics
Oklahoma State University
Stillwater, Oklahoma

Larry D. Abeldt
Grain Sorghum Producers
    Association
Hope, Kansas

Neal Bjornson
National Milk Producers Federation
Washington, D.C.

Robert Buck
Farmer
Waukee, Iowa

Milton Erickson
Economics, Statistics, and
    Cooperatives Service
U.S. Dept. of Agriculture
Washington, D.C.

Donald Frahm
American Soybean Association
Hudson, Iowa

Dale Hendricks
Mid–America Dairymen, Inc.
Bloomfield, Iowa

Gordon Leith
Farmland Industries
Kansas City, Missouri

Walter Minger
Bank of America
San Francisco, California

J. B. Penn
Economics, Statistics, and
    Cooperatives Service
U.S. Dept. of Agriculture
Washington, D.C.

Jerry Saylor
Deere & Company
Moline, Illinois

Lauren Soth
Journalist
Des Moines, Iowa

Lamar Spangler
Agricultural Division
American Bankers Association
Washington, D.C.

Aven Whittington
Farmer
Greenwood, Mississippi

COMMENTS BY A TASK FORCE MEMBER
NEAL R. BJORNSON

Domestic policy relating to the dairy industry is directed toward assuring the domestic production of an adequate supply of milk to meet market demand and maintenance of the productive capacity to meet future anticipated needs. The segments of the report dealing directly with dairy policy fail totally to recognize the basic facts regarding the existing policy structure—it has worked, it is working, and, administered in the manner intended, can continue to perform to meet the assigned task. It is ironic that, at a time when other major segments of agriculture have been under substantial economic stress, the report directs its most specific call for change at an area which is enjoying a relative degree of well–being.

The report's observation that import restrictions are damaging to consumers, counter to trade policy, and a potentially useful tool in securing concessions in international trade negotiations falls short of reality. First, it ignores the fact that the United States maintains the most open market of any major dairy producing nation in the world. Second, the lower–cost imports it suggests would be available to the U.S. consumer are primarily imports which enter this market from nations which make extensive use of subsidies to penetrate this or any other market. Given U.S. dependency on such supplies, these products would be substantially higher priced than domestic production. Third, it ignores the fact that in the 1978 multilateral trade negotiations the European Economic Community (the major source of U.S. dairy product imports) declared its Common Agricultural Policy—with its high internal prices, variable levies and export subsidies—to be non–negotiable, a position which U.S. negotiators accepted.

The report states that the 1953–1973 experience demonstrated that long–run supply–demand balance is maintained with milk prices about 75 percent of parity. A review of the historical prices paid farmers for manufacturing milk shows that in only one marketing year—1954–1955—did the price equal 75 percent of parity. In only five of these years was the average price level below 80 percent of the parity equivalent. Since August 10, 1973, the price support level itself has been set at 80 percent of parity or more, either under legislative mandate or by administrative action.

It is true that program costs for the 1976–1977 marketing year were substantial. On a constant dollar basis, however, these costs were substantially below those of many years of the program. Even so, the suggestion that the level of program cost is the prime factor to be considered ignores the basic legislative directive of the program. Milk production is not something that can be turned on and off or finely metered in response to changes in conditions. Commodity Credit Corporation stocks serve both as a reserve stock and a consumer price buffer. There is no quarrel with the recommendation that restraint be exercised in the setting of the dairy price support level. One of the most carefully studied questions among the leadership of the National Milk Producers each year is that of the recommendations to the Secretary of Agriculture regarding establishment of the price support level. These recommendations are tempered by recognition of actual and prospective supply and demand conditions, farm income needs and other factors relating to the production and consumption of milk.

The recommendations calling for removal of classified pricing used under Federal milk market orders demonstrates a misunderstanding of the purpose of the system. The fluid milk differential is the means of providing time, place and form utility to the product. Without the differential, it would not be possible to obtain the movement of milk in the quantities needed to meet the demand of fluid markets. This pricing system did not originate with market orders and some system of this nature would be necessary even in the absence of market orders.

The use of a cull–cow incentive payment program as a means of reducing production in times of excess supply has been carefully considered by the Federation. Its rejection was based on several considerations. First, it would require the development of a complex regulatory system if it were to be even moderately effective. Second, such a measure would mean the transfer of a problem of the dairy industry to the beef producers of the United States.

Rather than seeking to shift problems between the producers of various commodities, the federal involvement in agriculture needs to be aimed at the development of a national food policy which will provide adequate supplies of food for all Americans including recognition of the special needs of the young, the aged and the disadvantaged while providing stable markets where all farmers can receive reasonable returns on the capital, labor and management skills they have invested.

DISCUSSION

The formal discussants were: Irvin Elkin, President, Associated Milk Producers, Inc. (AMPI); Jim Kramer, farmer and American Agriculture Movement member; and J. B. Penn, Administrator for Economics in the Economics, Statistics, and Cooperatives Service, USDA.

Elkin said that the original intent of the dairy program was not to support incomes for dairy farmers but to assure an adequate supply of milk to consumers in the United States. The program has been administered quite well despite the complicated nature of the dairy industry, and AMPI favors continuation of the current program. Due to the ability of dairy producers to respond to price, the establishment of dairy support prices must be handled very cautiously. Prices higher than 85 to 87 percent of parity result in surplus production within about two years, while prices below 83 percent of parity result in inadequate supplies within about two years. Elkin said that the Task Force report was simply incorrect in maintaining that supply–demand balance is attained at milk prices equal to about 75 percent of parity, on the evidence of the 1953–1973 data. Elkin also said that the Task Force was made up of people unfamiliar with the dairy industry, and that dairy policy recommendations from such a group should not be taken seriously.

Kramer discussed the general position of the American Agriculture Movement (AAM) on farm policy. The concept of indexing agricultural prices to some measure of inflation, such as the cost of living, was suggested. Kramer indicated that if agricultural prices are supported at higher levels, the USDA would need to act as a supply control agent and as a guardian of reserves. The AAM does not favor Treasury payments to get parity but favors nonrecourse loans since they are repaid in cash or by turning the commodity over to the Commodity Credit Corporation (CCC). Finally, Kramer commented on the existing cash flow problem that farmers face, and asked that we work to stabilize forces that affect the agricultural economy. (A more complete statement of the AAM's views are contained in Chapter 7.)

Penn commented on issues related to international trade and on the need for new indicators of economic well–being for agriculture. He said that the current economic indicators are too aggregate or otherwise impaired to enable identifying the particular groups in agriculture that may be experiencing financial difficulties. He suggested efforts were needed to develop indicators that would enable determining the economic status of producers by type, size, geographic location, and other distinguishing attributes.

In the trade area, he suggested that if the current international efforts such as the Multilateral Trade Negotiations (MTN), the International Wheat Agreement (IWA), and others are unsuccessful, it may be appropriate to then consider alternative ways to market U.S. grain, such as the marketing board approach, bilateral trade agreements, and cooperative arrangements with other exporting countries.

Penn also commented on the economic structure of agriculture as related to policies and programs. He said a single national average price or income support for all producers, as under the 1977 Act, aids the largest producers, but may be of little help to small and medium-sized farms. Moreover, the cumulative structural effects of all policies—the income tax code, environmental, health and safety, and labor market regulation, federal lending programs, and taxation of intergenerational transfers—on the farm sector need to be taken into account. When considering the next farm legislation, alternatives may be considered that explicitly treat the structural issue and the international marketing problems as well as the traditional short-run price and income concerns.

COMMENTS AND QUESTIONS FROM THE FLOOR

It was generally agreed by the audience and the Panel that inflation is the number one problem facing agriculture at this time. Much of the discussion and some of the comments were concerned with this topic. In particular, farmers in the audience wanted to know how they were to pass on higher production costs, and who were the higher costs going to be passed on to. Tweeten responded that the current target price mechanism provides for an adjustment of prices to compensate for higher costs of production.

Several farmers in the audience expressed the view that deficiency payments, even though they are a means of passing on higher production costs, are a direct cost to the Treasury and thus akin to welfare. Generally, the subject of deficiency payments renewed old issues concerning direct payments, particularly problems such as whether there should be payment limitations, if so, how high to set the limits, and the feeling that these payments are viewed as welfare.

Several AAM members endorsed the use of the loan programs to index agricultural prices to a particular measure of inflation. Their reasoning was that CCC loans have historically been repaid, in cash or by turning over the commodity, in contrast to government payments being a direct cost to the U.S. Treasury. Opponents of this idea said that such a program would reduce exports from the United States. The main reason given was that the United States does not possess sufficient monopoly power in world grains and that higher world prices resulting from a U.S. loan program would encourage production abroad.

Several comments were made about Tweeten's inclusion of capital gains on farm land in his calculation of returns to agriculture. Some farmers felt that such gains should not be included because income from capital gains can only be realized by selling the farm land or by mortgaging it.

A few comments emphasized the uncertainty faced by agriculture. Most parties agreed that farm programs have tended to reduce market uncertainties; however, *ad hoc* programs that affect agriculture, such as the price freeze in 1973 and the grain export controls of 1974–1975 usually increase uncertainty faced by farmers.

The relationship between land prices and farm income was commented on by several participants. A particular issue was: what do existing data really show. Some noted that phenomenal land price increases have occurred since 1948 while commodity prices have actually declined. This point led to a discussion of changes in crop yield per acre, and the demand for land for nonagricultural purposes. Some of the discussion repeated points made in discussion of Castle's Task Force report, for example, the pros and cons of foreign investment in farm land in the United States.

The discussion returned to the topic of farm programs by addressing the question of what farm programs of the future would look like? No one had firm ideas to offer on the issue. It was suggested that in the future farm leaders should work for sound monetary and fiscal policy, i.e., hold expansion of the money supply to 6 to 7 percent per year and maintain a balanced budget. Also, these leaders should examine the benefits that could be gained from alliance with existing agricultural groups and nonagricultural groups, such as consumers.

TIM JOSLING*

CHAPTER 3

International Trade

Introduction

THE importance of international agricultural trade both to the national economy and to the world as a whole, if ever in doubt, has been underscored by recent events. In many parts of the world, where domestic production has barely kept pace with the increase in population, additional imports have had to fulfill the aspirations for an improved diet. The more affluent nations have continued to expand consumption of many livestock products which have to be either imported or fed at home on imported feed. Central–plan countries, faced with massive problems of variability and low productivity in their domestic production of basic foodstuffs have increasingly turned to the world market to assist in meeting the needs of their populations for a stable source of food supply. The major agricultural exporters, including the United States have in general been able to expand production to meet these requirements. This in turn has proved particularly beneficial at a time when the burden of energy and raw material imports has put strain on their own economies. Agricultural trade has filled these various needs and will continue to do so in the future. But in addition to its economic role, trade in basic foodstuffs is also of political significance. Indeed, maintaining the balance between the import needs of popu-

*The Task Force on International Trade met and discussed at length the questions touched on in this report. While the report is an attempt to pose the issues and discuss solutions in a way consistent with the tenor of our meetings, it is not limited to points of agreement. It remains a personal statement, albeit educated by the wisdom of the Task Force, and thus commits no one (except myself) to the views expressed. A list of Task Force members and their affiliations follows the report.

I would like to express my sincere appreciation to those who attended the Task Force meetings, commented on earlier versions, and contributed in other ways to content and presentation of this report.

lous developing countries and the exporting capacity of the developed world is itself crucial to the stability of the entire economic and political system.

It is against this background that policies influencing agricultural trade must be formulated and the performance of such policies judged. This report is intended to further discussion of these issues, and to provide the international dimension to the considerations of the various domestic agricultural problems contained in the other Task Force reports. The subject is too broad to allow detailed treatment of each individual issue. The report therefore concentrates on the major factors which will over the next few years determine the nature of the overseas market into which U.S. agriculture must sell, and on the trade policy directions which will influence its ability to make those sales.

The limitations of such policy must however be acknowledged. The nature of the foreign market for U.S. agricultural products is largely determined by the forces of income and population growth and by the development of agriculture overseas, modified by the activities of governments both acting alone and in cooperation with each other. United States policy can do little to influence population trends abroad, though the potential for affecting income growth and the development of agriculture in other countries may not be negligible. The more specific scope of U.S. agricultural trade policy has to do with actions at home to influence the ease with which overseas markets can be supplied, and to diplomatic activity to improve the prospects for such sales abroad. United States policy must in addition deal with the conditions under which imports can enter the country in competition with American farmers and processors.

Such international trade issues clearly cannot be treated in isolation from matters of domestic resource use, food and nutrition policy, and income support. Thus this report must touch upon such issues as the level of support prices, domestic food costs, and alternative marketing channels. But since these matters are the subject of other Task Force reports, these references will relate only to those aspects of the problems which are essential to the discussion of international trade policy.

The remainder of the report will be organized as follows. The following section will discuss the main elements which shape the world markets into which U.S. agricultural products must move, followed by an examination of policy issues at an international level. The place of agricultural trade in the U.S. economy will be considered in the light of these developments in the fourth section. The final section will attempt to outline the options together with some suggestions and recommendations relating to U.S. trade policy in agricultural markets.

World Agricultural Issues

THE ROLE OF TRADE IN WORLD AGRICULTURE

In one sense the most important aspect of world trade for a major exporter such as the United States is the future growth in the size of the market. Projections have an unfortunate habit of being wrong and no attempt is made here to give quantitative forecasts. It may be more useful to stand back from commodity and price forecasts themselves to see what forces are shaping the export markets of tomorrow. To do this it is necessary to consider the place of trade in the world's food system, and the problems that confront governments in the area of trade.

The world's agricultural economy is a system by which agricultural production in the world is mobilized to meet the needs of a growing population and the steady demand for dietary improvement. Though propelled by individual and national interests, the system is useful if these needs are met. On these criteria, recent performance has been generally satisfactory. Despite two years, in 1972 and again in 1974, when aggregate world production of the major crops declined, output has over the past 20 years been rising at a faster rate than population. There is of course no cause for complacency, nor will there be until levels of nutrition in the world have reached a more satisfactory level. Indeed the basic problem of an uneven distribution of food supplies remains as serious as ever. But the real constraint to the eradication of hunger is not present or impending shortages of food so much as the widespread incidence of poverty. In the lowest income countries the inability to purchase food implies the need to maintain an agriculture geared to the provision of basic necessities; in turn this perpetuates low productivity and limits further economic progress. Self–sufficiency may be a luxury for the rich; for the poor it is a burden, escape from which is only possible with a responsive and reliable system of international trade.

This defines the role for international trade in foodstuffs, the mechanisms by which natural production advantages are utilized and by which variability in production is offset, to the advantage of both developed and developing nations. It is clearly in the long–run interest of all countries that the world's agricultural resources be utilized in a way that minimizes the cost of providing essential foodstuffs. Present patterns of agricultural production do not satisfy that criterion. Three things in particular stand in the way of such an aim: the lack of trading opportunities for developing countries in the products that they could export; the perceived need to support farm incomes in relatively less efficient sectors of developed country agriculture; and the chronic instability in world agricultural markets which makes reasoned decisions on resource use particularly difficult and mistakes more costly.

DEVELOPING COUNTRIES AND FOOD IMPORTS

Developing country trading policies have in the past tended to downplay the role of food imports. The apparent drain on scarce foreign exchange, the presumed political vulnerability of dependence on other countries, and the difficulties of economic instability arising from fluctuating import prices are among the most often articulated reasons. But in addition, the absence in many cases of adequate internal transportation facilities, the existence of large peasantries unable or unwilling to work in nonfarm employment and the absolute lack of opportunities for such employment have often been as important in stimulating governments to emphasize domestic production of basic foods.

There are, however, forces which act to make such economies more open. Large scale subsidization of agriculture is prohibitively expensive for countries with up to three–quarters of their labor force on farms: indeed agriculture is as often as not seen as a major source of tax revenue rather than as a sector requiring support. Investment plans in developed countries call typically for expansion in industrial sectors which carry more prestige than is associated with basic agriculture. Production costs in farming become very high when output is stimulated in parts of the world poorly suited to such activity, and variability in output can itself be more severe when self–sufficiency levels are higher than warranted by natural soil and climatic endowments. Moreover, imports of production requisites and investment goods for agriculture can put almost as much strain on the payments position as would importing the foodstuff itself. For these reasons, despite the genuine aspirations of governments for more self–reliance in the area of food, a substantial expansion in the absolute level of food imports by developing countries seems likely in the years ahead to the extent made possible by their ability to earn foreign exchange.

DEVELOPED–COUNTRY FARM POLICIES

Actions of developed countries to support farm income also have tended to distort the ability of the system to generate food at the lowest cost. Almost by definition, government support gravitates towards those sectors of developed country agriculture which are least competitive. Support prices themselves often get out of line with world market conditions when based too much on domestic costs without due regard to international trends. This has been noticeable in recent years, particularly in the period up to 1972, when world market prices for many commodities were low and protection of inefficient domestic agriculture from the impact of these prices was considerable throughout the industrial world. As world prices rose domestic policy prices lagged behind and protection levels fell. Inflation continued, however, and agricultural policy prices were adjusted upwards. With the decline in world prices after 1975, protection has become once again significant enough to represent a major distortion in production patterns and hence to imply higher costs than necessary for basic foodstuffs.

It is of course possible to recite convincing political factors which appear to compel industrial countries to maintain protection for relatively less efficient domestic farm production. But there also are pressures which contain such action and modify its long–run impact. Taxpayers and consumers are taking a greater interest in the operation of farm programs as a part of the general trend towards more accountability of government programs and concern about inflation. Conflicts among domestic fiscal, foreign commercial, and agricultural policies are becoming more common with a weakening of the historically plausible assumption that agricultural factors will prevail. Such conflicts arise in all industrial countries, whether food exporters or importers, but it is in the importing countries where the credibility of traditional farm support programs seems likely in the future to be the most vulnerable to changes in attitudes.

MARKET STABILITY

The question of price and market stability has been high on the agenda in policy discussions for the past five years. An uncertainty of a different kind, however, was evident even before the events of the early 1970s. For a decade prior to that time, many world prices for major products had been heavily influenced by the marketing policies of governments, not least the storage and export subsidy programs pursued by the exporting countries. While this was in general a period of price stability, uncertainty centered on the concern that the price levels were scarcely enough to cover production costs even in efficient agricultural areas. Developing countries, whose imports of cereals began to rise rapidly during the 1960s, understood that the attractive terms under which these purchases were made possible only as a result of considerable subsidies in the form of farm programs and overseas aid. The price explosion which ended this era confirmed these fears. Those countries which had generated surpluses under domestic policies began to squeeze world supplies so as to soften the impact of harvest shortfalls on the rate of inflation at home. The impact of the dramatic rise in cereal grain prices during 1973 on attitudes towards agriculture throughout the world can hardly be exaggerated. The World Food Conference in 1974 marked an elevation in political priorities accorded to world agricultural production and trade problems. In developing countries, investment plans were revised and farm policies reviewed; in food–importing industrial countries, agricultural support was interpreted as a necessary insurance against shortages; in exporting countries the expectation grew that the higher price levels were the start of a period of economic prosperity and seller's markets. It now appears that these reactions were exaggerated, but they illustrate the fact that the uncertainty that accompanies price instability makes rational decisions on long–run resource deployment, both by governments and by individual farmers, unduly difficult.

These three aspects of the place of trade in world agriculture are thus related. Market instability is exacerbated by restrictive government trade policies, which in turn justifies further market intervention in affluent countries and promotes autarkic reactions in developing countries. The major trade policy challenge is to reverse this trend. International trade in agricultural products cannot of itself eliminate poverty and ensure food supplies to the needy. But improvements in the operation of the trading system can make a major contribution towards allowing countries to escape from the grip of poverty and participate in the international division of labor and share the fruits of economic progress.

International Policy Issues in Agricultural Trade

THE LIMITS OF INTERNATIONAL POLICY

Policies appear in response to problems in economic or social organization. This part of the report considers the development of international policy which arises as a result of the problems discussed in the previous section. International policy is, however, an imprecise concept. In the absence of any effective supranational authority, intercountry agreements rest entirely on the concurrence of national policy. International policy initiatives such as a United Nations (UN) resolution, the setting up of an international agency, the operation of a commodity agreement, are each premised on national policy actions. Thus any distinction between national and international policy problems must be to some extent arbitrary.

The most fundamental policy questions are, almost by definition, the most difficult to resolve. In the previous section the principal issue was described as the development of a food and agricultural system which provides in a more reliable and efficient way for the basic needs of the world's population. The interest of the United States in, and its obligation towards meeting such objectives are obvious, but the limitations of international policy are also significant. Many crucial factors, such as the rate of population growth and the internal distribution of purchasing power in other countries, are hardly subject to direct policy action at an international level. On such matters, intergovernmental contacts will continue to be of a discursive nature, a fact which concerns many who recognize their importance and frustrates those who regard these developments as inhibiting progress in other areas.

A number of less fundamental issues raise similar frustrations, including priorities in development plans and trade policies, preferences for particular national institutional arrangements governing trade, attitudes towards foreign ownership of and investment in industry, the choice of monetary and exchange rate policies, and the degree of discrimination in trading policies among sources of supply. In these matters, intercountry discussions may well have some positive outcome, but they remain essentially in the realm of domestic sovereignty.

Another set of issues, nationally important but by common consent more amenable to international action, relates to conditions of intercountry commerce and monetary settlements. In this category come the mainstream negotiating issues of tariff levels, nontariff measures which influence trade, bilateral and multilateral trading agreements, commodity price stabilization schemes, balance of payments facilities, international loans and grants, concessionary sales, and arrangements governing intercountry transfers of technology.

The "nuts and bolts" issues of international commerce—legal provisions, credit arrangements, shipping facilities, insurance services, quality standards and safeguards, and market information—complete the picture. Though often sensitive, these issues do not in the main require major policy decisions; they tend instead to reflect the general climate of commercial relationships, becoming irritants mainly in times of economic stress and being resolved when the climate improves.

The question arises of the extent to which actions taken by governments in concert can influence the broader objectives of world agricultural development. The belief which governs present U.S. policy, and that of other developed countries, is that such action is both valuable and essential, although opinions differ on both strategy and tactics. Central–plan economies appear unwilling to go as far, elevating the concept of national sovereignty to a point which diminishes their ability to participate fully in such discussions. Developing countries, in so far as they have a common view, at times attempt to broaden negotiations to include basic structural elements in trade traditionally held to be within national prerogative and at times emphasize domestic control over matters usually considered to be in the realm of international discussion. The resolution of this ambivalence by a group of countries increasingly important in world trade will have a great deal to do with the role of international policy in the future.

REQUIREMENTS OF THE TRADING SYSTEM

In agricultural trade, discussion and agreement on the conditions under which such trade takes place is particularly important. Most countries would subscribe to the aims of a trading system which actively encourages low–cost production, reasonable price stability, and a degree of security in food supplies, in turn allowing other economic and social objectives to be more easily obtained. An essential ingredient for the working of any trading system is *confidence* in the performance of that system. Developing countries should be able to plan their own development in the reasonable knowledge that the international food system will not turn against their interests. Exporters should be in a position to anticipate needs and develop markets without fear of arbitrary closures, unreasonable competition from heavily subsidized surpluses, or discriminatory trade policies introduced for short–term political gain. Importers should likewise be assured that temptations to exploit market shortage will be resisted and that world market conditions can prove a reliable basis for domestic resource–use decisions. Such confidence also would encourage central–plan economies to be more open as to their own requirements as the rewards from secrecy diminish.

Some factors, however, act to reduce the necessary confidence in the system. One example of this is the politicizing of agricultural trade; over the 1973–1975 period when concern was expressed as to the capacity of the trading system to handle agricultural problems, political issues such as the strategic use of food exports surfaced in a way that impeded the sensible discussion of the underlying market difficulties. Another is the growth of bilateral trade agreements which tend to tie up trade patterns and create problems for those left outside. A third is undue collaboration among exporters which might appear to limit availability by collusive decisions and price fixing.

The restoration and maintenance of confidence in the food trade system requires two major developments, both of which impose obligations on national governments. The first is to work towards a system whereby individual countries can afford to purchase foodstuffs on world markets when their own production is deficient. The second is that the world market be made sufficiently stable to allow its use as an alternative to domestic production.

BALANCE OF PAYMENTS FACILITIES

The extent to which countries can afford to buy extra imports is a function of their wealth and economic strength as well as their reserves of foreign exchange. In addition, provision of access to credit facilities materially helps such countries at times when their import require- ments are high. Balance of payments borrowing facilities already exist, both to help developing countries offset fluctuations in commodity export earnings and in general to assist in periods of crisis. But some people have suggested the establishment of a specific facility related to food imports to supplement these schemes and give particular impetus to the development of open food policies in developing countries. A variation on this theme has also been proposed which would set up a system whereby developing countries might insure against variations in their import requirements either with one or a group of developed countries. Payments from this "insurance policy," either in kind or in cash tied to import purchases, would follow shortfalls from domestic production trends, and in some variants of the proposal also would offset increases in world prices. This device would ensure that such aid would be granted when and where it was needed most, and improve upon the somewhat *ad hoc* methods of food aid distribution that now exist.

PRICE STABILITY

The other requirement mentioned above is the enhanced stability of world market prices. This too influences the willingness of develop- ing countries to pursue trade–oriented food policies. Three main ap- proaches to this problem have been discussed. One has been to regu- late world prices directly by means of accords among importers and exporters. Such proposals have superficial appeal by appearing to act directly on the problem: the danger is that they tend to treat the symptoms rather than the cause. Price variations are triggered by fluc- tuations in market balance, usually arising from variations in supply. Such fluctuations simply cannot be legislated away: they will have to show up either as variations in consumption or as changes in stock levels. Prices act as the means of promoting such stock and consump- tion adjustments. With unresponsive international prices, an elaborate system of quantitative trade obligations involving rationing in times of shortage and compulsory storage in surplus periods would be neces- sary. Individual governments can use trade policy to back up their own rigid price decisions: the international community as a whole has no such option since there is no one else with whom to trade.

Price stability on world markets can only be realistically achieved by *encouraging* variations in consumption and stocks to offset fluctuations in output. In this case, stable international prices are the outcome of the wise use of other policy instruments rather than being controlled directly. In market economies, the appropriate instruments are *domestic* price levels, which regulate both stock levels and use; in central–plan economies, consumption and reserves are controlled by the government. World market price stability thus requires that consumption and stock levels adjust in all or most trading countries to whatever extent is necessary to offset production instability in the world as a whole.

In recognition of this there has been an increased emphasis in recent years on the coordination of nationally–held reserves in products subject to price variability. As indicated above, significant variations in the level of reserves can achieve substantial increases in price stability if properly managed. The problems surrounding this approach have more to do with the costs of such schemes and the difficulties of implementation than with any doubts on its effectiveness. Complete price stability would certainly be costly, and this in itself would encourage governments to find ways of reducing their own commitments. Anything less than an agreement to defend a fixed price through stock purchases and sales would require complex management rules binding on individual governments or imposed by an international authority.

One attraction of such stocks management schemes is that they appeal to those who perceive problems arising from the concentration of grain exports in the hands of a few countries and a small number of private firms and state trading agencies within those countries. A major disadvantage arises from the tendency for stocks to obscure longer–run price trends necessary for the stimulus of production in appropriate quantities at appropriate locations. In other words, a stock scheme can be satisfactory so long as underlying policy decisions are taken which preserve market balance. If the added stability is taken to mean that governments can ignore market realities, then such attempts would be no more successful than merely setting trading prices and hoping for the best.

The most satisfactory attempts to provide market stability emphasize both consumption and stock adjustments. This implies the strengthening of the link between world and domestic market prices, most simply achieved by liberalizing trade. The essence of such an approach is that the less obtrusive government policy is in decisions relating to production, marketing, storage and consumption of agricultural products, the more the normal market mechanisms will be able to absorb unavoidable changes in supply. The fact that such a solution is consistent with the need to encourage a better allocation of productive resources gives it an added importance in international policy discussions, although for the same reason it also raises objections by interests adversely affected by such improvements. To be successful it requires a positive commitment on the part of governments to allow international price variations to impinge on domestic markets—not just in normal times but more importantly when such price movements are most necessary. It also requires that governments are sufficiently convinced of the longer–term benefits of such action to allow them to resist the temptation to intervene for shorter–run objectives.

MEASURES WHICH IMPAIR CONFIDENCE

If these developments are aimed at improving trading conditions and hence confidence in the ability of the trading system to perform satisfactorily, there are certain policies as mentioned above which act in the opposite direction. Bilateral trade agreements can often cause frictions which belie their apparent security; regional trading preferences can lead to excessive discrimination against outside suppliers; the use of trade restrictions as a means of applying diplomatic pressure on other countries increases uncertainty and inhibits market development; exporter collusion raises fears among importing countries and promotes autarkic responses; arbitrary and unpredictable trade embargoes weaken existing market links and raise serious problems for traders who find private contracts difficult to honor under such conditions. It seems inconsistent with the constructive nature of this report to treat these negative aspects in detail. But the task of maintaining an open trading system requires an attempt to guard against such regressions as well as the more positive aspects described above.

Agricultural Trade and the U.S. Economy

AGRICULTURAL TRADE AND DOMESTIC ECONOMIC POLICY

As foreign markets have become more important for U.S. farmers, so agricultural exports have been increasingly valuable to the economy as a whole. Agricultural exports are presently running at an annual rate of $28 billion, accounting for about 20 percent of farm receipts. Unlike most countries with a strong interest in agricultural export markets, the share of agricultural exports in total U.S. export trade has tended to increase over time. Significantly, this increase has been noticeable in the volume of trade, as well as in higher prices. It could not have come at a better time: the burden on the balance of trade arising from higher oil prices would have been even more difficult to bear without the buoyancy of farm exports. The link between agricultural exports and the economy as a whole is, however, somewhat more complex than might appear at first sight. Expanded exports of farm products bring some policy problems along with the undoubted benefits.

One such problem regards the stability of export earnings. Foreign demand for U.S. products depends crucially on harvest conditions in other countries. Whereas it is reasonable to expect that in many years these production variations will offset each other, the possibility still exists of the coincidence of large or small harvests in some major countries. As agricultural exports become more crucial to the balance of trade, the possibility of a destabilizing influence on the economy is enhanced. Insofar as agricultural export earnings influence farm incomes, this instability would be particularly severe in rural areas. Export growth brings with it some risks, and puts pressure on policymakers to take steps to ameliorate the uncertainty.

A second potential difficulty associated with a greater role for farm exports relates to the ease with which exchange rate adjustments can be expected to correct trade imbalances. A falling dollar should make U.S. exports more attractive and increase foreign exchange earnings, but this will only happen to the extent both that additional exports are available and that other countries are willing to buy them. The availability of additional exports, within a crop or livestock year, will depend on the ease at which supply can be diverted from domestic markets (or satisfied from reserves) and this will add to inflationary pressures at home. And the willingness of other countries to bid for those extra exports will in turn depend on the extent to which they allow the dollar's decline to increase competitive pressure on their own farmers. Additionally, countries holding reserves in the form of dollars may find themselves less able to buy imported foodstuffs as the dollar declines. Increased reliance on agricultural exports as an element in the balance of trade may possibly reduce the effectiveness of exchange rate changes, giving rise to greater problems of dollar instability.

TRADE COMPOSITION AND TRADE PATTERNS

One aspect of the growth of agricultural exports which requires particular attention by policymakers is the commodity composition of those exports. The major gains in the last few years have shown up in grains and oilseeds. The United States now provides 75 percent of the world's soybean exports, 50 percent of feed grains and 40 percent of wheat. Because grain production on modern farms is a highly capital–intensive operation, and since the natural resource endowment of U.S. agriculture relative to many other parts of the world so clearly favors extensive cereal grain production, this may indeed be merely a reflection of a cost advantage. But it also is possible that it reflects an implicit bias in domestic policy towards grain and feed exports.

Allied to this question of the composition of farm exports is that of their destination. Expansion of food grain sales has been in the developing country markets while feed grains and soybeans have gone more to industrial countries. Central–plan countries have purchased in both markets. Again, these trade patterns reflect in large part natural market developments, and may not in themselves reflect a particular export policy. It is important from the standpoint of the domestic economy to assess the relative benefits of exporting basic food and feed crops rather than items of higher value, such as livestock products, and the desirability of reliance on this particular geographical orientation of export outlets.

Policy options with respect to composition and distribution of exports will be discussed later, but some comments on the implications of present and emerging trade patterns for general trade policy may be appropriate at this point. Increases in demand for food grains in developing countries arise mainly from population and income growth. Their own production constraints serve to transfer much of this growth in demand to world markets. This market is vulnerable to a slowdown in economic progress in these countries and in particular to any adverse shift in their ability to pay for imports. Market growth in this area depends therefore upon the success of other trade and economic policies designed to maintain the momentum of development in the Third World, and to the establishment of confidence in the trading system mentioned above.

The rapid increase in the sales of animal feeds, and in particular soybeans and their products, to developed countries has been in spite of their generally adverse attitudes towards imports. Continued growth of these markets rests on the premise that their populations will continue to demand more meat and high–protein foods, that uneconomic livestock production in these areas will be subsidized at similar levels into the future, and that pressure on domestic resources will require additional animal feeds to be purchased abroad rather than being provided by domestic agriculture. Such markets are not constrained by balance of payments problems though they are responsive to economic growth. Development of these markets calls, among other things, for skillful negotiations on trade barriers which will include a willingness to purchase more from other countries.

Situated between the populous developing countries and the high–income developed countries are two groups of nations: the central–plan economies and the middle–income countries. They share some of the characteristics of both rich and poor, and they provide a new and somewhat uncertain element in the demand for temperate–zone foods. Middle–income countries include those that appear to have broken into the world of efficient industrial production on a scale large enough to provide serious competition to older developed countries. Reaction to this potential or real threat to employment and profits by industrial countries will largely determine whether the middle–income nations continue to stress growth through trade or whether they will be forced to adopt restrictive agricultural import policies in the face of shrinking export markets. United States agriculture has thus a real interest in the resolution of the many trade problems in the manufacturing sector.

Central–plan economies by their nature respond less predictably to world economic conditions and trends. Consumer desires surface slowly and the structure of production reacts to outside influence only to the extent allowed by the heavy hand of government planning.

Nevertheless, economic reality cannot be escaped by administrative control: over a period of time these countries place demands on world markets similar to those of market economies in a corresponding state of development. Their erratic incursions into world agricultural markets create significant problems, but it should not hide the longer–run potential for trade expansion in food grains, livestock feed and high–value consumer food products. Policy attitudes towards these countries, including willingness to purchase their export products, will again influence U.S. agricultural prospects. And, conversely, their desire to make use of American export potential will have significant implications for their attitudes in other areas of commercial and foreign policy.

In short, the role of supplier of food grains to developing countries, food and feed to central–plan and middle–income countries, and foodstuffs to industrial nations brings with it obligations in the field of general commercial relationships. Along with the possible implications for the stability of foreign exchange earnings and of the value of the dollar, this implies a need for coordination of decisions in trade and international monetary policies which recognizes the linkage between agricultural exports and conditions in nonagricultural markets.

IMPORT MARKETS

Emphasis on export markets, while appropriate in terms of their economic importance, should not exclude consideration of agricultural imports. Such imports are of considerable value in the effort to keep down domestic consumer food costs. Attempts artificially to constrain such imports have tended to weaken the competitiveness of U.S. agriculture as a whole, and encouraged resource use patterns which have had to be sustained by a continuation of government intervention and market control. Expansion of exports in itself has been hindered by policies which make import–competing sectors seem unduly attractive.

At the international level these problems have been magnified. Attempts to open up export markets have been jeopardized by policies which appear to restrict access of other countries to U.S. markets for those products in which overseas suppliers have a cost advantage. With respect to developing countries, expansion of their own agricultural exports of particular products would have allowed for greater purchases of U.S. farm goods. The situation is less clear–cut in the case of developed–country exports, many of which have been the result of surpluses created under domestic price supports and sold abroad with the aid of subsidies. Increased imports of these products may offer domestic advantage in the short run, but carry the risk of perpetuating distortions in resource use to the long–run detriment of agricultural trade patterns.

The recent expansion of agricultural exports has clearly had a major impact on the farm sector, as well on the economy as a whole. Export markets for grains and oilseeds have provided income opportunities of a kind not available from the domestic market alone. But the cost has been increased price and income instability. Grain price fluctuations add to the already serious problems of uncertainty in the livestock sector. As a result of a relatively open trading policy, the link between world price movements and farm incomes has been greater in the United States than in most other industrial countries. This causes significant problems for domestic policy formation and requires sensitivity in the making of trade policy. The next section discusses this problem in more detail.

U. S. Policy Toward Agricultural Trade

GENERAL ECONOMIC CONSIDERATIONS

The United States is at once the world's major industrial power and the largest exporter of foodstuffs. This paradox implies a set of opportunities and constraints which form the setting for U.S. policy and in large part shape the future of domestic agriculture. The farm sector in this country is dependent upon overseas demand for much of its growth. This demand, as suggested above will have to come largely from increased buying power in other countries. They will in turn increase their production of other goods, sometimes to the detriment of U.S. industry and industry in other developed countries. The profitability of agricultural sales abroad, and their rate of growth, also will depend on the level of costs faced by U.S. producers and hence on domestic inflation levels. In both respects, developments in the nonfarm economy vitally influence the outcome. Recognition of this fact provides a necessary basis for U.S. policy toward agricultural trade.

Economic growth in the world has been sluggish over the last five years. Persistent unemployment, inflation at an historically high level, and major imbalances in overseas payments have bedeviled industrial countries. In the developing world, those countries that do not have valuable energy or mineral resources have found that even the best and most ambitious development plans are difficult or impossible to implement without adequate investment funds and foreign exchange earnings. Despite these problems, a number of countries have managed to maintain an adequate economic performance and to improve living standards for their populations. A favorable turn of events in the next decade would see a period of renewed growth and relative stability, with inflation gradually being brought under control and unemployment falling to more reasonable levels.

Under such circumstances, policy conflicts among agricultural and industrial objectives are likely to be manageable. A strong demand for U.S. farm exports will assist the stability of the dollar on foreign exchange markets, thus helping to control inflationary pressures. Commodity program costs will be reduced, in turn allowing budget deficits to be contained and improving the opportunity for lower taxation and interest rates. Increased domestic output in the industrial sector also will tend to lower inflation, and income growth will generate the conditions for continued expansion, even in the face of increased competition in foreign industrial markets.

At the other extreme, depressed economic conditions, perpetuated among other things by policies in industrial countries aiming to correct payments deficits by restrictive domestic income and foreign trade policies, would create serious tensions in U.S. domestic policy. Stagnation in world trade would constrain the ability of other countries to purchase U.S. farm products, placing greater financial burdens on the government in the interests of income support. Other sectors too would require increasing access to public funds to make up for lost overseas sales, and any increase in employment through trade restriction would have as its basis not sound commercial opportunity but the artificiality of the protected market. Much of the progress of the postwar period could be jeopardized by a return to such restrictive policies.

The choice is then between outward–looking policies, based on a general expansion of economic opportunity, bringing with it a degree of liberalization of trade and capital movements and a reduction of government intervention, and inward–looking policies predicated upon an attempt to stimulate domestic demand by a combination of trade and domestic measures as an inadequate substitute for freely expressed consumer choice. The United States has consistently pressed in international circles for an outward–looking strategy, but such ideas have been coolly received by those countries with favorable balance of payments positions who fear the inflationary consequences at home of economic expansion. U.S. agriculture clearly has a major interest in supporting the more liberal approach to international economic cooperation, including but not limited to the reduction of trade barriers, both to stimulate markets and to control domestic inflation.

SPECIFIC TRADE POLICY ACTIONS

In addition to the participation and leadership in discussions on these issues relating to the performance of the trading system, the government can act on a number of trade matters more directly under its control. Some of these have to do with the trade process itself, while others influence trading conditions less directly. Of the more direct trade policies those relating to access conditions for imports, to export aids, subsidies and credits, and to government assistance in overseas marketing are particularly important. Indirect policies influencing trade of significance are domestic price supports, reserve policies, transportation regulations and quality controls, although almost every other domestic agricultural policy has some potential impact on trade. Nonagricultural policies, relating in particular to inflation, exchange rate movements, and imports of other goods, have a marked effect on agricultural trade but cannot be pursued in detail in this report.

The question of attitudes towards imports raises some difficult problems and must be squarely faced. Despite the impressive productivity achieved by much of U.S. farming, certain sectors are either unable to satisfy domestic needs completely or are operating at costs higher than those in some other countries. In such cases, the undue control of imports has serious implications. Import barriers raise the price of the product concerned to the consumer above that necessary to secure supply, and add to inflationary pressures. The higher price lures resources from other activities more securely profitable and retards adjustments which are in the long–run interests of the agricultural sector. Also, such protection leads to a dependence on government support which puts the sector at the mercy of changes in political alliances.

A policy to maintain the competitiveness of U.S. agriculture should not, however, disregard the welfare of those who presently produce import–competing goods under the umbrella of protection. Safeguards against market disruption from subsidized and unreliable foreign supply is consistent with sensible resource–use objectives. Programs to stabilize incomes should of course apply to all commodities whether produced for export or in competition with imports. But where import restrictions have become inconsistent with domestic and trade policy objectives, sensitive adjustments should be introduced with due regard to those who have devoted time and capital to the building of particular farm enterprises. And since the regional impact of such changes will be uneven, special attention should be given to problems in particular areas created by increased competition with imports. It is inconsistent to expect such changes in the nonfarm sector, to allow for an expansion of foreign sales of agricultural products, without recognizing the need to adjust within the farm sector itself to the possibility of greater imports.

A special problem exists with products where domestic production varies in a cyclical pattern. There has been considerable discussion recently on the use of trade policy in a "counter–cyclical" way, to allow more imports when domestic production is low and less when it is at its peak. It should be clear that trade itself is counter–cyclical. The question of the use of trade controls as such therefore becomes one of whether government action can improve on the stabilizing impact of trade. This is intuitively appealing, but in practice runs into difficulties. To stabilize prices beyond the situation implied by liberal trading policies can only be done by stabilizing *world* markets. By far the most direct approach to deal with cyclical problems is to reduce the instability in domestic production: manipulation through trade controls confers only temporary benefits on domestic markets while making the problems faced by overseas suppliers more severe. The end result may be less stability and higher consumer prices in all countries.

In terms of international negotiations, the difficulty faced by the United States in persuading other countries to allow more liberal trade while maintaining barriers against their imports cannot be ignored. If such import liberalization were contrary to U.S. interest, the problem might seem to be to locate some minimal "concessions" with which to purchase access abroad. This is not in general the case: improved overseas access and lower import barriers *both* confer benefits on the U.S. economy. The true link between them is that adjustments in import–competing sectors are made easier if expansion in other sectors is secured at the same time. While some import liberalization may be desirable on a unilateral basis, it is likely that the major opportunities will continue to arise in the context of general trade barrier reductions involving other agricultural and nonfarm products.

Government programs that encourage exports directly by means of subsidies, credits, and other aids, have a long history in U.S. legislation as in other developed countries. They have three justifications, not always easy to distinguish. At times they have been used as a way of helping an exporting sector over a period of temporary weakness, either due to a seasonal abundance, a fall in demand, or aggressive competition from other suppliers. Though such motives seem eminently reasonable, there are drawbacks to these policies. Adding the weight of the U.S. Treasury through export subsidies pushes world market prices still lower and accentuates the original problem. The benefits of the export subsidies spill over to foreign consumers leaving domestic taxpayers with the check. The export subsidy policies of other countries are made to appear more necessary and respectable. Fortunately the change in U.S. policy under the Agriculture and Consumer Protection Act of 1973 to place more reliance on target prices to underwrite farm returns has largely removed the need for such export subsidies.

A second motive is to support farm incomes by regular, as opposed to temporary, export aids. Though widely used in other countries, they have not been a part of recent U.S. programs. Any return to such ways of creating artificial markets would place agriculture on a risky footing, dependent on government support, alienating taxpayer and consumer interests, and undermining the U.S. position in negotiations with other countries. Export aids can, however, be used more positively for market development, where commercial sales are expected to follow. Export credit assistance is the most direct way of making such a policy specific to particular markets and avoiding the problems inherent in general trade subsidies. This should, however, be coordinated with similar policies relating to other export items, and not be considered as primarily an agricultural policy matter. Care should also be taken to avoid futile credit–term competition with other exporters.

Nonpecuniary export assistance, through the provision of market information, the activities of government agencies overseas and the servicing of trade missions, are important in expanding export markets. It is difficult to evaluate their contribution, as in their absence private trade organizations would fulfill many of these functions. But the dominance in many countries of the government in trade decisions probably requires a considerable level of diplomatic support for U.S. exporters. Since the cost of these facilities is usually not great relative to the value of trade, they appear to have a secure place in agricultural trade policy. Recent policy developments along these lines appear to be soundly based.

The question is sometimes raised as to whether the government should actually involve itself in the sale of commodities directly, much as some other exporters have marketing boards to dispose of the domestic crop. This has been suggested both by those who fear that the present private marketing firms are using their position in the trade to appropriate revenue which would otherwise accrue to farmers and by those who consider a government selling agency to be a better place to deal with foreign governments. Besides the numerous political issues raised by such proposals, outside the scope of this report, the main economic question is whether a government selling agency could materially raise the price over a period of years. It is not clear why this would be the case. Market power comes essentially from the ability to control supplies. Given the likely reaction of other countries, such supply restriction has a limited long-term value. Even if some other exporters agreed to participate in such a scheme to raise prices— implying export restrictions—the benefits are likely to be quickly dissipated by expansion in other countries. With the exception of the marketing strategies of the oil producing nations, agreements that rely on exporter collusion have generally rebounded against their proponents.

TRADE POLICY AND DOMESTIC AGRICULTURAL POLICY

Much more contentious is the indirect relationship between domestic policy decisions and foreign trade. Though this relationship differs by commodity, two major issues can be isolated. These key questions refer to the *price levels* set under domestic support policies and the *stock policies* pursued under the same programs. In this respect the increased flexibility provided by the 1973 Act through the ability to set target prices with income objectives in mind and loan rates with an eye to market conditions has lessened the actual or potential conflict between domestic policy and overseas trade.

For the United States, more than for other countries, domestic policy making has to take account of world market conditions. This is clearly seen in the grain market. To a significant extent the loan rate for grains sets the lower limit to the international price. Other countries know that this price represents a floor below which U.S. production would tend to be accumulated by the Commodity Credit Corporation (CCC). It is thus improbable, for example, that any price negotiated internationally under a new International Wheat Agreement (IWA) could be below the U.S. loan rate, since an arrangement for other countries to accumulate reserves only below the floor price of the major exporter would quickly prove unworkable. Price rises are also conditioned by U.S. policy, since the Food and Agriculture Act of 1977 specifies a minimum level of 115 percent of the loan rate at which CCC stocks can be sold, and when the farmer–held reserve program is in operation, CCC stocks can only be liquidated at 150 percent of the loan rate. The present legislation appears to put strict limits on the extent to which exports from these stocks can be subsidized, thus implying a commitment to hold stocks until such time as prices improve. Under such conditions, world grain prices might be expected to remain somewhat above U.S. loan rates, but will tend not to rise much above 150 percent of such levels unless supplies are extraordinarily short. Therefore, U.S. policy in a real sense sets the range of normal international prices, as well as constraining any administered price levels which might be agreed to under a new IWA.

U.S. target prices for grains have a different impact on world markets. Though not directly influencing selling prices in a particular year, they will almost certainly affect the future market balance. They determine relative profitability of grain in the world's most prolific producing region, and hence underwrite a large part of world trade. In terms of international policy the level of U.S. target prices is as important in the long run as the loan rate is in the short run. Future administrations will face a dilemma. From the standpoint of program costs there will be pressure to keep down target prices. But unless inflation is controlled in the future, target prices are destined to rise along with farm costs. This will bring upward pressure on loan rates, risking the loss of competitiveness abroad. Thus the additional flexibility offered to U.S. policy makers in moving target and loan rates independently may prove illusory.

Acreage limitations may under these circumstances seem to be a way out of this problem, but these may now have little effect as a means of raising prices, both because other developed countries can merely expand their own production and also because developing and middle–income country export markets may be quite price–responsive. Acreage restraint in the future could result in serious market loss and detract from agriculture's contribution to the balance of payments.

The management of stock schemes also is constrained by international factors. A number of different reserve programs have emerged in recent years which pose new problems for this aspect of policy coordination. In addition to the farmer–owned reserve stock scheme, and the Emergency Wheat Reserve, the United States will if negotiations are successful have to play its part in the management of an international stock system under a new International Wheat Agreement, possibly together with an additional emergency reserve to supplement multilateral food aid efforts. Whereas a greater level of reserves than has been held over the past few years might add to stability, too high a carryover in the United States and other countries can itself be destabilizing to the market. It remains to be seen whether countries can act more responsibly in the field of stock management than has been evident in other aspects of agricultural trade. U.S. policy in stocks, as in supply restriction and pricing, faces some significant challenges in the years ahead: action without due regard to international market consequences could prove very costly.

POLICY CONCLUSIONS

Developments in the world agricultural economy appear to favor an expansion of trade. Pressures on the U.S. economy make it more desirable than ever for farm exports to increase into profitable markets. Modifications to U.S. domestic farm policy have provided an opportunity for the maintenance of an internationally competitive agricultural sector. A strong and consistent approach by government, understood and accepted by industry and farm groups, could consolidate the enhanced position of agriculture in the economy and enable the benefits of these developments to be fully exploited. A strong approach need not be inflexible, however, and it should emphasize those aspects of policy where public action is most productive. This involves continued pressure through negotiations at the international level with greater coordination on matters of domestic policy among the interests involved.

The acceptance of responsibilities and obligations at the international level is vital to the establishment of a trading system both profitable to U.S. agriculture and capable of feeding the world. Other countries and in particular other industrial nations should be encouraged to participate fully in the improvement of trade conditions. While protection in importing countries is unlikely to yield to diplomatic pressure alone, the aim should be to produce a climate in which reductions in such protection can be made. This implies obligations restricting the use of export subsidies in the United States as well as abroad. National policies should be accepted as subject to international scrutiny as to their effects on other countries. While this is likely to be more difficult a prescription for others to follow, the United States has a major interest in its success and should therefore take the lead.

A cautious and pragmatic approach to international commodity agreements is appropriate. They represent no guarantee of success, but could be useful if they contain provisions which constrain domestic policies to take into account world market conditions. Wherever such agreements meet this criterion, they should be supported. Bilateral trade deals on the other hand often give the illusion of security and access but are likely to hinder the process of improving the trading system as a whole. Attempts should be continued to integrate central–plan economies in the mainstream of world trade and discrimination against these countries should be reserved as a last resort if such accommodation is not possible.

The continued expansion of world trade in other products, the resolution of conflicts regarding competitive industrial imports, and the development of a stable world monetary system are all vital to the growth of agricultural trade. Many of these developments will have as much impact on agricultural markets as measures more directly aimed at farm trade. In particular, developing–country trade needs will increasingly dominate world agricultural markets and these will be sensitive to issues such as foreign exchange availability and the pattern of their own agricultural development. Imports into more affluent countries are likely to continue to be important, in particular for animal feedstuffs. But the prospect exists also of sales of high–value products. Expansion in this direction requires the identification of such markets and the willingness to take the risks involved in their development. Government has a role in such information and export market promotion. Such government aid is more specifically required when selling into markets controlled by state trading agencies.

To support these commercial and diplomatic efforts, domestic agricultural policy must above all remain flexible and consistent. Support prices in particular should represent an evaluation of that level which will encourage the production of saleable commodities. Too low a level denies farmers the security necessary to plan ahead: too high a level will reawaken concern by taxpayers and force the government to raise loan rates or restrict acreage, and hence threaten export market competitiveness. Consistency and equity requires that producers of both export goods and those which compete with imports be treated alike. Price supports in import–type goods should also be reviewed in terms of their competitiveness. This not only retains the essential support of consumer and food industry interests, it allows an export–related strategy to shape production patterns at home and to find more acceptance abroad.

The expansion of U.S. agricultural exports has undoubtedly been a strong point in the economy in the past five years. It may continue irrespective of the state of the economy, but prospects will be enhanced if the problems of inflation, employment levels and income growth are brought under control. A strong economy with stable prices can resolve conflicts which appear in times of economic stress. U.S. agriculture can assist in economic recovery by remaining competitive, searching out markets, and orienting its production to emerging opportunities. Agricultural policy should have this as a major objective. In turn agriculture should receive the benefits of such developments through more stable costs and a more secure basis on which to plan ahead.

Summary

Exports of U.S. agricultural products are climbing to record levels at a time when international confidence in other aspects of U.S. trade performance is at a low ebb. This renewed importance of agricultural trade to the economy is matched by its increased significance for farm incomes. Export markets, however, bring with them uncertainty as well as opportunity. Their continued growth depends on economic conditions and governmental policies in other countries. U.S. policy instruments, limited as they are in directing market growth at home, have even less influence on foreign demand. The search for policies that will sustain the growth and profitability of international market outlets is complex. It involves actions at the national level relating to market support, reserve management, transportation facilities, information systems and export promotion. It includes negotiations at an international level on trading and monetary systems, on the implications of national support policies, on attempts to improve market stability and on the enhanced security of world food supplies. All this in turn must be set in the context of changing international political relationships which often seem to frustrate the task of meeting the world's food needs from the most appropriate sources.

On the basic question of the future of agricultural trade there is little doubt that, short of a disastrous collapse in the world economy, the combination of income and population growth coupled with the constraints on agricultural production abroad will lead to an increase in U.S. exports of foodstuffs over time. Variability in output both at home and abroad will continue to contribute to market uncertainty. The pressures inhibiting such trade, the desire for greater self–sufficiency in developing countries, the shortage of foreign exchange earnings in those countries, and the autarkic tendencies of industrial–country agricultural policies, will continue to distort the flows of products from efficient suppliers to willing consumers. Demand from the needy will continue to be restricted by the widespread existence of poverty. But the imperatives of adequate nutrition and of food supplies at affordable prices will continue to overcome the reluctance of governments to see an expansion of agricultural imports.

The main task for U.S. policymakers is to press for the development of a trading system in agricultural products which will reduce those concerns of other governments that presently inhibit a more open approach to trade. This involves the conclusion of sensible arrangements at an international level to prevent violent fluctuations in price and availability of basic foodstuffs. This is most directly accomplished by ensuring that adjustments in both consumption and stock levels are widely spread among those who can afford them, rather than being forced on a few major exporters or borne by the world's poorest consumers. A greater degree of flexibility in the farm policies of developed countries coupled with agreed conventions on reserve holding must be a priority in international discourse. Such an approach also implies flexibility on the part of U.S. policy both to ensure the cooperation of others and to demonstrate commitment to the improvement of the trading system. Longer-term modifications to the allocation of agricultural resources in the interests of more reliable supplies of foodstuffs at reasonable prices will themselves follow more easily if the problems of year–to–year instability are overcome. Continuous scrutiny and international discussion of agricultural policies relating to price levels, investment, marketing and trade can be constructive if basic objectives are kept in mind.

Policy developments in other areas also will have a bearing on these agricultural questions. Countries will not be able to afford food imports unless they too can sell their goods abroad. In the short term, adequate financing must be available for the coverage of abnormal purchases when domestic production is low. This facility might be tied to food imports directly or relate to the broader payments position. Variations on the theme of food aid which stress insurance principles should be explored. In the longer run only an opening up of markets for foreign goods can ultimately allow other countries to take full advantage of the opportunities of trade in agricultural products.

On the domestic level, two approaches are necessary. The need to ensure that market information and marketing facilities are adequate to take timely advantage of overseas requirements is clearly an important part of policy. Equally significant is the implication that domestic market and income support policies be kept consistent with overseas trade realities. This requires difficult decisions affecting the market for imported commodities as well as the sensitive operation of price supports on export goods. Recent policy changes have given the flexibility needed to keep domestic agriculture competitive. The benefits of expanded commercial markets abroad can be maintained only if domestic policies are made consistent with these developments. The rewards are to be found in the widespread acceptance of the contribution of agriculture to the U.S. economy, the necessary degree of political and economic stability to encourage the full development of agricultural potential, and the contribution to the problem of feeding a hungry world.

List of Task Force Members

INTERNATIONAL TRADE

Tim Josling (Chairman)
Food Research Institute
Stanford University
Stanford, California

Don Anderson
Agricultural Investments
  Consultants, Inc.
Lubbock, Texas

Fred Bond
Flue–Cured Tobacco Cooperative
  Stabilization Corporation
Raleigh, North Carolina

John Brinker
A. O. Smith Harvestore
  Products, Inc.
Arlington Heights, Illinois

Carl Campbell
National Cotton Council
  of America
Washington, D.C.

Bill Collins
Massey Ferguson
Des Moines, Iowa

John Curry
National Corn Growers
Knoxville, Illinois

Irvin Elkin
Associated Milk Producers, Inc.
Amery, Wisconsin

Baxter Freese
U.S. Meat Export Federation
Wellman, Iowa

D. Gale Johnson
University of Chicago
Chicago, Illinois

Leo Mayer
Office of the Special Trade
  Representative
Executive Office of the President
Washington, D.C.

Carl F. Schwensen
National Association of Wheat
  Growers
Washington, D.C.

Darwin E. Stolte
U.S. Feed Grains Council
Washington, D.C.

Joe Swanson
Farmer
Windom, Kansas

Robert S. Swift
Minister (Commercial)
Embassy of Australia
Washington, D.C.

George Voth
Far–Mar Co., Inc.
(Former President)
Hutchinson, Kansas

COMMENTS BY A TASK FORCE MEMBER
Carl C. Campbell

The report gave more attention to agricultural policy regarding food and feed commodities than it gave to international trade. In addition, while the report mentions the problems of financing, foreign exchange, transportation, etc., concerning exports of U.S. agricultural commodities, it does not discuss these matters in detail. Such factors are quite important to international trade and more attention should have been given to them.

While I agree with some of the comments and suggestions in the report, I think that it includes too much academic and theoretical thinking and unproven concepts. It seems to me that the Chairman used the report of the Task Force more to communicate his thinking and ideas than he did to report on the discussions that took place during the sessions of the Task Force or to report on the information that was submitted to him by members of the Task Force for possible inclusion in the report of the Task Force.

The report infers that the primary purpose of U.S. agricultural exports is "to feed the hungry world." While I do not object to having U.S. exports feed hungry people, I do not think that this is the basic reason that we export food and feed commodities. Rather, we need to export our agricultural commodities in order to have a viable agricultural program in the United States, in order to provide work and income to our farmers and exporters, and in order to assist our country in maintaining reasonable balances of trade and payments. Achieving these objectives is in our best interests, and these are the reasons why we try to maintain and expand our agricultural exports. At the same time, we understand and appreciate that some of our exports feed hungry people all around the world.

The report indicates that it would be in the best interests of the United States and other developed countries to maximize the liberalization of their trade, and it opposes actions that might be taken to restrict or control trade. While I understand and appreciate the benefits that can accrue in many instances through more liberalized trade, I think that there must be some limits or controls placed on trade in certain products. For instance, in the case of most developing countries which are trying to expand their economic activity, the first industrial activity that they undertake is the production of textiles, and most of them develop their textile industries with the intention of exporting a considerable volume of their production. Since most developed countries already have textile industries which can generally supply their requirements of textiles, and since the developing countries make little effort to expand the consumption of textiles in their own countries or in other developing countries, this oftentimes results in a surplus of textiles being available in the international market and this depresses the textile industries in all countries and weakens the pricing structure for textiles in general.

To protect the interests of textile workers and industries in the developed countries, some mechanism to reasonably control the trade in textiles and other significant import–sensitive products is required. The Multifiber Arrangement and the Bilateral Agreements thereunder are means of accomplishing this objective in regard to trade in textiles. The Orderly Marketing Agreements authorized by the U.S. Trade Act of 1974 are means through which trade in other import–sensitive items can be reasonably controlled in order to preclude severe adverse economic and social impacts on U.S. workers and industries. If imports of sensitive items were allowed to come into the United States at uncontrolled levels, it would result in serious unemployment, social, and economic problems which would ultimately develop into political problems that would force our government to undertake even more restrictive measures than are taken under the present arrangements and agreements.

For international trade to expand and develop as desired in the long term, it will be necessary for effective demand (buying power) to be built up significantly in the densely populated developing countries. This can only be accomplished by a speed–up in the economic development of these countries in order to provide increased per capita income for their people. In many countries, this speed–up in economic development cannot take place until the literacy rate in such countries is significantly improved, because a reasonably educated work force is a prerequisite for economic expansion in any country. In view of this consideration, more efforts should be directed towards improving the educational level of the people in the developing countries.

The developing countries make significant efforts to expand their exports to hard currency countries and give relatively little attention to developing their home markets or expanding their trade with other developing countries. I understand and appreciate their desire to generate needed foreign exchange in order to pay for their imports from the developed countries. However, it would appear that they should and could develop trade among themselves through the use of clearing accounts under bilateral agreements. There is no question but that in the long term, trade between the developing countries will have to expand significantly if such countries are to establish and maintain viable industrial sectors in their economies.

DISCUSSION

The formal discussants were: Tony Dechant, President, National Farmer's Union; and Walter Minger, Senior Vice President, The Bank of America.

Dechant's main point was that farm prices simply must be increased substantially, and that the report had not come to grips with this problem. He thought that the report was wrong in its pessimistic view of international commodity agreements. Such agreements had in the past been quite successful in some cases, and in others had not really been allowed to work. He said the idea that action to raise prices would lead to undesirable consequences for exports reflects the textbook viewpoint but not the real world in which the "free market" does not exist, and international grain trading companies manipulate prices. In wheat the United States sets the world trading price, and should take the leadership in establishing stable and higher prices. He argued that we could set a floor price around $4.00 per bushel, with no harm to our export capability, under a new International Wheat Agreement.

On trade liberalization, Dechant said that there is not much evidence that the remaining tariff barriers applying to agricultural products are a major hindrance to trade. World demand is the force behind expanding exports, not trade policy or domestic price support policy. He closed by saying that protectionism is a natural response to chaotic markets and low prices. Those who criticize protectionism abroad or at home need to do more than recite textbook arguments. They need to provide an alternative policy to improve the current situation in what is largely a political market, not a free market.

Minger said the Task Force report is a good general statement, but does not help much in providing recommendations for improving the environment for international trade. He had some specific suggestions for promoting trade. First, there are some simple steps such as removal of "blocked assets" by legislation, which would facilitate expanded trade with China, and removal of restrictions requiring certain amounts of trade to be carried in U.S. flagships. More generally, Minger thought that using food stocks as a political weapon, and mixing up social and commercial policy was economically harmful to the United States. On a related matter, concessionary sales and credit programs may be helpful, but it should be recognized that there are inherent problems in providing long–term credit for commodities consumed as quickly as food products. For facilitating future commercial exports of U.S. products it might be better to assist in development of the infrastructure of less–developed countries, to avoid waste of products abroad and to enable the handling of large quantities of imports.

Another step that should be considered is encouraging foreign ownership of U.S. agribusiness. While foreign purchases of U.S. farmland are creating some nervousness, joint ventures with countries such as Japan have promise in helping to give foreign buyers the feeling of confidence in U.S. supplies that we all recognize to be extremely important in promoting U.S. trade.

In closing, Minger mentioned a matter of longer–run concern: the attitudes and beliefs of the general public in regard to international trade. In Japan, so heavily dependent on food imports, an appreciation of the benefits of trade is widespread. In the United States it is not so. We need to educate the public on the importance of exports and trade to our economy, and on the idea that expanding U.S. exports will involve some responsiveness on our side in permitting increased imports. On the issue of the free market raised by Tony Dechant, Minger thought it important to recall that perhaps the best remaining case of relatively free markets is the internationally traded agricultural products. While the bulk of the trading is by private treaty, such trading as is done by open bidding has a very important role in price discovery if for no other purpose; and in any case there is no reason to expect farmers, lenders, or anyone else to find themselves better off under a regime of state trading as compared to current arrangements.

Josling responded to Dechant's comments by saying that the report had not taken a rigid free–market view, but was concerned with the very real question of how far farmers could go in attempts to turn world prices in their favor. He said that the history of commodity agreements can be put in two ways: one can either say that most of them have failed or one can say that a few have not failed. The chances of success are not high. He agreed that the International Wheat Agreement had appeared "successful" but said that this had been due largely to the actions of the United States and Canadian governments prior to 1967. The problem with the International Commodity Agreement (ICA) approach in general is that if an agreement does not have the full support of the nations involved, then it will fail; but if it has the necessary support, then the agreement as a formal structure is probably unnecessary. Such agreements are not often successful at persuading countries to act against their interests. In the case of an agreement to support wheat prices at $4.00, the required coincidence of interests does not seem to exist; and an attempt to operate such an agreement would result finally in the United States having to undertake domestic supply management or other measures to maintain the floor price. This would before long be found to involve unacceptable program costs. On the other hand, if market support prices are maintained more closely in line with longer–term realities, domestic policies are much more viable. Longer–term stability is promoted by policies which are sustainable instead of policies that lead to periodic crises and the turning off and on of a government tap.

COMMENTS AND QUESTIONS FROM THE FLOOR

An AAM member said that pricing agricultural commodities "competitively" meant competing with countries that exploit their labor and have much less product regulation than in the United States, and that this was not competing on an equal basis. Josling responded that this point is often of concern with respect to imports of nonagricultural goods, but that for the major agricultural export products the more serious problem is competing with countries that have high internal support prices and that use their treasuries to subsidize the export of the resulting surpluses. He said that this aspect was discussed fully in the report.

A question was raised about what kind of trade relationship should be sought with the Soviet Union when the current agreement expires. Dechant said that he did not like bilateral agreements, although they may be better than nothing. It would be better to make a real effort to get the Soviets into a multinational grains agreement. Minger indicated that he was still uneasy about trying to replace the current market system with a system of state trading. He pointed out that informal bilateral agreements containing price ranges were commonly breached when prices rose in 1972–73, and was skeptical about the practicability of any agreement containing minimum and maximum prices.

Finally, a comment was made that the United States exports and imports many agricultural products besides grains, yet the session focused almost exclusively on world grain trade. Josling responded that in fact the grains are the big trade issue, although this may not be the case in the future. Meat, dairy, and vegetable issues currently just do not carry the international and national impact that the major grain crops do.

C. Peter Timmer and Malden C. Nesheim*

CHAPTER 4

Nutrition, Product Quality, and Safety

Introduction

THE American supermarket is the envy of the world. Other societies, rich and poor alike, marvel at the amount, diversity, quality, convenience, and relative cost of the items available at literally thousands of neighborhood food stores across the United States. No other major society spends so small a fraction of its income for food as we (and the Canadians) do, and the sheer availability and appeal of the American food supply offer a substantial bonus to consumer welfare.

At the same time that the modern supermarket and the ten thousand or so items that stock it were evolving to their present state, the American diet and health–care system were contributing to longer life expectancies and larger physiques. Figure 1 shows that since 1900 the major gains in life expectancy have been among the younger and nonwhite parts of the population, but those are precisely the groups likely to benefit from better nutrition, control of infectious diseases and improved maternal care.

With such a record the American public might well be expected to show great satisfaction with their food system, content in the knowledge that our diet is healthy and safe. And indeed there are many satisfied consumers who used the great variety and quality of foods available in the United States to choose a diet of excellent nutritional quality, high taste appeal and moderate cost. To the consumer who has the *motivation*, *knowledge*, and *financial means* the American food system offers a diet as healthy, safe, and appetizing as any in history.

Despite this potential for great consumer satisfaction, it is not the

*A list of Task Force members and their affiliations follows the report.

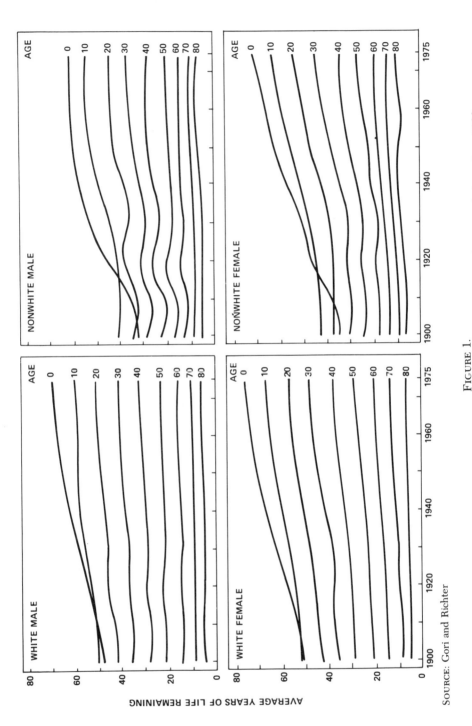

FIGURE 1.

Life Expectancy at Different Ages for U.S. White and Nonwhite Populations since 1900.

SOURCE: Gori and Richter

AVERAGE YEARS OF LIFE REMAINING

prevailing mood in America's supermarkets and kitchens. An under-current of uncertainty, frustration and outright fear of much of the food in the American food supply has caught much of the public. Heart disease, cancer, diabetes, "tired blood" and reduced sexual vigor, we are told, may be caused by ingredients which we put into our foods, or take out of our foods, or both. At the same time certain foods or food components are held in almost magical awe. For example, vitamins C and E, brewer's yeast, rose hips, and almost anything "organic" are thought by some to cure disease and prevent aging, cancer, and the common cold.

In this atmosphere of belief, uncertainty, and fear, many in the American public are looking for reassurance and direction in the form of simple rules. Which foods are unsafe? How much vitamin C and E? Are eggs good or bad? In scientific and public policy forums government, industry, and university experts have attempted to respond by describing the complexity of the scientific evidence and the range of statistical uncertainty, but to many this smacks of cover-up or self-serving propaganda. The nutrition messiahs, with their instant dietary salvation, have found a massive audience by playing off the public's fears against the imperfect scientific evidence.

This paper attempts to define the nutrition, product quality, and safety issues in the context of their potential economic impact on the farm sector. We review some of the scientific evidence that is the basis for the controversy as a mechanism for presenting the policy issues that are distinct from the scientific issues. Inherent in the distinction is a fundamental dilemma for the American democratic system—when private choices, even if fully informed, lead to public health problems, who shall decide on the nature and extent of remedies?

The Issues

Our understanding of human requirements for various nutrients evolved in the context of pathological changes that were traced to particular nutrient deficits. Understanding the mechanisms of the classical nutrient diseases of scurvy, beriberi, pellagra, goiter, xerophthalmia and rickets provided the foundations of biochemistry and modern nutritional science. The elimination of these diseases in modern societies is one of the great achievements of science (although widespread improvements in economic well–being deserve much credit as well).

It was natural in the context of concern over nutrient inadequacies that recommended intake levels would be set sufficiently high to meet the needs of nearly everyone, and much less concern was devoted to the effects of excess nutrient intake, either singly or in combinations. However, epidemiological evidence, animal feeding trials, and basic biological research on mechanisms of nutrient utilization now point increasingly to significant health problems at both ends of the intake spectrum. Figure 2 illustrates the broad range of intakes possible and their health impact. How wide the range of health is with respect to nutrient intake depends very much on the nutrient in question as well as on a variety of other factors unique to the individual—genetic makeup, activity levels, tobacco and alcohol use, and other aspects of lifestyle.

The important point is that a possible relationship between diet and chronic illnesses has been indicated by several types of scientific evidence, and the search for specific causal mechanisms based on animal and human models is well under way. The idea that dietary practices are a risk factor in the development of heart disease and other vascular diseases, for example, will continue to be debated within the scientific community, among government policy makers, and the consuming public, but the issue is unlikely to be resolved in the negative.[1]

Dietary practices that have been linked to the development of vascular diseases involve the consumption of high levels of dietary fat, particularly saturated fat and the consumption of diets rich in cholesterol. Since the major sources of these components of food are animal products—beef, pork, milk, butter and eggs—government actions in

[1]Max Kellough, National Cattlemen's Association: This paragraph would be much more objective if worded as follows: Some types of scientific evidence have indicated a possible link between diet and certain chronic diseases. That evidence is largely epidemiological. It points out the need for continued research based on animal and human models to determine specific causal mechanisms, but it does not at this time justify efforts to stimulate diet alteration among the general public. The concept that dietary practices, other than the consumption of excess calories, are a risk factor in the development of heart disease and other vascular diseases is being debated within the scientific community, among government policy makers and the consuming public. Until the issue is scientifically resolved, the federal government should represent both sides of the controversy equitably, letting the public make the final determination regarding diet modification or alteration.

FIGURE 2.

Relationship Between Nutrient Intake and State of Health

INTAKE	Functional Deterioration Deficit			Minimum Requirement	Maximum Allowance	Functional Deterioration Excess		
HEALTH	Disease and Death	Clinical Signs	Bio-chemical Changes	Low Tissue Stores	Tissues Replete	Bio-chemical Changes	Clinical Signs	Disease and Death

SOURCE: Calloway.

the name of public health that would tend to reduce consumption of these products are likely to have direct economic implications for agriculture. An examination of the scientific issues involved in this particular issue is important because of the direct impact on the farm sector from diet modification. The concern is real because surveys show substantial numbers of consumers modifying their diets for personal health reasons, presumably with small risk and costs.

A similar review of safety issues, especially with respect to possible carcinogens added to the food supply during processing, would also be useful, but the implications for the farm sector are not so direct and immediate. Changes here will be felt primarily through government regulation and intervention which will probably require much clearer scientific evidence before being implemented and made effective.

Evidence from the U.S. Center for Health Statistics shows that in 1974 heart disease and stroke were responsible for 48.7 percent of all deaths among men in the United States. Cancer, with 19.1 percent, was the next–highest cause of death in the same year. Infectious diseases accounted for relatively few of the deaths; only 2.9 percent of the deaths were from pneumonia and influenza. The incidence of heart disease is not the same in human populations throughout the world. In the age range of 45 to 55 an American male in 1964 was seven times as likely to get a heart attack as a Japanese male of the same age. The differences in incidence between Japanese and American men are much reduced in Japanese–Americans living in the United States. The data in Table 1 show some of the differences in incidence of heart disease among men between the ages of 45 and 54 among various countries. Since the countries are all relatively developed countries, the differences cannot be ascribed to differential mortality from infectious disease.

Many aspects of lifestyle differ among the populations of the countries shown in Table 1, one of which is diet. The evidence supporting various dietary practices as being risk factors in the development of coronary heart disease (CHD) has been summarized recently by Glueck and Connor, as well as by Stamler, and these reviews should be consulted for specific references that document evidence summarized here. Epidemiological studies of populations have shown statistically significant correlations between foods consumed by the populations studied and coronary heart disease mortality rates. Several

TABLE 1.

Mortality Rates for 22 Countries Ranked by Mortality Rates for
Coronary Heart Disease (Males, Age 45–54), 1964

Country	1964 Mortality rates per 100,000 population		
	Coronary heart disease (CHD)	All cardiovascular diseases (CV)	All Causes
Finland	442	579	1,120
Scotland	359	463	933
U.S.A.	354[a]	477[a]	964[a]
Australia	324	425	821
No. Ireland	324	465	804
Canada	311	385	752
New Zealand	293	386	758
United Kingdom (Eng. & Wales)	254	341	734
Israel	214	302	572
German Fed. Republic	182	275	772
Denmark	181	248	613
Norway	164	218	566
Netherlands	162	222	582
Austria	159	263	823
Belgium	159	302	820
Czechoslovakia	151	263	738
Switzerland	134	210	658
Italy	133	239	717
Venezuela	131	235	897
Sweden	124	189	522
France	74	202	863
Japan	51	251	733
Mean	212	315	762
Standard Deviation	±103	±109	±145

SOURCE: Inter–Society Commission for Heart Disease Resources.

[a]For white males only, mortality rates are: CHD = 355, CV = 450, all causes = 900.

food groups showed positive associations with CHD and dietary constituents such as saturated fat, cholesterol and total energy have been positively correlated with CHD in several epidemiological investigations. Studies of individuals within population groups show a significant correlation of serum cholesterol level and subsequent risk of

CHD. Genetic differences between populations do not seem to be shown responsible for variations in CHD since populations in the U.S. that come from various countries do not maintain the differences in blood lipid levels or CHD that have been shown by country studies. For example, Japanese men residing in the United States develop blood lipid levels and CHD rates resembling American men.

The epidemiological data, although extensive, are not sufficient to implicate diet directly in the development of CHD. In essentially every species of experimental animals studied, including subhuman primates, dietary cholesterol and saturated fat have been important for the development of experimental atherosclerosis.[2] The nature of the arterial lesions produced in experimental animals by dietary means lends further support to the idea that serum cholesterol levels influence the development of the lesion.

Dietary cholesterol and saturated fats raise serum cholesterol in experimental animals and replacing saturated fat with poly–unsaturated fat reduces blood cholesterol in such experiments. When human subjects are studied under controlled conditions, dietary cholesterol, at least in levels between 0 and 300 to 600 mg per day, has been shown to affect serum cholesterol. Higher levels of dietary cholesterol may not raise blood cholesterol further. Similarly, in human metabolic studies enriching a diet with saturated fats has been shown to elevate blood cholesterol while replacement of saturated fat with unsaturated fat tends to reduce blood cholesterol levels.

Human population groups within the United States with certain dietary habits also differ in serum cholesterol values. Vegetarians have considerably lower serum cholesterol levels than non–vegetarians. In a study of Seventh Day Adventist men, the strict vegetarians had mortality rates 77 percent below that of the general population.

The epidemiological data, animal studies, and human metabolic studies have led many research workers to the conclusion that alteration of dietary practices to reduce saturated fat and cholesterol consumption and to increase poly–unsaturated fat consumption would be

[2]Max Kellough: In fact, Kummerow shows that intimal thickening in the pig (changes in the arterial tissue during development of atherosclerosis) occurs spontaneously in time on low–fat, cholesterol–free diets during the aging process. Other factors also involved are excessive levels of Vitamin D_3, oxidized cholesterol that develops in deep fat friers, and *trans* fatty acids from hydrogenated oils.

desirable for the U.S. public. It is due to this type of evidence that the U.S. dietary goals were developed by the U.S. Senate Select Committee on Nutrition.

These views are subject to controversy, however, and some nutritional scientists do not support the idea that recommendations for marked changes in the U.S. diet are warranted. Such dissenting views have recently been published by Reiser, Mann, Harper, and Leveille.[3]

Much of the controversy comes from the difficulty in doing direct human experimentation in this area. It is not possible to divide homogeneous populations into groups that follow specific dietary practices over a lifetime and then draw conclusions as to effects of these diets on CHD. Thus epidemiological, animal, and human metabolic studies must be carried out and conclusions from these investigations must be translated into population dietary recommendations. Individuals draw different conclusions from basically the same body of data.

One controversial area involves the level of serum cholesterol that constitutes a risk. If the level of serum cholesterol represents a risk factor over a broad range of cholesterol levels, a case can be made that intervention to lower serum cholesterol throughout the range may alter risk of CHD. Reiser has held that serum cholesterol and CHD risk are correlated only when serum cholesterol values exceed 250 mg. This category of serum cholesterol values represents about one–third of all American males. Glueck and Connor, however, cite evidence supporting a relationship between CHD and plasma cholesterol over the entire cholesterol distribution. Such an interpretation of the literature has a major effect on the number of U.S. men who may be considered at risk due to serum cholesterol levels and thus the number of individuals who would be helped by broad public health measures taken to influence dietary practices.

An additional difficulty in assessing the epidemiological data in-

---

[3]Max Kellough: The specific objections of these men should be mentioned. Reiser, for example, finds, "The data relating diet to coronary heart disease, when critically examined, clearly show that there is a normal spectrum of blood serum values, and that normal persons do not develop pathological levels upon the ingestion of eggs and other cholesterol–containing foods. The data also show that a small fraction of any population have pathological levels upon the ingestion of large amounts of cholesterol–containing foods. Average data obtained from mixed populations of normal and pathological blood lipid values should not be used to advise the normal majority of that population."

volved in the diet–heart question involves studies of individual dietary practices in relatively homogeneous populations. These studies have consistently failed to demonstrate significant associations between individual nutrient intakes, as determined by dietary recalls, blood lipids and coronary heart disease risk. This lack of correlation has led to skepticism as to the benefits to CHD risk that may be obtained from dietary alteration. The methodology for obtaining dietary history on individuals is weak and Stamler has pointed out that most studies that have attempted to consider this question have not obtained data with sufficient precision to permit the within–population correlations that have been attempted.

A further area of controversy involves the assessment of what benefits would be obtained if a population at risk actually changed dietary practices. Some data from studies of populations that have had dietary practices altered for a period of time are available. Generally the results suggest that risk is lowered by dietary intervention, but, in most of the studies, the data are not as yet unequivocal.

Controversy in this area then reflects the need for more definitive data that assess dietary practices in relation to coronary heart disease risk. This controversy also leads to different assessments of the public policy steps that should be taken for improvement of public health.

The public and scientific debate relative to the diet–health relationships will continue and the relationships have neither been completely proven nor discredited as some would claim. Both individual decisions and public policy moves in this area may require economic adjustments by segments of U.S. agriculture, particularly those groups involved in the beef, dairy and egg sectors. These adjustments will be less disruptive if they do not come abruptly and by surprise. Hence it is important that the U.S. agricultural system in general and the livestock sector in particular understand the level of scientific support for the idea that dietary practices and CHD incidence are related. A survey of 211 scientists working in the lipid or atherosclerosis field by Norum showed that 188 of these individuals thought there was a connection between diet and CHD. One hundred seventy–six of these scientists thought there was sufficient knowledge to recommend a moderate change in the diet for a population in an affluent society. Most of these researchers had altered their dietary practices on the basis of their knowledge.

Although science is not conducted by ballot, the survey does show that scientific agreement in this area is greater than some would have us believe. The implications of such agreement for public health policy are quite significant. Gori and Richter have assembled data that cross–tabulate preventable factors influencing mortality rates in the United States with specific causes of death. They roughly assess the influence of each factor on each cause of death, with the results shown in Table 2.

The message of Table 2 is unmistakable, despite the honest uncertainty over exact levels of influence of each factor on each cause of death. First, smoking and diet make very high contributions (roughly 30 percent by Gori and Richter's judgment) to three of the five major causes of death, and both contribute at that level to the two most important killers, cardiovascular renal disease and cancer.

Second, our social priorities with respect to reducing mortality are not consistent with the pattern of causation shown in Table 2. Gori and Richter (pp. 1125–6) state that " . . . massive government organizations and funding preside over an unprecedented regulatory effort to protect the environment. Yet, important as this is, it would seem reasonable to think that human health gains from these efforts are likely to be modest, because the epidemiologic record of modern diseases in the United States indicates that an even more determined and massive action is required in respect to diet, smoking, alcohol and drug abuse, and automobile and occupational safety. Such action of course presents greater difficulties than do simple engineering approaches to environmental preservation, because it calls for a conscious commitment to modify life–styles . . ."

The third and perhaps most important point from Table 2 is its emphasis on the multiple causation of most of the major causes of death. Life expectancy depends on a large number of variables, only some of which can be consciously controlled by the individual. Moreover, over a certain significant range some choice variables can substitute for others in a manner illustrated by Figure 3. It must be emphasized that Figure 3 shows a hypothetical relationship only. Medical evidence is not yet as precise as the diagram would indicate. But the direction of interaction of dietary restrictions and physical exercise is well accepted by the medical community even if the extent of synergism between the two (and with smoking, another very important variable in the relationship) is not well understood.

Figure 3 illustrates both the individual and the policy dilemmas

TABLE 2.

Influence of Selected Preventable Factors on Mortality[a]

Factor	Cause of death				
	Major cardio-vascular-renal diseases	Malignant neoplasms	Accidents, motor vehicle and other	Respiratory diseases	Diabetes mellitus
Smoking	VH	VH	L	VH	VL
Diet	VH	VH	VL	VL	VH
Occupational hazards	VL	L	VH	H	VL
Alcohol abuse	L	L	VH	L	L
Drug abuse	VL	VL	H	VL	VL
Radiation hazards	VL	L	VL	VL	VL
Air and water pollution	VL	VL	VL	L	VL
	(number of premature deaths)				
In 1973	395,000	90,000	44,000	16,000	24,000
In 2000[b]	595,000	127,000	71,000	33,000	30,000

SOURCE: Gori and Richter.

[a]Very high (VH), 30 percent; high (H), 20 to 30 percent; medium (M), 10 to 20 percent; low (L), below 5 percent.

[b]If current trends remain unchanged.

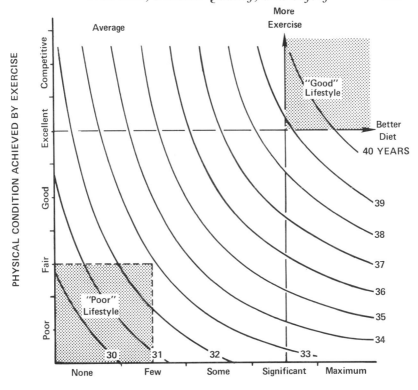

FIGURE 3.

Hypothetical Relationship Between Physical Condition from Exercise, Diet Restrictions, and Expected Number of Years Free from Chronic Disease for a Forty Year Old Nonsmoking Adult

inherent in the likely link between diet and disease. A "good" lifestyle includes sufficient physical exercise to maintain an "excellent" rating for aerobic capacity as well as significant dietary restrictions to maintain low risk levels of serum cholesterol and other blood lipids (and other restrictions on total caloric intake, simple carbohydrates, and highly processed foods). This particular example also includes no smoking as a lifestyle element. The years of freedom from chronic disease at age forty that can be anticipated with this lifestyle combination can also be achieved, however, with somewhat less exercise and more stringent dietary restrictions or by more exercise and fewer dietary restrictions.

A greater risk of chronic disease is likely with reductions along both axes.

The private dilemma is the cost an individual is willing to pay now (e.g., at age forty) for an uncertain but probably higher quality of life thirty to forty years in the future. Are the "pleasures" of the "poor" lifestyle subset of Figure 3 worth the likely, but by no means certain, price that may be paid from heart disease or other chronic illness in later years? It would seem extremely difficult for society to make this choice for the individual, and yet extremely important to society on humanitarian grounds that the choice be informed by the best scientific evidence available.

But society's interest in this decision extends beyond humanitarian concern. Even if sufficient information were available to indicate the probable benefits of the "good" lifestyle, many in society will continue to choose the "poor" lifestyle for a variety of personal reasons. Although the individual who chooses the "poor" lifestyle pays part of the costs through more chronic disease and higher medical costs, not all of such costs are private. Society pays an important share of such costs through losses in productivity of workers and through partial public financing of medical costs. That is, there is a strong social investment in the individual's "lifestyle" decision, and some mechanism is needed to reconcile the difference between private and public costs and benefits to alternative dietary/lifestyle decisions.

It is here that the substitution possibilities inherent in Figure 3 present enormous policy implications. Health may be improved through various combinations of lifestyle changes, including exercise, diet, and smoking. To some individuals alteration of one component of lifestyle, e.g., exercise, may be much more acceptable than alterations in other components. The opportunity exists for individuals to substitute movement along the "more exercise" ray for movement along the "better diet" ray while maintaining a personally satisfying expectation of future health.

What should society do when faced with such a dilemma? An economist would be tempted to answer that society should spend its educational and regulatory money where it will get the greatest marginal gain, and scientists should do research to determine if that is in exercise or diet or smoking, or other factors. Such an answer would be naive in three ways. First, our society may not have mechanisms for making sound decisions in such scientifically controversial areas. Second, scientists are not able to quantify these relationships with sufficient precision for public policy making to take the "facts" as given. Third, lifestyle, including dietary practices, is immersed in and grows out of a complex American social and political economy. The American food system, in particular, has a very large stake in policy decisions aimed at altering the composition of the American diet for health and safety reasons. Many citizens, including many knowledgeable consumers, would feel much more comfortable achieving significant health gains through improved lifestyles than through increased regulation of the American food system and greater restrictions on what may be eaten with good conscience. The Quelch and Clayton survey, for example, showed that 98 percent of respondents felt that consumer lifestyles were an important detriment to *nutritional* well–being.

What are the implications for the farm sector? Despite the adequacy or inadequacy of the present evidence linking diet to health problems, Jones (p. 28) reports that about half the 1400 households surveyed by U.S. Department of Agriculture (USDA) in the spring of 1976 were "altering their diets due to health concerns, either to alleviate existing health problems or to avoid potential ones. Diet changes were more likely in higher income households, where families were larger and the homemaker more highly educated." The most common dietary changes involved reductions in sweets and snacks, fried foods, fatty red meat, ice cream and soft drinks. The main additions were lowfat milk and cheese, lean red meat, fish, fresh fruits and vegetables, poultry, and broiled and baked foods. Fried foods, butter, eggs and fatty red meats were avoided in households reporting a high–cholesterol problem. Households with diabetics avoided sweets and snacks, soft drinks and sugar.

Whatever the merit of the scientific evidence linking diet to health problems (and it is the strong opinion of the authors that it will not disappear) this market evidence is what counts for the American food system and ultimately, the farmer. The issue of changing dietary patterns for health purposes is not restricted to a few vegetarians and health food enthusiasts but has entered the consciousness of the average American consumer. This consumer votes both at the ballot box *and* the market place, and has an impact on the farm sector both directly and through impetus for governmental intervention into nutrition, quality, and safety issues.

A fair process for deciding on policy directions and governmental interventions in the food sector is desperately needed. Many Task Force members felt that establishing this process for reaching decisions in the nutrition, product quality, and food safety areas was the most important goal for the entire Farm Summit. The producer activists in particular felt great concern that consumers, and especially consumer organizations, were so distrustful of information emanating from the food industry that no meaningful communication could take place. The consumer activists felt that producer activists considered them to be biased and uninformed. Some channel of communication in an atmosphere of trust is urgently needed to avoid further factionalization and fear in the food arena.

Alternative Paths for the Food System

The Task Force discussed four alternative paths for the U.S. food system. No consensus emerged as to which was preferable, but various members strongly urged that each possibility be identified with a "fair" assessment of costs and benefits attached.

LESS REGULATION

Several food producer representatives on the Task Force made a strong plea for *less* regulation of the U.S. food system as a means to improve both producer and consumer welfare. Such a view is consistent with the Quelch and Clayton finding that 55 percent of food manufacturers sampled and 54 percent of farmers felt that reduced governmental intervention would improve the nutritional well–being of the population. Table 3 shows that this view is not widely held by other interest groups in the food system, but there are some strong elements to the position. First, the Delaney amendment that prohibits the addition to the food supply of any material known to cause cancer in man or animals was enacted in an era when analytical methods were far less sensitive that those in use today. A logical case exists for modifying the Delaney amendment so that the tolerance is not zero, but some very small amount. However, it was noted in comments on a draft of this report that the basic food and drug legislation requires that all additives be "safe." Even in the absence of the Delaney amendment it

TABLE 3.
Agreement With Actions Government Might Take to Improve the Nutritional Well-Being of the Population

Actions	Consumer Activist	Food Mfg.	Food Retailer	Farmer	Gov't. Program Admin.	Nutritionist (Gov't.)	Nutritionist (Industry)	Nutrition (Academic)	Other Academic	Nursing Profession	Other	Overall Agreeing Percentage
						(percent)						
Control food advertising to children	95	65	70	73	91	98	74	87	89	93	93	85
Mass media nutrition programs	97	79	95	82	97	98	90	93	94	100	93	92
Increase enforcement of nutrition standards	90	33	58	64	87	87	56	81	86	91	85	76
Increase nutrition research funds	94	85	86	78	92	96	95	97	100	88	94	92
Increase community nutrition centers	87	57	71	40	81	94	68	89	82	79	81	77
Mandatory nutrition education	88	83	90	76	87	95	93	90	83	88	90	88
Reduce government intervention	18	55	37	54	21	24	47	26	24	51	30	33
Nutrition label information in food advertising	92	29	38	77	87	87	60	82	87	95	88	77
Percentage of ingredient information	97	34	64	74	86	85	67	73	78	91	83	77
Restrict food stamp foods	66	58	64	94	77	83	84	65	77	88	72	76
Restrict school lunch foods	98	71	81	96	91	94	93	86	92	93	92	91
Simplify nutrition label	92	88	92	92	91	80	54	74	88	92	98	86

SOURCE: Quelch and Clayton.

would be extremely difficult to show that a known carcinogen was safe.

Second, the prohibition does not permit a cost–benefit assessment of whether certain chemicals might cause more good than harm, nor does it permit the consumer to make that decision on an informed, individual basis. The cases of saccharin, cyclamates, nitrites, and other commercially important additives, coloring agents, and so on illustrate how real and difficult the issues are. Despite the fact that it seems silly to ban the use of a chemical whose social benefits outweigh its social costs, present scientific evidence on health costs and benefits is so slippery that even technical assessments of the issue are almost impossible. A recent report by the National Academy of Sciences finds claims for *any* benefits from saccharin unsubstantiated. From an economist's perspective the availability of sugar–free products does expand the range of consumer choice (where to "spend" his or her calories) and hence contributes to greater consumer welfare. The controversy is over any association of *medical* benefits (such as weight loss) with these *consumer* benefits. In general, there is no recognized decision–making process for fairly deciding when costs outweigh benefits and vice versa. At the moment Congress seems intent on legislating the issue on a chemical–by–chemical basis, and many scientists would prefer the Delaney clause as it stands to such an *ad hoc* public decision–making process with respect to the safety of the foods we eat. It is not surprising that our Task Force could not agree that less regulation was in the public interest, in the absence of a prior agreement on a mechanism for settling disputes in this area.

KEEP THE PRESENT RULES

A second alternative that had significant appeal to some members of the Task Force was to do nothing at all in terms of intervention, but to leave the food system to find its own path in the context of changing technology, consumer tastes, and present regulations and standards.

This position emphasized the extremely wide choice of foods available to most American consumers and the potential to enjoy the safest and highest quality food supply in the world. But the position also recognized that the American food system is not static, and mere failure to enact new public regulations will not result in a status quo situation. Indeed, there was considerable desire from the defenders of this alternative that at least the broad trends likely to emerge from a "no more regulation" scenario be outlined.

The first is that the trend to more processed foods using a wide range of substitutes is likely to continue and possibly accelerate. The substitutions include vegetable protein extenders for meats (when prices are right, as they are likely to be for several years), synthetic substitutes for foods thought by some to cause health problems, such as eggs, whole milk and cheese, sausages, and perhaps shellfish, and the use of manufactured or synthetic products to make convenience or "instant" foods, e.g., instant soup mixes and the like. As this trend continues, the existing product identity standards (now covering 205 food products) will come under further pressure from manufacturers to permit substitutes and synthetics to manufacture a product similar in nutritional quality to the original. The stake of individual parts of the farm community in such decisions is very great (e.g., the dairy industry for dairy standards of identity), but it is not so clear that the overall impact on the farm sector will be significant since the substitution tends to be of one farm–produced commodity for another.

A continued trend toward more highly processed foods created from mixtures of ingredients unique to human evolutionary experience worries many consumers, nutritionists, and health practitioners. Their concern for the long–run safety of an increasing proportion of the American diet is distinct from the health concerns about the composition of the diet from more or less traditional foods—meats, eggs, dairy products and the rest. The safety issue revolves around the possible long–run carcinogenic impact of small amounts of chemicals that are new to the human digestive system. *Consumer Reports* recently prepared a thoughtful review of these issues: it is included as Appendix A to this report. The impact of substantial changes in permitted additives would have much more impact on the manufacturing sector than on the farm sector, but the major impact might be on current lifestyle trends for many consumers who rely on the instantaneous aspects of many processed foods to free time for other pursuits.

NUTRITION EDUCATION

The third alternative the Task Force discussed was extension and improvement of nutritional education. On one of its rare points of unanimity, all members felt improved nutrition education was important. Since 93 percent of respondents in Quelch and Clayton's survey of nutrition interest groups saw inadequate consumer knowledge as a barrier to nutritional well–being (see Table 3), the Task Force was representative of a much broader constituency.

The appeal of more and better nutrition education has several reasons. First, and perhaps paramount in many people's minds, it does not intervene in the freedom of choice of individuals, either directly or indirectly, as regulations and price manipulations do. If both the public and health policymakers are assured that consumers are truly well–informed about current nutritional issues, including the public health dimensions of private dietary decisions, then food choice can and should be left to the responsibility of the individual consumer. Maintaining and increasing this individual responsibility received major emphasis from many, but not all, on the Task Force. The concern of the dissenters lay in a recognition of the realities of factors actually affecting food choices in today's society. The $3 to 5 billion spent annually for food advertising significantly influences what we want and choose. Few would argue that the major thrust of this advertising has the intent or effect of improving diets and nutritional status.

The second reason for the appeal of programs to improve nutrition education is that sufficient knowledge now exists to recommend healthy diets, but the knowledge is inadequate to justify more massive interventions into the food system to change substantially current dietary practices. Many people in the United States are now in excellent nutritional health, and if others simply imitated these role models, they could enjoy similar nutritional benefits. No major breakthroughs in scientific understanding would be necessary although understanding the epidemiology of such good lifestyle patterns would be extremely important, especially to help clarify the trade–offs and substitutions among the various dimensions of chronic disease. Accurate information of the sort hypothesized and modeled in Figure 3 would be an important component of a nutrition program because it deals specifically with the critical question for such programs: what is the message?

The controversial aspect of this approach is how to bring about behavioral change. Even with agreement on a message, and the example of good nutritional role models, our understanding of how to make nutrition education *effective* is seriously inadequate.

The third reason for widespread support for nutrition education is that, at least as traditionally conducted, the programs are relatively inexpensive. It is hard to find $100 million spent each year by governments and nutrition groups to improve nutritional understanding, while food advertising now is $3 to 5 billion annually.[4] Even major expansions in nutrition education programs will leave the dollar volume spent to improve the public's understanding of good nutritional practices and their motivation to use them as only a tiny fraction of the dollar volume spent to persuade consumers to buy specific products of the food industry.

The authors feel a fourth factor also accounts for the widespread popularity of nutrition education programs. As traditionally conducted these programs do not threaten anyone's vital (economic) interests because they may not in fact change food consumption behavior in any significant way.[5] The objective of much nutrition education has been to ensure consumption of a variety of foods that provide the required nutrients in adequate amounts. When nutritional educators begin to mount programs aimed specifically at reducing the intake of foods thought to be associated with major public health problems such as coronary heart disease, cancer and diabetes, then opposition and widespread controversy erupt quickly.

Notwithstanding the widespread agreement from the Task Force that better nutritional education was desirable in order to allow individual consumers to make nutritionally responsible dietary decisions, there was major controversy over what the nutritional education message should say. Part of the controversy revolves again around the separate perspectives of public and private, and another part between *nutritional and health risks* associated with a dietary recommendation and the *economic risks and costs* associated with its adoption.

For instance, the *Dietary Goals* urged that Americans consume fewer highly refined, processed foods, more fruits, vegetables and

---

[4]Richard E. Hagen, National Food Processors Association: The linkage of the food advertising budget to government nutrition spending is an improper comparison. It is true that food companies spend substantial sums competing against each other for market share, but to suggest indirectly that food advertising causes poor eating habits is a leap which the data do not justify.

[5]Richard E. Hagen: This statement is inconsistent with survey results cited earlier in the report which show that substantial numbers of Americans have, indeed, modified their eating habits in recent years.

whole grains, less saturated fats, dietary cholesterol, and sugar, and fewer calories in total (U.S. Congress, Senate). This was not intended as an individually prescribed diet and would not be adequate for such purposes for many millions of Americans with specific nutritional problems. However, it is the strong opinion of the authors (from which several Task Force members dissent) that as a population—wide average into which individuals are free to fit as their knowledge, preferences, needs (and doctor's advice) dictate, such dietary changes *in aggregate* are considered likely to cause significant health improvements at relatively little health or nutritional risk.

Advocating such dietary patterns as the basis of an expanded nutritional education program is controversial *not because of widespread fears of substantial health risks associated with the new diets but because of the economic costs and dislocations should they be widely adopted.*[6] In short, the critical issue for nutrition education is the content of the message and whether the private sector can agree on a message that makes public—health sense as well as economic sense.

The stakes here are quite substantial for both the American farmer and the food processing sector, in both the short and long run. Reducing consumption of many animal products will further reduce the farmer's share of the consumer's food dollar, since these are products that return a much higher proportion than the 35 to 40 percent average (see Table 4). Reduction of highly processed foods, or further restraints on permitted additives, will disrupt the high—profit part of the food processor's line and may substantially reduce both profits and growth opportunities. Despite the widespread appeal of nutrition education, its potential for disagreement and widespread controversy is as great as other issues in the nutrition, product quality, and safety arena. Once

---

[6]Max Kellough: This is simply not true. Agricultural producers are justifiably concerned that their livelihood may be undermined by allegations which are unfounded in fact, which may have a long—term detrimental effect on public health, which are unlikely to reap any widespread benefit, and which they believe will be eventually disproven. Moves to alter the food system should be avoided unless and until a product is proven harmful. There is no proof that mass diet modification to reduce cholesterol and saturated fat consumption would benefit the public health. There is, in fact, evidence that radical and extreme efforts at diet modification could be detrimental. Clear scientific evidence should be required in all cases affecting the nation's health or wealth. At no time should such public policy be determined on supposition or a prevailing view developed by exposure to only one side of a controversy. Economic factors should not be the sole determinant if the public health is unquestionably at stake.

TABLE 4.

Farmer's Share of the Consumer's Food Dollar for Selected Foods, 1975–1977 Average

Product	Farmer's share	Product	Farmer's share
	(percent)		(percent)
Unprocessed foods[a]		Processed foods	
Animal products:		Animal products:	
Eggs	66	Butter	65
Pork	60	Milk, fresh	54
Beef, choice	59	Cheese, American	48
Chicken, frying	56	Milk, evaporated	48
		Ice cream	35
Crops:		Crops:	
Beans, dried	42	Vegetable shortening	40
Tomatoes	41	Peanut butter	37
Onions	38	Margarine	34
Lettuce	34	Orange juice, frozen	32
Apples	30	Flour	31
Oranges	23	Rice, long grain	38
Grapefruit	21	Peaches, canned	24
		Peas, frozen	20
		Potatoes, french	
		fries, frozen	18
		Tomatoes, canned	13
		Cookies, sandwich	12
		Bread, white	10[b]
		Corn flakes	8

SOURCE: U.S. Department of Agriculture 1978, June.

[a] Some processing is involved for almost all products. Foods classified as unprocessed are sold mostly in fresh form in contrast to the foods classified as processed which are derived mostly from animal products and crops.

[b] For wheat only; all farm ingredients were 16 percent.

again, the most urgent task is for a mechanism for resolving controversies. The Farm Summit, by airing such controversies in a search for areas of consensus, is an important first step in identifying agreeable decision–making frameworks.

MORE ACTIVIST INTERVENTIONS

Even a major increase in traditional nutrition education activities is regarded by many specialists as a non–interventionist approach to what they see as America's nutritional problems. To make more rapid progress in changing dietary patterns, this group, which was represented on the Task Force, would like to see consideration of more activist interventions. These range from extension of nutrition labeling to significant restrictions on food advertising aimed at children, from introducing food grading with consumers in mind to altering the relative prices of various foods and food products so that their private costs (at the supermarket) would more accurately reflect what is currently known about their public health costs. The Task Force discussed these issues in the context of a sequence of progressively stronger interventions, but no agreement could be reached on which alternatives should be discussed and clearly none were recommended.

Despite the unhappiness of the producer representatives on the Task Force that such interventionist alternatives are being contemplated and analyzed, the farm sector would be badly misled if it felt that either (1) the scientific evidence that gives rise to the concerns over the nutritional health and safety of the American diet has been (or will be) entirely discredited, or (2) that all consumer activists who urge enactment of more stringent regulations and interventions to change eating behavior do so for personal reasons and do not represent significant grassroots interests.

The USDA survey noted above found fully one–half of American households altering their diets for health reasons. The concern among the American population exists and is real. The consumer activists are merely tapping this concern and using it as a political force to create what they feel would be a safer and healthier diet. There is honest disagreement over whether such steps are necessary or desirable, and at what cost, but questioning the motives of people who seek such change will only exacerbate the tensions and distance between the consumer movements and producer interests. If disputes are settled in the political arena, then political solutions will be imposed, no matter who is right. But we should keep in mind that everyone is a food consumer, and only a relative few are food producers.

A new mechanism for resolution of food issues is urgently needed. The most important aspect of such a mechanism would be the ability to engage in dialogue without the fear of economic disaster on one hand or of widespread and immediate health risks on the other. Both parties, but especially those groups responsible for generating and evaluating scientific evidence with respect to health risks and safety of our food, must show great restraint in how their positions are presented. The press is constantly looking for sensational stories and much economic damage can be done by creating unjustified fears in the public mind and subsequent pressure for ill–considered public policy interventions.

Economic Impact on the Farm Sector

It should be clear that the Task Force, despite substantial internal disagreement on the nature and extent of the issues and on their resolution, strongly agrees that the farm sector has an enormous economic stake in how the public policy issues with respect to nutrition, product quality, and food safety are handled and resolved. However, the economic stake in each of the above three areas is different for different producing sectors. It is useful to summarize the impact separately for each area.

NUTRITION

The primary public policy question in the nutrition area is the possible contribution of dietary patterns to major causes of disease and death among the American population. The national and international epidemiological evidence has been indicative of such a linkage for nearly three decades, and the scientific evidence from animal feeding trials and laboratory models of human metabolic mechanisms, although not conclusive, is certainly supportive of the epidemiological evidence. This combination of evidence provided the impetus for the formulation of the *Dietary Goals* which called for a significant restructuring of the American diet. These goals, and the extent of nutrition interest group agreement with them, are summarized in Table 5, taken from Quelch and Clayton.

Any success in achieving the goals calling for reduced consumption of butterfat, eggs, fatty meats, other sources of saturated fats, and sugar is likely to have negative repercussions on the animal sector of the U.S. farm economy. A number of these commodities, especially the high-grade meats, eggs and dairy products are not extensively traded to foreign markets, and so market losses in the United States are not likely to be offset by gains internationally.

Just the opposite is true for those farm items that the dietary goals would have increase in consumption—whole grains and fruits and vegetables. Many of these, especially the grains and fresh fruits, are sold extensively overseas by U.S. producers, and larger market opportunities domestically are likely to come through reductions in exports, at least in the short run, with relatively little benefit to substantial parts of the farm community. However, for commodities currently having large stocks and production restraints under government programs, notably wheat, an increase in consumption could come out of a reduction in stocks and a relaxation of set-asides, to the benefit of both farmers and consumers/taxpayers. In addition, localized producers of many fruits and vegetables might show significant gains.

If consumption of livestock products were to drop substantially, significant amounts of feed grains would become available for human consumption or export. Since the United States is the largest supplier of such commodities internationally, substantial increases in export availability would probably cause lower international prices and quite possibly lower overall foreign currency earnings.

The pressing question for the farm community is how to be part of the decision-making process without appearing to speak from a position of vested economic interest. There is a natural tendency to listen more favorably to scientific evidence that defends the economic position of interest, the tobacco industry and growers being a prime example. Since scientific evidence in the dietary area is unlikely ever to be as clear-cut as the evidence linking smoking to lung cancer and heart disease, the potential for finding agreeable scientists and evidence will be substantial.

The authors feel it would be a mistake for the farm community to

TABLE 5.
Agreement With Food Consumption Goals Corresponding to Dietary Goals

Dietary Goals	Consumer Activist	Food Mfg.	Food Retailer	Farmer	Gov't. Program Admin.	Nutritionist (Gov't.)	Nutritionist (Industry)	Nutrition (Academic)	Other Academic	Nursing Profession	Other	Overall Agreeing Percentage
					(percent)							
Decrease consumption of butterfat, eggs, and other high cholesterol sources	86	69	73	31	82	81	44	68	75	79	80	71
Decrease consumption of foods high in fat and partially substitute polyunsaturated fat for saturated fat	97	74	84	46	92	94	51	77	85	91	91	82
Decrease consumption of meat and increase consumption of poultry and fish	90	67	74	20	74	87	46	69	78	76	78	71
Decrease consumption of salt and foods high in salt content	97	83	88	63	93	94	84	82	95	88	90	87
Decrease consumption of sugar and foods high in sugar content	97	77	88	77	94	98	86	84	98	95	92	90
Increase consumption of fruits and vegetables and whole grains	99	98	99	93	99	99	97	97	99	100	98	98
Substitute nonfat milk for whole milk	81	61	71	35	66	74	38	71	77	73	63	66

SOURCE: Quelch and Clayton.

take this approach in dealing with possible diet–related disease and mortality factors. A more constructive approach would be to interpret the existing (and future) evidence as a statistical assessment of possible risk factors and to urge that any intervention strategy consciously recognize the statistical (and hence uncertain) public health benefits in the context of more definable economic costs. If the farm sector can have the public policy issues framed in this manner, it is likely to receive widespread sympathy and support for any assistance needed to cope with economic dislocations.

FOOD QUALITY AND STANDARDS

Several members of the Task Force were concerned about the economic implications of proposed changes in the manner in which fresh and processed foods are graded for quality and in the need for changes in standards of identity as new food substitutes and combinations reach the marketplace. Official USDA grades were designed to facilitate trading between farmers and processors or between processors and wholesalers. These grades tend to reflect visual appearance of most foods rather than eating quality or nutrient content which tend to vary as much within a given USDA grade as they do from one grade to another. The current system has worked well to facilitate trading, but consumers do not use USDA grades for making many important purchase decisions. Consumers do not want a U.S. Prime chuck cut for a pot roast,[7] and they do want apples to be crisp and juicy, not mealy even though unblemished and bright red. Since ripeness, firmness, sweetness, and flavor are normally not part of the grade for fruits and vegetables, there was considerable sentiment on the Task Force for a set of consumer–oriented grades that would more adequately allow a rational judgment in the marketplace. A recent Office of Technology Assessment report on grading concludes however, that such consumer–oriented grades, especially if they are to include taste and nutrient content, may not be feasible given present knowledge of causes of taste and nutrient variation and the present marketing system (U.S. Congress).

[7]Max Kellough: Cattle feeders recognize this because consumers, in making free choice purchase decisions, have told them so; and cattle feeders have responded by producing less prime beef. In the last 3 years, the production of prime beef has dropped 36 percent.

Substantial controversy existed over proposals to change product standards of identity to permit substitutes in the manufacture of many common foods. The proposal to use sodium caseinate in the manufacture of ice cream, for example, illustrates many of the issues. Consumers are apprehensive over such changes because they would not know if they were getting "real" ice cream or not, whereas producers agree that substantial cost savings are possible (some of which would be passed on to consumers as lower prices), but they know few consumers will buy "Frozen Sodium Caseinate and Other Chemicals that Taste a Lot Like Ice Cream."

It is not clear what the stake of the farm sector is in such proposed changes. Presumably the dairy sector will sell more milk if it is the only ingredient allowed in ice cream. But if it is, the cost may become so high that the total market will be smaller. Permitting some adjustments in the standards of identity may or may not be in the interests of the farm sector.

SAFETY

The issue of the long–run safety of the American food supply must be divided into two components to unravel its potential impact on the economic interests of the farm sector. The first is the set of issues arising from production practices on the farm itself, and the second is whether the increasing degree of processing and prevalence of "manufactured" foods in our diets has long–run safety implications.

Safety of Farm Production Practices. The increasing use of chemicals in farm production practices has given rise to serious questions about the ultimate safety of the foods that result from such practices. The use of pesticides that would clearly be toxic if consumed by humans in large quantities is condoned on the basis that no detectable residues are found in the resulting foods and because the cost savings are so great. The use of antibiotics and hormones in animal feed is justified on similar grounds.

If evidence accumulates that such production practices result in long–run safety problems either through a carcinogenic effect or through the development of antibiotic–resistant bacterial strains, the short–run dislocation would be severe, but it is unclear what the ultimate economic impact would be. For commodities where American producers receive a price dictated by international market forces, an upward shift in U.S. cost curves will cause economic hardship. For commodities where U.S. producers face an inelastic demand curve and the backward shift in supply curves causes a significant reduction in output, the new equilibrium price may result in higher gross and net revenues to farmers, but at substantial costs to consumers (USDA 1978).

Significant concerns have been expressed that U.S. producers must meet quality and safety standards that foreign competitors do not meet. There is concern that diseased livestock from Mexico and other countries and pesticide–contaminated foreign fruits and vegetables are being imported into the United States. In addition to much stricter inspection to ensure equal rules for all competitors, many U.S. producers want "country of origin" labels affixed to foods sold in supermarkets.

Safety of Processed Foods. The ultimate safety of a diet composed of increased amounts of highly processed foods made visually appealing and tasty with artificial ingredients, storable with preservatives, and convenient to handle with other additives is unknown. There is no evidence suggesting a clear and present danger. However, many of the individual compounds have not undergone long–run safety tests, and very few have been tested in combinations used commercially to examine any synergistic impact. Similarly, many micronutrients are removed during processing, and only a handful are added in enriched formulation. Although nutritional science knows a good deal about human nutrient requirements, it is a certainty that not everything is known. Diets made up entirely of highly processed foods may have long–run nutritional health implications that are not now apparent.

What will the economic impact on the farm sector be if evidence accumulates implicating a highly processed diet in significant health problems? A significant reversal of present trends toward such processed diets and an increase in consumption of less refined foods should have a positive impact on the farm sector, as it would reap a larger share of the consumer's food dollar, but the implications for processors would be immediate and drastic. Much of the commercial strategy of modern food processors is oriented toward achieving gains in market share through advertising of company–unique products that emerge from research and development laboratories. A return to a less–processed diet could drastically reduce the number of food products now on supermarket shelves and radically narrow the marketing options open to food processors in their search for larger markets.

Conclusions

It would be nice to conclude with a set of recommendations aimed at improving the nutritional value, quality, and safety of the American diet that all members of the Task Force felt was consistent with the available evidence and with the best interests of the farm sector. Such a set of recommendations may be feasible, but this Task Force could not find it. Fundamentally different perspectives and values precipitated useful, frequently even enjoyable and humorous interaction, but those differences precluded resolution of the issues.

However, one major item of agreement came through unanimously and clearly—the need for new decision–making mechanisms to resolve disputes in the food nutrition, quality and safety arena. Present mechanisms in which all evidence offered by the producing sector is considered suspect because of the "profit motive" and all evidence from the consumer organizations is rejected because it is "politically motivated" do more to exacerbate problems than to resolve them. The Task Force agreed that it was important for the farm sector to participate in the new decision–making process although it would not be able to dictate the results.

References

Consumer's Union of the United States, Inc. November 1978. *Consumer Reports.*

Calloway, D. 1978. Personal communication with the authors. Department of Nutrition, University of California at Berkeley.

Glueck, C. J. and W. E. Connor. 1978. "Diet–Coronary Heart Disease Relationship Reconnoitered." *Amer. J. Clinical Nutr.* 31: 727–37.

Gori, B. B. and B. J. Richter. 1978. "The Macroeconomics of Disease Prevention in the United States." *Sci.* 200: 1124–30.

Harper, A. E. 1978. "Dietary Goals – A Skeptical View." *Amer. J. Clinical Nutr.* 31: 310–15.

Inter–Society Commission for Heart Disease Resources. 1970. "Primary Prevention of Atherosclerotic Diseases." *Circulation.* 42: A55–A95.

Jones, J. L. 1977. "Consumer Research Developments." in *National Food Situation.* USDA–ERS–NFS159, March.

Kummerow, F. A. 1979. "Nutrition Imbalance and Angiotoxins as Dietary Risk Factors in Coronary Heart Disease." *Amer. J. Clinical Nutr.* 32: 58–83.

Leveille, G. A. 1978. "Establishing and Implementing Dietary Goals." in *Family Econ. Rev.* USDA–ARS–Consumer and Food Econ. Institute, NE–36.

Mann, G. 1977. "Diet–Heart: End of an Era." *New Eng. J. Med.* 297: 644–50.

National Academy of Sciences. "Saccharine: Technical Assessment of Risks and Benefits." forthcoming.

Norum, K. R. 1978. "Some Present Concepts Concerning Heart Diet and Prevention of Coronary Heart Disease." *Nutr. Metabl.* 22: 1–7.

Quelch, J. A. and A. G. Clayton. 1978. "Nutrition and the American Consumer, A Survey of Interest Groups." *Food Products Development.* 12: 80–4.

Reiser, R. 1978. "Over–Simplification of Diet: Coronary Heart Disease Relationships and Exogenated Dietary Recommendations." *Amer. J. Clinical Nutr.* 31: 865–75.

Stamler, J. 1978. "Life Styles, Major Risk Factors, Proof and Public Policy." *Circulation.* 58: 3–19.

Timmer, C. P. and P. Rankin. 1978. "Problems in Defining a U.S. Nutrition Policy." Paper prepared under a grant from the Ford Foundation, mimeo.

U.S. Congress, Office of Technology Assessment. June 1977. *Perspectives on Federal Retail Food Grading.* OTA–F–47.

U.S. Congress, Senate. 1977. *Dietary Goals for the United States.* Select Committee on Nutrition and Human Needs. Washington: U.S. Gov't. Printing Office.

U.S. Department of Agriculture. June 1978. "National Food Review." ESCS, NFR–3.

U.S. Department of Agriculture. September 1978. "The Economic Effects of a Prohibition on the Use of Selected Animal Drugs." ESCS.

U.S. Department Health, Education and Welfare. 1978. *U.S. Center for Health Statistics, 1978.* Health Resources Admin. Nat'l. Center for Health Service.

ADD A PINCH OF GUAR GUM, A DOLLOP OF BHT, A DASH OF SORBITOL

If you've ever read the ingredients list on a package of instant dried soup mix, you can appreciate the cover of this issue. It reads more like a chemical glossary than a food ingredients list.

Whatever happened to the Good Old Days when food was really food? The Industrial Revolution happened, and population growth. Migration from farms to cities. All those things helped change the way people eat.

Food additives are a result of America's altered lifestyle. If it weren't for additives, you'd have to shop for less food more often. You'd also have to pay more for it to compensate for spoilage losses. Your diet would often be limited to seasonal foods. And a simple bowl of soup might take half a day's time.

Additives perform a variety of functions. Some are preservatives. Some are colors, flavorings, or agents to affect the consistency of foods. Some additives are foods in their own right: honey, sugar, salt, and vinegar, for example. Some, such as pectin or citric acid, are a natural constituent of foods. Other additives are manufactured chemical compounds. Some additives are necessary; some aren't. Some may be of questionable safety.

Additives can be divided into five broad categories, according to how they're used in food products:

Preservatives. These keep foods edible for long periods. Antioxidants such as ascorbic acid, BHA, and benzoate prevent foods from becoming rancid and developing peculiar colors or flavors. Antimycotics, including propionates, sorbates, and propylene oxide prevent mold growth that could spoil foods. Chelating agents such as EDTA, calcium phytate, and sodium phosphate bind to metallic impurities in foods so they don't contribute an off–color or off–flavor; unfortunately, they also bind to metals that are nutrients, such as calcium and iron. Antibacterials such as benzoic acid, calcium sorbate, and erythorbic acid minimize dangerous bacterial growth.

Consistency–Improving Agents. These include emulsifiers, stabilizers, anticaking agents, firming agents, and moisture–retaining agents. Some consistency–improving agents are mono– and di–glycerides, polysorbate, lecithin, guar gum, silicates, propylene glycol, and carrageenan.

Flavoring Agents. This group includes spices and the oils derived from them, salt and salt substitutes, sugars, and synthetic sweeteners and flavors. Some flavoring agents are glutamic acid, saccharin, sorbitol, corn syrup, and salt.

Coloring Agents. Several coloring agents have been removed from the market because they have been found to be carcinogenic. Many agents are still used, however, though not all have been adequately tested.

Nutrition Supplements. Vitamins, minerals, proteins, fats, and carbohydrates added to foods are legally considered additives. If the added nutrient was not originally present in the food (or if it was present in much smaller amounts), the food is "fortified." If the nutrient was present but was diminished or lost in processing, the food is "enriched" when the lost amount of nutrient is replaced.

Assessing Some Additives

Dried soup mixes are highly processed products. Their manufacturers use marginal amounts of food (dehydrated chicken, beef, vegetables, noodles), then add a battery of additives to make sure the product has a long storage life and some palatability. On the labels of the soups tested for the accompanying report, we counted 125 different ingredients and additives. A dried soup mix might have food ingredients such as dehydrated chicken, carrots, parsley, onions, and so on. But it might also have salt for flavoring, MSG for flavor enhancement, mono– and di–glycerides and sometimes polysorbate 60 as emulsifiers, guar gum as a stabilizer, phosphates as chelating agents, silicates as anticaking agents, and thiamine hydrochloride as a nutritional supplement or flavoring agent. And it might have added coloring to make the mixture look more appealing than it sounds.

Most of the additives in dried soup mixes are on the U.S. Food and Drug Administration's GRAS (or "generally recognized as safe") list, meaning either that they have been tested and proved safe or that they have been in use for a long time without causing any known ill effects. Other additives in the mixes are not on the list and usually can be used only in specific amounts.

Many of the additives in the soups are natural and are derived from other foods, but some are completely synthetic. Here's an assessment of some of the more common additives in the dried soups, based on sources Consumer's Union believes to be reliable.

Disodium Inosinate and Disodium Guanylate. These are sodium salts that have been hydrolyzed from proteins. They have no taste of their own and are used as flavor enhancers. There is no evident hazard connected with their use.

Butylated Hydroxytoluence (BHT) and Butylated Hydroxyanisole (BHA). These are widely used as preservatives and antioxidants, yet their addition to foods has been criticized as unnecessary. Some allergic reactions have been reported, and the chemicals have had adverse effects on experimental animals as well as on tissue cultures. Neither has been adequately tested for safety by long–term animal studies. The FDA proposed in 1976 that BHT be removed from the GRAS list until further studies either condemn it or clear it. Nothing has come of that proposal.

Propyl Gallate. This is an antioxidant that's often used with BHT and BHA because together the three have a synergistic effect in keeping fats from going rancid. Like BHT and BHA, the chemical's use has been criticized as unnecessary. It has not been adequately tested for safety by modern, long–term animal studies.

Mono– and Di–glycerides. These additives prevent oil separation, prevent starch from crystallizing, and may improve the stability of the dried soup mixes. They comprise about 1 percent of the normal food fats in the diet. As additives, they represent no evident hazard.

Phosphates. Sodium methaphosphate, sodium triphosphate, and tricalcium phosphate are all used in the dried soups. They act as chelating agents, buffers, and emulsifiers. They also help retain juices in cooked meat and poultry. Phosphates in the amounts used in today's processed foods represent no evident hazard.

Silicon Dioxide. A stabilizer, thickener, and anticaking agent, silicon dioxide is basically sand and represents no evident hazard in the quantities used in foods.

EDTA. This additive is used as a chelating agent to bind traces of metal, which might, if free–floating, contribute to rancidity and discoloration. It has been tested in long–term tests on several animal species and found to represent no evident hazard.

Polysorbate 60. An emulsifier and surfactant. Animal tests have shown it to be safe at the levels consumed in foods.

Propylene Glycol. An antimycotic and an emulsifier, this additive helps maintain the desired texture of the soup. Animal tests have shown it to represent no evident hazard.

Potassium Carbonate and Sodium Carbonate. These alkalis are used to neutralize acidity in the soups. They represent no evident hazard in the amounts used.

Dextrin. When starch is treated with acid, heat, or enzymes, it breaks down partially to form dextrin. This is used as a thickening agent in the soups and represents no evident hazard.

Sodium Silico Aluminate. An alkaline anticaking agent used to keep the dried soup mix free–flowing. It has been tested extensively and found to be without evident hazard to humans.

Sorbitol. This is a "sugar–alcohol" with a sweet taste. It improves the body, or texture, of a food. A number of studies on animals and humans have shown that small amounts of sorbitol represent no evident hazard.

Artificial Colorings and Flavorings. These are used to make dried soup more like real soup. The colors don't contribute anything, and consumers could well do without them. The added flavors are probably necessary, since few natural flavorings remain after processing, and none are really strong enough to make the soups appetizing. A number of coloring agents have been banned in the past. Most of the colorings and flavorings in use today have not been adequately tested by modern test protocols. (Caramel coloring is in some of the tested soups and is suspect, since it's thought that caramelized sugar could form carcinogens. Caramel coloring is on the FDA's priority list for testing.)

Alternatives?

Some of the additives in dried soup mixes are safe, and some may be worrisome. According to the report on dietary goals of the Senate Select Committee on Nutrition: "Although food additives as a category may not justifiably be considered harmful, the varying degrees of testing and quality of testing and the continuing discoveries of apparent connections between certain additives and cancer . . . give justifiable cause to seek to reduce additive consumption to the greatest degree possible."

If you want to consume fewer additives, you may want to reduce your consumption of dried soup mixes and similar highly processed foods. Raw or lightly processed foods (fresh or frozen fruits and vegetables, meats, cheese, milk, butter, whole grains and whole–grain flours) and moderately processed foods (canned vegetables, fruits, and meats, margarine, some baked goods, and some salad dressings) can provide a varied, balanced diet. And there's a fringe benefit: you'll get used to eating foods that taste a lot like they did in the Good Old Days.

List of Task Force Members

NUTRITION, PRODUCT QUALITY AND SAFETY

C. Peter Timmer (Chairman)
Dept. of Nutrition
Harvard School of Public Health
Boston, Massachusetts

Jane Anderson
American Meat Institute
Arlington, Virginia

William Boehm
National Economic Analysis Division
U.S. Dept. of Agriculture
Washington, D.C.

Jim Coddington
National Wheat Institute
Washington, D.C.

Wayne Crain
Florida Fruit & Vegetable
  Association
Orlando, Florida

Carol Forbes
Dairy & Poultry Subcommittee
House Agriculture Committee
Washington, D.C.

Susan Fridy
National Milk Producers Federation
Washington, D.C.

Ellen Haas
Community Nutrition Institute
Washington, D.C.

Richard Hagen
National Food Processors Association
Washington, D.C.

John Huston
National Livestock and Meat Board
Chicago, Illinois

Max Kellough
National Cattlemen's Association
Friend, Nebraska

Betty Majors
Women Involved in Farm Economics
Osceola, Nebraska

Malden C. Nesheim
Division of Nutritional Sciences
Cornell University
Ithaca, New York

Ann Norman
National Pork Producers Council
Des Moines, Iowa

Jerry Stein
Food & Nutrition Service
U.S. Dept. of Agriculture
Washington, D.C.

Catherine E. Woteki
Office of Technology Assessment
U.S. Congress
Washington, D.C.

COMMENTS BY A TASK FORCE MEMBER

Max Kellough*

After reading the Timmer and Nesheim paper, the image of the Senate Nutrition Committee's *Dietary Goals* report comes back into focus (U.S. Congress). While the paper acknowledges the existence of a legitimate controversy, it does not present any of the large amount of evidence contradictory to the authors' views. Consequently, the reader is led to conclude that meat is detrimental to good health. Unfortunately, many people accept these conclusions as final and factual, when in reality they are preliminary and unproven.

The input of members of the Task Force demonstrated that the diet–health relationship issue is highly controversial. Timmer has a right to his own opinion; but, more importantly, he also has a responsibility to represent in the report a true picture of the controversy which was readily acknowledged by the Task Force. The report, however, is more reflective of the authors' views on the diet–health issue than of the sentiments of the Task Force.

As long as the diet–health issue is so controversial, there is no justification for the federal government to advocate a course of action based on only one side of the controversy. By the same token, certain food manufacturers should not seize upon a medical controversy as an aid in selling their products.

Harper (p. 312) has written:

... the diseases for which the dietary goals have been prescribed ... are all diseases of complex and not clearly understood etiology. There is great disagreement over how important nutrition is as a factor in their development. When those who work actively with this problem disagree so completely, there can be no sound basis for recommending radical changes in the composition of the U.S. diet.

Olson (p. 6) has stated:

Epidemiological studies of coronary artery disease have shown statistically valid associations with dietary fat, protein, sugar, cholesterol, plasma cholesterol and various lipoprotein fractions, smoking, obsessive–compulsive competitive (Type A) personality, lack of exercise, soft drinking water, family history of heart disease and *the per capita usage of television.*

*John Huston, National Livestock and Meat Board, wishes to be associated with this statement.

Epidemiological studies are not, of themselves, sufficient evidence to assume cause–and–effect relationships. Olson recently described eleven large–scale clinical trials of the Lipid Hypothesis in some 5,000 men comprising about 40,000 years of observation. Diet trials were carried out in London, Oslo, Helsinki, New York City, New Jersey and Los Angeles. In addition, three trials of hypocholesterolemic drugs were carried out in England, Scotland and the United States. In none of the investigations was there a positive effect of a high–polyunsaturated fat, low–saturated fat, low–cholesterol diet upon mortality. There is no evidence, Olson said, in the 5,000 men studied thus far that diet modification affects their overall survival rate, and thus it provides no support for a large public health program aimed at control of atherosclerosis in general and coronary heart disease in particular through diet or hypocholesterolemic drugs.

As the incidence and mortality rates of infectious diseases decline, the incidence and mortality rates of cardiovascular disease and cancer increase, both the total numbers and in percentages. In many countries of the world, India for example, people die at an earlier age from infectious diseases or nutritional deficiency diseases, and simply do not live long enough to die from degenerative diseases such as CHD and cancer.

A recent trial at Texas A&M University involved 30 professors and four diets which included red meat and no visible eggs, red meat and three visible eggs, poultry and fish and no visible eggs, and poultry and fish and three visible eggs. The result, according to Reiser and O'Brien (Vance, p. 42) was that, "Statistically as a group, not only was there no significant build–up of cholesterol, but most of the participants recorded a slightly lower serum cholesterol content when on the red meat diets than when eating fish and poultry." These researchers added that eliminating foods containing cholesterol makes it difficult for people to get well–balanced diets.

A recent paper by Enig, Munn and Keeney (p. 2219) concluded, "If there is a relationship between dietary fat and cancer, our analysis indicates that processed vegetable fats should be more carefully investigated." They point out that most of the total increase in fat intake from 1909 to 1972 was a result of an increase in unsaturated fat, an increase that is four times the increase in saturated fat. They also point out that more saturated fat in the diet has come from vegetable fat than from beef since 1929.

Hegsted (p. 10), recently named head of USDA's Human Nutrition Center, was quoted as stating, "The first indication that a change in diet would be beneficial came out of Norway after World War II." Hegsted cited reduced consumption of animal products and increased consumption of grains and vegetable products as primary contributors to a "remarkable reduction in death rates."

Conversely, however, McMichael wrote,

Professor Jens Dedichen of Oslo has admitted responsibility for the attempt to control coronary artery disease by alterations to the diet following observations 25 years ago on the decline of recorded coronary deaths in the war years, which might have been related to dietetic deprivation. From 1955 he strongly pursued a policy to reduce fat intake and stuck to a low–fat diet himself, criticizing colleagues who would not support these ideas. He now realizes that in spite of the Norwegian effort there is no fall in coronary mortality, but rather a steady increase. He regrets the anxiety created by this advice in the population. Soybean oil consumption in Norway increased five–fold but there was an increase in coronary mortality. During these 25 years, Professor Dedichen says, it has become 'increasingly clear that we are on the wrong track'. . . Professor Bengt Borgstrom of Lund says that pursuit of these policies of fat reduction and more unsaturated fats is irresponsible, as it would have far–reaching economic, agricultural and psychological effects. There might be quite unknown consequences of altering the nature of our dietetic fats. Even now we can be sure that a diet rich in polyunsaturated fats will increase the risk of gallstones.

The case against animal products is not fairly represented by listing beef, pork, milk, butter and eggs as the major source of cholesterol. According to the U.S. Department of Agriculture (p. 146) many other foods, including chicken, turkey and some marine foods, are as high or higher in cholesterol as beef. Fluid milk is quite low in comparison. Data published by Feeley, Criner, and Watt give the cholesterol content of beef and other meats, fish, milk, cheese and poultry, along with total fat, saturated fatty acids and unsaturated fatty acids. These values are not significantly different statistically from one another to warrant the statement in the paper that "beef, pork, milk, butter and eggs are major sources of cholesterol and saturated fat."

The American Heart Association's Nutrition Committee (Glueck, Mattson and Bierman) wrote that "A reasoned resolution of the controversy (diet–heart) is not currently possible." However, Timmer and Nesheim conclude that the issue is unlikely to be resolved in the negative. Such statements only serve to stimulate polarization, ignore other scientific data indicating no relationship between dietary cholesterol and heart disease, and exemplify the counter–productive practice of presenting theory as fact. To do so is not in the best interest of science, consumers or the industry, nor does it reflect the feelings of most members of the Task Force.

There are some diet and other lifestyle guidelines that people can and should adopt to improve and maintain their health. Suggested guidelines include (1) reduce—cut back on calories from all sources, (2) become more physically active—walk, jog, exercise, swim, ride a bicycle and do these regularly, (3) cut back on smoking, (4) eat a variety of foods, consume moderate amounts, (5) learn to deal with stress, and (6) have regular physical check–ups. These recommendations will not make headlines, but will deal with many known risk factors, instead of only one which is unproven.

Excessive calories from all sources are probably the major dietary risk factor. Other dietary factors are unproven health factors for the vast majority of Americans. Of all the risk factors, attempts to lower serum cholesterol will probably have the least significant impact on reducing heart disease and may result in other detrimental effects if carried to the extreme—some known, others unknown.

I must vigorously disagree with the statement in the paper that the farm sector would be badly misled if it felt that either the scientific evidence that gives rise to the concerns over the nutritional health and safety of the American diet has been (or will be) discredited, or the consumer activists who urge enactment of more stringent regulations and intervention to change eating behavior do so for personal reasons and do not represent significant grassroots interests.

I *do* believe that much of the evidence, most of which is epidemiological, is being and will be largely if not entirely "disproven." I *do* believe that the American food supply is the most wholesome, nutritious, most abundant and least expensive in the world today. Further, I do *not* believe that many consumer activists represent significant grassroots interests.

This, obviously, is a dissenting comment. It is not meant to imply disrespect for the Task Force Chairman, for any of the members of the Task Force, or for their views and ideas. The sole purpose of this comment is to register disagreement with many of those views and ideas, and to provide some scientific data pointing out the extremely controversial nature of the diet–health issue.

I do believe we have established an open line of communication and that we will now be able to talk *to* each other instead of *about* each other. That can only result in positive benefits.

References

Enig, M. G., R. J. Munn and M. Kenney. 1978. "Dietary Fat and Cancer Trends — A Critique." *Federation Proceedings* 37: 2210–20.

Freely, R. M., P. E. Criner and B. K. Watt. 1972. "Cholesterol Content of Foods." *J. Amer. Dietetic Assoc.* 61: 134–49.

Glueck, C. J., F. Mattson and E. L. Bierman. 1978. "Diet and Coronary Heart Disease: Another View." *The N. Eng. J. Med.* 298: 1471–74.

Harper, A. E. 1978. "Dietary Goals–a Skeptical View." *Amer. J. Clinical Nutr.* 31: 312.

Hegsted, D. M. 1978. "Optimal Nutrition." *Nutrition Today* 30: 10.

McMichael, J. 1977. "Dietetic Factors in Coronary Disease." *Euro. J. Cardiology.* 5/6: 447–52.

Olson, R. E. 1978. "Is There an Optimum Diet for the Prevention of Coronary Heart Disease?" Proceedings of the National Cattlemen's Association meeting on *Nutrition Information,* Denver, Colorado.

U.S. Congress, Senate. 1977. *Dietary Goals for the United States.* Select Committee on Nutrition and Human Needs. Washington: U.S. Gov't. Printing Office.

U.S. Department of Agriculture. 1975. "Composition of Foods." *USDA Handbook No. 8.* Agricultural Research Service.

Vance, J. E. 1979. "High Cholesterol Creates No Problems for Texas A&M Professors." *Beef.* 15: 42.

DISCUSSION

The formal discussants were: Richard Lyng, President, American Meat Institute; Jim Turner, Board of Directors, National Consumer's League; Wallace Warren, Southwest Region Administrator, Food and Nutrition Service, USDA; and Raymond Reiser, Emeritus Professor of Biochemistry, Texas A&M University. The main points made by the discussants were as follows.

Lyng thought that the report focused too much on our nutritional problems as opposed to nutritional accomplishments. The latter have been considerable, especially in the past 10 to 15 years. Domestic feeding programs for the disadvantaged, for example, are on the whole a major success story in striving to eradicate poverty–caused hunger and malnutrition. However, he said that he believed the report was correct in taking seriously the distrust that exists among the consuming public with respect to nutritional issues. Lyng put himself in the category of those who favor less regulation in the food area, particularly in the meat area where the costs of regulation seem out of proportion to benefits. More generally, he thought it important to preserve freedom of choice by consumers.

Turner agreed with two important points made by the Task Force: (1) there are two very different arenas for food policy, the scientific arena and the public policy arena, and arguments in the two should be carefully distinguished, and (2) nutrition issues are permanently on the policy agenda, and given this agenda the central problem is the absence of a forum for discussion and decision on the issues.

Turner thought it was easy to draw misleading conclusions from the statistic that only 16 percent of U.S. consumer income goes to the food budget. The figure represents more the rise in U.S. incomes than the cheapness of food prices. Food prices have doubled at least twice since 1939, and once since 1968. Moreover, many low–income people spend 40 to 45 percent of their incomes on food. Similarly, the aggregate life expectancy data are misleading. The gains in life expectancy have been made primarily at younger ages through the decline of infectious diseases. When we have one–half our population dying of coronary–related disease and 20 percent dying of cancer, there is bound to be great concern over the apparent diet–related aspects of these causes of death.

On the two substantive areas that the report focuses on — nutrition and safety — the consumer movement is divided on many issues but it is united in opposition to those who deny any evidence of a relationship between diet and health. In the safety area, Turner thought that the Task Force did a disservice. The Delaney Clause is not the central issue in food safety regulation. Zero tolerance for cancer–causing substances would remain even if the Delaney Clause were repealed. The basic law says no substance can be added to the food supply unless it can be shown to be safe. The key point is that zero tolerance will never be taken out of the law until some forum more satisfactory than either Congress or the existing regulatory agencies is created to establish safety guidelines for food. In addition, the idea that long–term cancer causing agents in food are the main future food safety issue may not be correct. The range of disease problems in which diet is being implicated is growing, e.g., currently the neurological diseases. If these diseases begin to be related to chemicals in the food supply, then the current problems with carcinogens may turn out to be small in comparison. The problem areas include long–term irreversible genetic damage that would carry over even to future generations.

Reiser emphasized that in the area of diet and health, simple answers will not do. Diet is only one of many factors implicated in coronary heart disease. The role of cholesterol is far from clear. For those without a genetic predisposition for problems (80 percent of the population), cholesterol in the diet may not be a serious issue. He said that nutrition education was too involved a process to be obtained from short messages or reading product labels. For the general public, the best advice is to follow the old rule that one should eat a variety of foods, in moderation.

COMMENTS AND QUESTIONS FROM THE FLOOR

Several members of the American Agriculture Movement talked about laxity in the enforcement of quality and safety standards for imported food products. They expressed special concern about imports of vegetables and beef from Mexico. In general, the inspection of imported products was said to be inadequate. It was recommended that all imported food products be required to be labeled as such. It was said that efforts are currently being made to have wines produced outside California but imported into that state subject to the same quality standards imposed on the growers of California. It was suggested that general legislation of this type would be desirable.

Among the statements made in response to the comments and questions about health dangers from imports were the following. Lyng said that current law for meats applies the same standards to imports and domestic production, and he thought it might be mistaken to try to establish trade barriers in this area unless it could be shown specifically that a health or safety problem exists. Several respondents said that certainly the existing laws should be enforced. Robert Swift, Minister (Commercial) of the Embassy of Australia, thought that the charges of substandard imported products were much overstated, and he said he resented the idea that his own country's inspections were thought to be so inadequate as to require oversight from U.S. inspectors. He suggested that the very existence of U.S. inspectors in foreign countries with powers to oversee domestic inspection any time at any place has a powerful impact.

There was general discussion of coordinating efforts that exist to affect the tradeoffs between price and nutrition in the policy–making process, and of what changes, if any, should be made to settle public issues in this area. Timmer responded that the issue is basically that of finding a *process* with which all interested parties will be satisfied even if they disagree with particular outcomes of the process. We need a decision–making process not governed by a person's political ambitions or the profit motive, that searches for the general interest and treats all interests fairly. Timmer said that the Task Force was *not* able to come up with a blueprint for such a process, but was able to reject all the readily available alternatives, e.g., the Food and Nutrition Board of the National Academy of Sciences (which, however helpful on scientific issues, cannot resolve policy issues). Turner said that the primary place where issues about price and nutrition are and must necessarily be resolved is the marketplace. In this context, the government's proper role is to set minimum standards (such as keeping known poisons out of food), and not to try to move society to some kind of optimal diet. In addition, Turner thought that it was generally agreed that whatever process was established must involve *all* interests and be perceived by all as a fair process to have the credibility necessary for success.

The question was raised: Is it in the public interest to pay for testimony at hearings on food quality and safety, particularly if the government pays for testimony in support of its position? Could those testifying be objective in such circumstances? Lyng said that he strongly felt that the government should not pay for testimony, especially when public officials making the regulatory decision also hire the testimony. Turner said that it is unwise to leave the decision–making procedures on any issue in the hands only of those who can afford to spend time in Washington on a regular basis. Lyng responded that in instances where important interest groups cannot afford to send a representative to testify, an independent authority should choose the witness, not the government. Warren pointed out that the Food and Nutrition Service had formerly paid witnesses but was now prohibited by law from doing so. He also said that holding hearings out in the country rather than in Washington helped to get broader participation.

In response to Turner's statements about the 16 percent of income spent for food in the United States, an AAM member said that in 1948 all the basic food commodities were higher–priced than they are today. Turner replied that he never asserted that the price of food is "too high." His point was that we should not try to convince consumers that food is really cheap, which they will never accept. The truth, he said, is that good food is expensive, and well worth it.

JOHN KRAMER*

CHAPTER 5

Agriculture's Role in
Government Decisions

The Problem: Perceptions of Weakness

HAVE American farmers completely lost the political power to affect their economic future? Their impression is that their ability to control government decision–making involving agriculture is constantly diminishing. Over the period of the last forty years, American farmers have come to believe and operate on the assumption that their voice in Congress, in the White House, and in the United States Department of Agriculture (USDA) is listened to less and less. They complain that the political system has, instead, become more responsive to non–agricultural interests and values in the form of labor, consumer, urban, environmental, budgetary, and anti–inflationary concerns.

Farmers have always been subject to the unpredictable vagaries of weather and overseas harvests of competitive crops and products. Now their margin of subsistence also appears to be at the mercy of a political process whose outcome they cannot accurately forecast or effectively dominate. Or so they perceive.

Are these perceptions valid? Do they understate the continued strength of productive agriculture vis–à–vis governmental actions impacting upon farmers' livelihoods? Has the old farm policy agenda been totally displaced? And how helpful have the reactions of producers been to what they view as their precarious political situation? Are there more fruitful approaches than retreating to anti–governmental ideology or isolation in opposition to the forces proposing the new agenda or outright confrontation? What can farmers realistically do, if not to

*A list of Task Force members and their affiliations follows the report.

restore their old hegemony, at least to increase the prospect of implementing some policies beneficial to their needs?

Our answers to these questions are necessarily tentative. But we are united in condemning as fruitless the more characteristic protests of the farmer as King Canute against the waves invading his shore. We offer some suggestions for future action that seem more promising than railing at reality. The suggestions are worthy of active exploration even if they do not guarantee a return to the pre–1970's situation of agricultural policy–making of, by, and for the farmer.

The Extent of the Limitation of Political Power of Agriculture

THE EVOLUTION OF POWER

Until the late 1960's, there was no debatable issue as to how much of a role farmers had in government decisions affecting their lives. They essentially called the tune through their general farm organizations and commodity lobbies and their allies in Congress and the Department of Agriculture.

Price supports for specific crops such as wheat, corn, and cotton first came into being as a result of legislation in the 1930's. Around this legislation there developed strong commodity interest groups that became the "primary vehicle of farmer political influence on agricultural commodity policies" (Bonnen) through lobbying relationships with the commodity–specific subcommittees of both the House and Senate Agriculture Committees and the program executives in the Department of Agriculture. (See also, Barton; Brown and Wiggins; Grommet; Hajda; Hardin; Heinz; Paarlberg; Peters; Porter; Stucker, et al.) This relationship has been characterized as a "triangle of power," giving the producer a monopoly of influence over the policies affecting his interest and generally excluding even the Secretary of Agriculture and the President from any meaningful decision–making roles.

Businesses involved in providing fertilizer, machinery, and other inputs for agriculture, as well as food processors and distributors, broadened the policy power base by the late 1950's, creating a four–way sharing of power and transforming farm policy into food and fiber policy. The decision–making process increased its complexity even further in the 1960's as the commodity interests fragmented, disagreeing with one another and with agribusiness, making formulation of any national policy a difficult task. The bargaining situation among agricultural interests and, for the first time, labor and consumer groups, became crucial to passage of farm legislation in the Congress. Decision–making in the Executive Branch gravitated upward, starting with 1961–1963 grain legislation and continuing with the 1965 Agriculture Act and sugar legislation, from program administrators to the Secretary and, ultimately, to the President and his staff, resulting in the involvement of the Council of Economic Advisers and the Bureau of the Budget (now the Office of Management and Budget).

Even then, no matter how multi–sided the decision–making in the Congress or how concerned the White House had become with food policy, farm bills still took a day, not a week, to pass the House of Representatives. The Secretary of Agriculture did not have to play second fiddle to the Director of the Office of Management and Budget or the Chairman of the Council of Economic Advisors or the staff of the Domestic Council in proposing legislative programs. The Secretary of State did not set farm export policy.

There was a time when agricultural producers were a world unto themselves, when even the Secretary of Agriculture could not override the commodity interests, when there was no need for them to bargain with organized labor or environmentalists or consumer groups. That world has gone forever. It was on its way out in 1964 when wheat and cotton needed to acknowledge the existence of food stamps in order to guarantee the passage of their programs without deleterious amendments. It was clearly no longer the same in 1970 when payment limitations were averted only through carefully evolved trade–offs with coal mine safety (black lung) and occupational health and safety legislation. The population had shifted. Rural congressmen, either reapportioned out of existence or required to represent increasingly suburban or even urban constituencies, were in the minority and had to maneuver to be certain that they could still command majority support on any crucial vote.

The political balance of power change that became visible in the 1960's accelerated in the 1970's. A combination of bad weather, poor harvests in foreign countries, and massive purchases of grain by the Soviet Union in the first years of the decade contributed to substantial increases in the cost of food in the United States. Food cost inflation created a vocal and powerful constituency of consumers involved for the first time with the impact of agricultural policy on their lives. Almost simultaneously, other interest groups focusing on the use and exploitation of natural resources, food quality and safety, the rights of farm labor, and the food needs of the poor in the United States and abroad developed increased concern about food policy. What had once been a private affair quickly became a very public matter subject to increased political uncertainty. The Secretary of Agriculture was only one of many voices in the Executive Branch, and negotiating farm bills through Capitol Hill became a fine art.

It is no wonder that the farm community believes itself to be increasingly powerless and expresses frustration that its ability to dictate farm policy has vanished. The political facts of farm life in 1978 cannot be ignored. The farmer cannot afford to live in the political past when his authority went virtually unchallenged. Nor, on the other hand, should he overestimate the changes wrought in the 1970's and lavish self–pity upon his perceived weakness.

THE CURRENT LEGISLATIVE BALANCE SHEET

A more balanced assessment of the credits and debits of the political situation reveals significant limitations not quite offsetting underlying and continuing power if not to control policy, then, at least, to influence it favorably. There have been undeniable losses in the Legislative and Executive Branches: price supports that were rejected, and regulations that were imposed. But these have been alloyed with unquestionable advances, particularly toward productive agriculture's goal of higher prices, although success has been more meager when aimed at securing exemption from regulations raising the cost of production.

A payment limitation was finally imposed upon feed grains and cotton. But in practice the limitations did not significantly hamper production or profit. Cotton almost lost its checkoff. But, ultimately, it did not, and Cotton, Inc. thrives. Dairy lost an increase in its price supports to a Presidential veto and the Senate Budget Committee's opposition in 1976, but dairy producers' economic interests are currently well served by price supports and marketing orders. Tobacco lost its bill to a Presidential veto in 1975, but then less than eight members of Congress ever voted for the bill in person on the Floor of both Houses, and tobacco has managed to survive every attack on its favored position, whether from the export or research point of view.

Sugar was defeated in its drive to increase prices through domestic processor payments in 1978, but it will achieve part of the same ends in 1979 by way of Executive–imposed import fees and quotas, and further legislation is probable. Wheat and feed grains could not overcome a veto to raise target prices and loan rates on an emergency basis in 1975, but they still managed to secure an absolute majority of 63 votes, which certainly does not denote feebleness, and they fully met their goals in the 1977 bill. In 1978, they lost an alliance of flexible parity with prices considerably in excess of cost of production, which was too much for the budget or consumers to swallow, but they did salvage better wheat prices.

With respect to regulatory legislation, the accomplishments of agriculture in avoiding the imposition of undesired environmental or safety controls have been less notable. While agriculture was always certain of being totally exempted from such laws as minimum wage in the 1930's through the late 1960's, that is no longer the case. Nevertheless, agriculture still retains some clout sufficient to relieve it of the full burden of regulation imposed upon other productive enterprises. For example, the minimum wage in agriculture was not fully equal to that in industry until 1978. Occupational health and safety legislation, which once threatened to restrict the family–size farm, no longer significantly applies to farmers with 10 or fewer employees. The use of pesticides is more regulated than ever, but more power resides with the states than before to permit local variations. Clean–water controls affect, but do not substantially inhibit, farming.

The political picture is, thus, not unrelievedly bleak. If anything, it is slightly positive. The rumors of agriculture's death in Washington are definitely exaggerated. The rhetoric of weakness and isolation is belied by the record, which reveals considerable residual strength both alone and, more significantly, in combination with other forces. The hard truth is that the way the policy–making process actually has functioned in the recent past is more progressive and favorable to the farm than the farmer has been led to believe.

THE SENATE

In particular, it probably is fair to state that productive agriculture and especially the largest farms and related agribusiness firms essentially own the Senate of the United States. Because almost every Senator has some substantial crop that is raised in his state, no Senator can afford to turn his back upon an economic bloc of votes no matter how relatively small, since dedicated single interest groups often decide closely contested elections. The main problem in the Senate is forestalling foolish overreaching. If the Senate comes in too high, no amount of compromising with the House can both save the Senate's face and escape unoverrideable White House vetos. The 1978 farm bill would have failed in that fashion had not defeat in the House forestalled any conference. The 1975 farm bill would have won less than a majority on override instead of a strong majority (but less than two–thirds) had the Senate not caved in on every dollar figure. Excess plus pride could prove to be a disastrous political combination. The strength of the farm bloc in the Senate thus puts to shame the perennial lament of minority status, but needs to be tempered with wisdom.

THE HOUSE OF REPRESENTATIVES

In the House, the situation is different. In the absence of logrolling (the 1973 farm bill), negotiated compromise (the 1975 emergency farm bill), or simply moderation (the 1977 farm bill), farm legislation dealing with price and supply cannot hope to obtain a majority if the Administration objects or if inflation is a topical issue. The consumer–labor axis clearly wields the balance of power. When it supports such legislation (e.g., 1973, 1975, 1977), it passes, although never by a supermajority necessary to overcome a veto (e.g., 1975). Alliance is quintessential in the House. Agriculture has to do everything in its capacity to appeal to a substantial bloc of suburban (pro–middle class consumer) Republicans and urban liberal Democrats in order to accomplish its legislative program.

Where regulatory legislation is at stake, agriculture seems to be able to afford to be somewhat more intransigent. In the past, however, agriculture has often been unaware of the full implications of such legislation until long after the underlying law has taken effect and the initial enforcement efforts have occurred (Occupational Safety and Health Administration [OSHA], pesticides, Environmental Protection Agency [EPA]). Then it is normally too late to repeal the basic law in the face of the consumer–labor bloc. Whether or not agriculture might have prevented passage of the original bill is a moot point.

Agriculture, acting on its own and in defiance of the consumer–labor bloc, has, however, effectively (with some exceptions) utilized several devices to undermine the regulatory regime. The most successful devices have been appropriations riders (language in an appropriations bill restricting the use of funds where no restriction applies in the underlying authorizing statute), and denying funds for regulatory enforcement whether it be Federal Trade Commission (FTC) rule-making on television advertising of sugared products aimed at children or OSHA regulations on cotton dust.

A similar tactic is a rider to an authorization bill or restrictive language in a committee report, for example, a rider concerning the use of "super donuts" in the school breakfast program. The agricultural lobby is focused on these single–shot issues and controls the timing of the assault, placing the consumer–labor bloc in the dark as to where or whether to be on the defensive.

The ultimate weapon for negating statutory authority is the one-house legislative veto, i.e., legislative provisions permitting either the House or the Senate to prohibit the implementation of regulations proposed by the Executive Branch. While the Senate seems to be adamantly opposed to its use, a clear majority of the House favors it in some, if not all regulatory agency and departmental contexts. Recently, the House, by its intransigence on the matter, has either prevailed or halted the passage of authorizations that fail to contain the one–house veto provision. Agriculture and all components of the food marketing system appear to support such provisions. Since agriculture has considerably better access to Congress than to the regulatory agencies, resort to this approach is likely to grow in succeeding years as regulatory lobbying moves back from the agencies to Capitol Hill.

It should be noted that all of these mechanisms, from appropriations rider to legislative history restrictions (language inserted in a committee report or a staged dialogue between Congressmen or Senators limiting the meaning of language contained in the Bill) to one–house legislative vetoes, raise the likelihood of increasing confrontation in the future with the very groups agriculture needs to court to achieve its pricing goals. Their use should not be indiscriminate, since they result in division, not coalition.

The Range of Ideology

THE RHETORIC OF IDEOLOGY

One way to deal with a decrease in political power is to challenge it rhetorically by denying the validity of government intervention in the farm marketplace, and by claiming that farm policy only inhibits the farmer. Too many American farmers pay too much lip service to the myth of rugged individualism. They like to view themselves as working to earn a living opposed by the hostile forces of nature, suppliers, processors, retailers, labor, environmentalists, and consumers. They identify the enemy as the government and, indeed, any other group that does not share their exclusive emphasis on production and prices. They need no help from the government in order to survive. The government, beholden as it is to urban and labor forces only hurts, not helps. They can do better by going it alone.

The image is reassuring. But it is false. It is not in accord with the more complex reality of a food production system that is as dependent as any major industry upon the assistance of the federal government, whether it be for income support, availability of credit, disaster insurance, research, or export aid. The cattleman can proclaim his freedom from socialism until it comes time to invoke statutory authority to permit a dues checkoff referendum, to promote the consumption of beef, to protect against packer defaults, or to inhibit the importation of foreign beef. Nor does the insistence upon self–sufficiency accurately reflect the inextricable linkage of producers to those in the market chain to whom they sell and, beyond, to those who are the ultimate users of their products.

The image and the ideology it represents are dangerous. They are as responsible as any other factor for productive agriculture's inability to develop an effective process for dealing with the legislative and executive branches of government so as to shape future farm policy.

The vision of the farmer against the world only serves to hamper the
pragmatic forging of meaningful coalitions and the development of
successful short–term and long–range political relationships between
the farmer and those social and economic interests to whom his future
is inevitably wed. Ideological demagoguery represents the problem,
not the solution. It operates not to expand the potential role of agriculture in government decision–making, but to contract it further and to
guarantee agriculture permanent and debilitating minority status.

THE PARANOIA OF ISOLATION

There is a standard opening to any speech on "the farm problem"
delivered to agriculturally oriented audiences. Each succeeding Secretary of Agriculture, the various Assistant Secretaries, leading commodity producers, and even members of the House and Senate authorizing
and appropriating committees responsible for agriculture rely heavily
upon it to unite their listeners.

They begin by lamenting that, in 1978, farmers comprise less than
_____ percent of our nation's population (and they fill in the percentage depending upon whether they count hired hands and persons
who earn more from nonfarming than farming sources, but they keep
the figure at five percent or less). They proceed to note that the
number of Members of Congress who come from rural districts is less
than _____ (and they fill in the number based upon their definition
of rural, which can focus on the residence of the majority of the
population or the area's chief source of income or employment, but
either way the count stays below 50 districts out of 435). They sound
the theme of the increasingly frail political status of agriculture.

Such a speech is well designed to intensify the audiences' paranoia
about the forces that allegedly threaten to overwhelm them in the
political marketplace, the legislature, and the executive departments.
The message is sometimes understood (if not intended) perversely:
since we are so few, the only way we can survive is to go it alone.

Unfortunately, such a speech is not calculated to relieve the illness
it inaccurately diagnoses. It downgrades agriculture's existing political
power, particularly in the Senate. Its vision of agriculture as a be-
leaguered minority may just as readily induce the draw–up–the–
wagons–in–a–circle syndrome, often on a fragmented, commodity–

by–commodity basis, rather than efforts to reach out to accommodate diversity within the producer sector (including small as well as large farms, the farm worker and renter as well as the owner–operator) or to find common ground among specialized commodity interests. It tends to nourish the "we–they" syndrome of the nearly three million farm owners or operators versus the over six million persons employed in the food marketing system, a stereotype all too attractive to farmers aware that they secure an average of only 41 percent of the proceeds from the sale of their produce and livestock, while those who transport, process, package, and market obtain the bulk.

Even as it reinforces divisions within agriculture and the food chain, the message that agriculture is increasingly a less significant part of the American economy often functions to obviate coalition politics by reinforcing the image of the farmer opposed by the rest of society. Consciousness of being isolated does not necessarily result in any concerted attempts to negotiate or compromise with the economic main stream. Instead, it sharpens the ideological drive constantly to oppose nonfarm groups concerned about issues labeled "consumer," "labor," "urban," or "environmental."

No cure should aggravate the disease. If the agricultural establishment is weakened, it cannot grow stronger by disdaining to deal with other sectors of the economy simply because of a lack of identity in short–run economic self–interest or by reacting with hostility to every critic, rather than recognizing the legitimacy of some non–production oriented concerns.

THE STYLE OF CONFRONTATION

Some groups of producers have adopted a strategy of direct confrontation as the preferred means of dealing with a government that refuses to meet their demands for prices sufficient not merely to meet production costs, but rather to enable them to boost their purchasing power to its 1910–1914 equivalent. Within seven brief months in the fall and winter of 1977–1978, the American Agriculture Movement (AAM) was conceived and delivered in Colorado, replicated in many states, and partially interred in Washington, D.C. It thrived on such tactics as blocking highways with tractors and other farm equipment, threatening to burn half the crops of anyone who planted as usual, releasing goats on the steps of the Capitol, marching on the White House, and relieving the Secretary of Agriculture of his office for a day.

The resemblance to the activities of a whole host of groups representing what they believed to be minority status in the 1960's and 1970's, whether it be civil rights, women's rights, gay rights, anti–Vietnam, or pro–marijuana was said by some to be purely coincidental, although other AAM activists were pleased to be labeled as militants. In the minds of most Americans, tired of a decade of similar protests, only the ages and income of the protesters had changed. It was more of the same.

But the style of lobbying by direct challenge did work. A Congress that might never have acted in the absence of the constant, irritating pressure of hundreds of insistent men and women demanding parity at least enacted some form of legislation. Confrontation bore some fruit. The adoption of intransigence rather than compromise as the primary method of dealing with agricultural policy–making may succeed once. But it cannot be sustained. It is hard for its perpetrators to repeat year in and year out. The Congress and the White House, may be caught off guard once, but they quickly learn to adapt and become immune to constant ultimatums, consistent noncooperation. The tactic that may be good for a quick victory in a battle cannot last through an endless campaign.

What is to be Done?

This background indicates that the three most readily adopted approaches of the farm community outside of Washington to deal with the perceived decline in the political status of producer agriculture in the federal government's decision–making process are, if not bankrupt, at best, not helpful. They have not been fruitful nor will they be. Agriculture does best when it rejects all three, as it has increasingly in recent years. The background further suggests that, although weakness is postulated, the reality more readily suggests surprising political resilience, with producer agriculture exhibiting considerable strength in the Congress under certain conditions.

To turn those conditions into a political program is not easy. But they do help delineate the range of possibilities for effective future action. While no one solution is guaranteed to work and while some struggles (for example, for 100 percent of parity) may be forever unwinnable, no matter what the strategy, there do exist opportunities for more political success than the sheer weight of voting numbers would indicate to be likely. The key to those opportunities can be succinctly stated. In unity and only in unity can there be meaningful strength. The unity to which we refer encompasses both unity within agriculture between producers and among the related sectors of the agricultural economy, as well as unity outside of agriculture among a variety of constituencies that can combine on a transitory, *ad hoc* basis to form viable coalitions.

The best answer, we think, rests in the careful and pragmatic creation of coalitions with open recognition of the cost–benefit balance that appeals to each group's self–interest and sensitivity to the volatility of any such collaborative effort as the balance changes from issue to issue.

It is time, therefore, for American agriculture to ignore the thermometer reading of population percentages and rural districts and recognize that it is not at all impotent or puny, but neither can it invariably prevail when dealing with the Congress and the President unless it carefully cultivates both internal and external allies.

Pragmatism has to replace ideology. Agriculture has to be prepared to expand its internal political base, by acknowledging instead of merely waxing rhetorical about the needs of the family farm and the farmworker; by seeking a more integrated agriculture–wide approach to legislation and regulation instead of encouraging each commodity to solve its own problems by unilaterally dealing with its own controlled legislative or bureaucratic constituency; by combining forces with other interests in the food marketing system. This does not mean that, from time to time, it may not be preferable to deal with problems on a special–interest basis or to challenge rather than cooperate with, for example, the truckers and the food chains. It is simply that the presumption should be to seek a unified approach, instead of automatically to go it alone.

Agriculture, further, must forge a broader external political base, learning to exploit coalition politics to achieve its ends. There are many issues upon which labor and agriculture can either share or trade–off perspectives. Every farm household is a consumer, be it of pesticides, machinery, or processed food. Those who seek food safety or promote nutritional quality are not invaribly hostile to agriculture. They may well be trying to save it from itself. To view every public policy from the perspective of food and agriculture may be one method of achieving the type of integration that enables the five percent to assert the leverage of 51 percent.

This does not mean that agriculture may not have the ability in any given situation to act strictly on its own behalf, without compromise or coalition, and to employ tactics ranging from confrontation to focused organization relying on craft and timing to secure particular objectives. Such an approach may prove successful on occasion as it has in the past, but it is not in the overall best interest of agriculture or of the country.

AGRICULTURE—INTERNAL DIVERSITY

Farming is not a monolithic enterprise composed of units that share common economic goals. Like medieval England, it is a collection of often—warring baronies, each seeking to advance its conception of its own self—interest, even at the expense of other farmers.

The trouble begins within individual commodities. Although the public may believe that cotton is cotton, California cotton growers, blessed with perenially favorable climate, spur production, while Mississippi cotton growers stress price at the expense of production. Arkansas and California rice growers do not see eye to eye. Northwestern wheat growers look to the Asian market; Midwestern ones, primarily to Europe. Many cotton and wheat farmers fail to understand the need for commodity prices to remain at a competitive level to secure sales in the export trade and, additionally, in the case of cotton, to avoid being undercut domestically by manufactured chemical fibers. Sugar beet and sugar cane growers do not naturally share the same policy perspectives. It takes work to bring them together to agree on the details of sugar legislation.

This fragmentation of policy concerns accelerates when it crosses commodity lines. It may not be possible to expect ranchers or poultry growers to back higher loan rates or target prices for feed grains. Their economic interests seem opposed rather than allied if price is the only policy issue. That does not mean, however, that they must disagree with every aspect of agricultural policy or that the livestock producers will necessarily exercise their political influence to assure low feed grain costs. Some compromise may still be achievable.

More often, a particular commodity interest thinks that it can do better for itself in the legislative arena divorced from the burden of other commodities. Individual commodity organizations do tend, in most instances, to be more effective politically than the general farm organizations that represent numerous commodity interests. The reasons for this may include: greater ease of organizing a position around one commodity, the greater sophistication of Washington commodity group representatives, their superior ability in directing campaign contributions to supporters, the more natural focus of farmer constituents on one crop when expressing political views, or the narrow commodity orientation of subcommittees in the House Agriculture Committee and, hence, members of the full Committee.

Accordingly, in recent years, without waiting for inclusion in a general farm bill, dairy, rice, tobacco, and sugar have sought to promote their own single–shot bills, without notable success in the case of dairy, tobacco, and sugar and with success in the case of rice only because the particular legislation at stake appeared to reduce rather than increase government market controls and budget costs. When cotton agreed to oppose escalation of wheat and feed grain prices in 1973 in order to avoid a stringent payment limitation, it lost and had to resort to a bargain with labor interests to avert humiliating defeat. When the individual commodities go their own way they do not invariably achieve their special goals, but they do reduce the extent of the support for a broad farm bill.

The economic clashes that translate into more serious political differences, where agricultural policy–making is concerned, occur between farmers of any and all crops and those with whom they deal in the economic chain en route to the final production of food and fiber. Even though almost every major commodity is ultimately the subject of processing before it reaches the consumer and, thus, farmers' economic well–being is tied to every other component in the food marketing chain, there are many more political clashes than agreements between farmers and farm labor, farmers and warehousers, farmers and processors, farmers and exporters, farmers and retail food chains.

These clashes within commodities, among commodities and across the agricultural economy are long standing, but their more recent manifestations have been politically self–destructive as each agricultural group asserts its own rights at the expense of others, with the split permitting the nonagricultural interest groups more readily to control the balance of power. There have even been recent instances of turf fights between established agricultural lobbies and those who prefer direct action traditional techniques for influencing legislation, despite some agreement on economic aims.

This wide divergence of views within the farm community itself raises a question about whether farmers can agree on anything, let alone persuade others to adopt their perspective. The need to develop a better mechanism for airing, even if not resolving, these differences should be obvious.

It ought not to follow inevitably that divergent economic interests, however conflicting, refuse to seek some common ground or to compromise some portion of their short–run desire in return for somewhat more in the long run. Sugar cane and beet growers and sugar processors and refiners bargain and agree on a daily basis in the marketplace. Why is this impossible in the world of politics? After all, corn producers who market their product for processing into corn syrup know that they benefit from higher sugar prices and act accordingly on sugar bills.

If each commodity–specific group or each general farm organization seeks to press its own narrow view, the consequence may be (as it has already been from time to time) that the combined attempt to farm the government till by providing government protection for the income of all either fails because of political resistance by the politicians who are not primarily accountable to those involved in the food supply or leads to the loss of markets to foreign suppliers anxious and ready to compete.

It is very difficult for a single commodity group or even two to muster a majority in Congress (let alone the two–thirds necessary to override a Presidential veto) for a program change that lacks support either from all of the other commodities through an omnibus bill or from the nonfarm bloc. Tobacco failed in 1975; sugar lost in 1974 and 1978; and cotton could not override in 1975 when it was perceived as the primary beneficiary of so–called omnibus emergency legislation. Divided they fall. This is not to imply that any of these individual commodities would have triumphed in unity through a genuine general farm bill, but only that the votes were not there and may never be there to enact significant price–increasing laws on a single commodity basis.

Agriculture: Prospects for Internal Cooperation

THE GENERAL FARM ORGANIZATIONS

It might seem logical to turn to the general farm organizations to supply the missing cohesion in the role of farmers in agricultural policy–making. After all, the American Farm Bureau Federation, the Grange, the National Farmers Organization, and the National Farmers Union are voices for more than specific commodities and represent broad interest groups among farmers through the local members who pay them dues. From time to time, these four major organizations have coordinated lobbying efforts to present a united front. In 1977, for example, 34 farm groups united to present a joint compromise on price levels under the banner of the National Farm Coalition.

Unfortunately, however, the general farm organizations are not as well suited to this task of coalition as might appear on the surface. The reasons are that they focus much of their effort on membership retention through the delivery of services (information, insurance, etc.), resolve policy stands through exceedingly lengthy lists of resolutions, some of which may deter potential political allies from joining with them on specific agricultural issues, and have strong ideological identifications in the public mind ranging from conservative to populist that also cause potential allies to hold back from being identified with an unwanted label. The general farm organizations could serve as the cement, but they have not, and there is no indication that they will come to view that as their primary purpose.

THE SEARCH FOR COMMON GROUND

Are there other alternative ways to take this Tower of Babel with tens of conflicting voices and translate them into a coherent and effective political language? Perhaps not all at once or in every instance. But certainly there is room to do more along the lines of communication among and compromise of these divergent views than is being done now. The opportunity for progress exists. The rigidity of the traditional differences between agricultural interest groups discussed above is beginning to break down somewhat as the economics of production change and producers recognize the value of minimizing disunity and opposition. The existence of this very Farm Summit symbolizes the recognition that something must be done to seek broad–based solutions to the economic problems confronting all of American agriculture. Where regulation of agriculture is the issue, be it EPA or OSHA, there is a distinct common interest that overrides economic differences. The program for this Summit describes it as "a challenge to reach beyond the old divisions— . . . to find the common ground . . . to identify and define the important areas of agreement."

A three–day meeting once a decade is not enough. Something more permanent and more structured is called for in order to begin to build a feasible, viable cohesion among the various agricultural interests. Perhaps the most useful way to begin would be through the informal exchange of information on a fairly regular basis. We propose that careful efforts be made to develop an open–ended agricultural coalition that meets at least monthly in Washington, D.C., excluding no active participant in the food production system. The object would not necessarily be to forge a lobby binding everyone to promote particular programs and policies. Such efforts in the past have been notably unsuccessful, with nonparticipation by the National Farmers Union on one side and the American Farm Bureau Federation on the other. Rather the focus would be on exchanging points of view and opening a dialogue with the Executive and Legislative Branches well in advance of the need to take positions and testify.

Meaningful intra– and inter–commodity political communication has been rare in the past. It could conceivably lead to adjusting and negotiating trade–offs that would sufficiently satisfy each distinctive economic interest so as to permit the maximum degree of public unity and the minimum of splintering. If there proves ultimately to be no common ground on some matters, efforts to locate one can only bear fruit in other areas through a stronger sense of mutuality.

These efforts might well commence on a commodity–by–commodity basis and broaden thereafter, although, since the objective is to unify all of agriculture as much as possible, splintering at the outset might not be advisable. The existing forums and luncheons simply do not meet the need. There have been some attempts to bring limited groups of lobbyists together on an *ad hoc* basis to form a coalition on a specific farm–related bill, but these have been too narrow in scope and too limited in duration to approximate what we think to be most valuable. The model to which we aspire might be the education lobby called EFFORT, which has successfully conducted regular breakfast meetings of every group with a Washington office that has an interest in education legislation, culminating in an agreed–upon package of appropriations amendments for committee and for Floor action encompassing the most diverse educational programs. We recognize that there are substantial differences. Government programs in agriculture have a profound effect upon and critically interact with market conditions. In education, the market is predominantly public. But the model is viable and ought to be seriously considered and revamped to fit the circumstances of agriculture.

One mechanism to be explored, therefore, should be the institution of a series of breakfast meetings, on a set day each month, of the Washington representatives of all agriculture–oriented associations to listen to speakers from the Administration or Congress and then to discuss specific forthcoming legislative or regulatory matters of common concern or even broader agricultural topics in an effort not to achieve consensus, but to develop the understanding of each individual group's bottom–line position that is the precondition of any future negotiation and conciliation. The objective would be to bring the groups together on a social and, hence, more relaxed basis so that all of the representatives might become personally acquainted in a less competitive environment. Where these meetings and discussions might lead we cannot confidently predict. We can state that, without this type of undertaking, the prospects for building a significant and lasting coalition among agricultural interests by exploring and staking out common ground will be dim.

RESPECT FOR NEWLY EMERGING VOICES

As part of any effort to bring about a more unified voice of the producer in agriculture, the existing lobbying groups will have to be more willing to welcome competition. To achieve any level of cooperative action in agriculture, the old–line, established farm organizations, whether commodity–oriented or general, are going to have to be willing to work with new groups, however brash their tactics may seem. It is hard for those who have been entrenched in and accustomed to the subtle style of Washington for as many as 40 years to avoid being contemptuous of those who would unleash goats and dump grain on the streets. History repeats itself. The Grange was considered radical in the 1880's; farmer holidays were viewed as Communist–inspired in the 1930's; and NFO calf kills and milk dumps were deplored in the late 1960's. Yet, each in turn has become part of the establishment.

The rapid growth of the American Agriculture Movement (AAM), beginning in late 1977, ought to be a signal to the establishment that those economic segments that believe they are unrepresented by the major groups (in this instance, predominantly, but not exclusively, young men involved in large–scale farming enterprises subject to large mortgages because of increased land–holdings and heavy equipment debt) have to be listened to. If the establishment pays attention only to the more traditional forces, it will compel the new voices to create their own sources of organizational strength and the fractionalization that has already undermined the political base of agriculture will continue.

Responsiveness to all farming constituents, indeed, increased attempts to explore the full, if previously silent, range of their constituencies ought to be a major thrust endorsed by the general farm organizations. There is no reason to turn one's back on collections of farmers and mock the validity of their contentions simply because they start out leaderless and unrealistic. Successful farm pressure groups in the future will be those that can harness the raw power of anger and make it plow somewhat more productive political ground. The AAM may have failed because it sought too much too quickly (although part of its loss on the House Floor was the unfortunate conjunction of its drive with a particularly sharp rise in inflation and public concern about that), but it accomplished more through its techniques of harassment and dogged persistence than the establishment could have by relying on contacts and finesse. We do not suggest that these techniques should be repeated or expanded, indeed, they may well have become counterproductive after the spring of 1978, particularly in terms of the massive, sustained presence of farmers in Washington. We only wish to acknowledge the power of energy and concern when channeled into lobbying activities. The agricultural community is perhaps as well represented in Washington as any other economic group in terms of the knowledge of the effective access points by its representatives and their political acumen. They, however, need the political backup of the farmers throughout the country to maximize their clout.

Among the new forces in agricultural lobbying that must be taken into account is the advent of farm women in the form of WIFE (Women Involved in Farm Economics), a wheat–oriented group that worked hard in the House on the 1977 farm bill, the female members of AAM who were a very visible presence in 1978, and American Agri–Women, a national coalition of farm and ranch women's organizations. Women have always been farmers or else unpaid farm labor, but now they are appropriately vocalizing their perspective on farm policy and demanding to be heard. Their potential power as a decision–making force remains to be tapped.

RESPONSIVENESS TO THE ENTIRE CONSTITUENCY

While it is useful for established agricultural organizations to acknowledge and even hail the arrival of the newest and most lively in order to reinvigorate their own efforts, it is equally as important for farm organizations to encourage, through vigorous outreach, participation in policy formulation, by the broadest possible range of growers.

If, as is all too often the situation, a growers' organization is responsive only to those who own or manage the larger farm units and who, therefore, can afford to delegate some day–to–day farm supervision to others in order to devote time to the organization, the danger of underrepresentation or nonrepresentation of family farming is substantial.

Since the family farm accounts for 90 percent of all farms and 60 percent of total cash receipts from farming, the failure to take its perspective into account in formulating farm policy is harmful. Slighting the needs of the family farm not only evidences disrespect for what everyone acknowledges to be the genius of American agriculture, but also leads to a farm policy that hastens the demise of that very genius. To neglect the medium–sized and small farm in organizational politics can only speed the trend to larger and larger farmland holdings by fewer and fewer people with diminishing opportunities for entry into agriculture and, concommitantly, because individuals vote according to their number, a smaller political base for the commodity. AAM's rigid demand for parity may have been distasteful to the establishment, but it spoke more directly to the perceived economic needs of the majority of farmers, who felt excluded from meaningful political activity. Appropriate compromise of product pricing and other goals is only possible when unintentional exclusion of some points of view is replaced by the conscious effort to bring participation by all. Seeking to bring more farmers into politics will yield the additional benefit of a larger pool to solicit Political Action Committee (PAC) political contributions to support sympathetic candidates as well as more voters to build up the single interest bloc. Thus, each organization should conscientiously strive to be more responsive and sensitive to the needs of all its members (thereby avoiding the all–too–typical organizational syndrome of a Washington–oriented executive board or secretary increasingly out of touch with local constituents) and hold open to all the opportunity to move up the organizational ladder to positions of prominence.

SUPPORT ACROSS THE FOOD MARKETING AND DISTRIBUTION SYSTEM

The need to seek effective broad–based coalitions extends beyond the growers or producers of one or more commodities to those who handle the commodities at any point in the food distribution chain. Again, there will be times when the self–interest of the grower–producers dictates that cooperation is out of the question. Indeed, in the current state of inflation, it is incumbent upon growers to perform better in educating the consuming public about the responsibility for price increases in food so that the entire blame and public disfavor is not directed at the farmer.

At the same time, whatever educational campaign is conducted has to be as fair and factual as possible to prevent burning any bridges with the other sectors of the food marketing system, such as labor, with whom alliances may be essential in the future. The public is becoming increasingly aware of the fact that labor accounts for a slightly larger portion of a household bill for food consumed at home than the raw foodstuffs themselves, but the public should know that transportation costs went up faster from 1967 to 1977 than labor costs, which might appropriately transfer part of the negative public relations burden for high food costs from the farmer to our system for regulating trucking.

The economic education of the consumer requires clear pinpointing of responsibility for food price hikes. But it should not necessarily foreclose political trade–offs between components of the food marketing system that function to fulfill the goals of each component. For example, sugar cane growers, who, among other things, need higher price supports in order to meet their cost of production are not ready and willing simultaneously to raise that cost by boosting the wages they pay to their field workers. If, however, that is the price of labor support for a better sugar bill, then there is no choice. Substantial and stubborn delay in entering into such an agreement led to the demise of the sugar program in 1974. The lesson was learned and bargaining with labor in 1978 concluded well prior to, rather than considerably after, moving the bill to the Floor of the House. This may not have been sufficient to assure passage, but it was necessary.

The approach of increasing public understanding of the responsibility of each segment of the food marketing economy for the value added in each step of the food chain from field to market, while still enabling the segments to engage in cooperative ventures of mutual interest, will be difficult to sustain. The balancing act is a delicate one. The sheer economic power of the food retail stores and the transportation companies cannot be overlooked in support of policies desired by farmers any more than can the proven political strength of food marketing–related unions, including the meat packers, retail clerks, and teamsters. Everyone involved in the chain—and that encompasses over 10 million workers if farmers and hired hands are combined with the employees of the distribution system—has a distinct stake in the well–being and survival of any link that may, when convincing arguments are presented about the need for unity, overcome the natural instinct to buy cheaply from the prior connection and sell dearly to the next.

To date, there have only been a handful of conferences convened by consumer groups that have brought the various links together to consider national food policy. There are many issues on which common interests across the chain should be obvious (e.g., advertising of sugared products on television). But there needs to be a concerted, structured attempt within the food industry to forge a continuing coalition to analyze and seek some middle ground on all public policies, regulatory or subsidy in nature, the impact anywhere along the chain, with potential ripples up and down the line. Agriculture, which, ironically, is now the smaller portion in numbers of personnel and dollars of value added in the food industry, should take the lead in creating a food system task force or lobby.

On the other hand some Task Force members are doubtful that consolidating farm power into a relatively unified bloc, with or without other components in the food system, would be wise or in the best interests of agriculture. It is possible that a united agriculture would impose too many demands on the government and seek to transfer too much enterprise risk from the market to the federal treasury, resulting in a loss of markets and an overall loss of income even after government subvention. The farmer's short–run concept of his welfare may not be in his best interest in the long run.

Agriculture: External Coalition

THE NEW AGENDA OF FOOD AND NUTRITION POLICY

Numerous analysts of our food system have spoken in favor of developing, on both an executive and legislative level, a national food and nutrition policy that would deal with food–related issues in an overall, consistent framework rather than on an *ad hoc* basis. A national food policy would seek to resolve the various conflicts among interest groups concerned with the production, distribution and consumption of food (agricultural, consumer, labor, rural, environmental, religious, scientific, medical) in such a way as to assure what Assistant Secretary Foreman has labeled "an adequate supply of safe, high quality, and nutritious food at reasonable prices, while providing a reasonable return on investment to those who produce and distribute food, and assuring some assistance to those at home and abroad who cannot afford an adequate diet even at reasonable prices" (Foreman, p. 778).

There is no doubt that developing and implementing such a policy is a tall, if not visionary order. It constitutes what Paarlberg would term the "new agenda of farm policy," expanding it well beyond the issues the agricultural establishment has long felt comfortable with, that is, the economic returns available to the farmer (supplies, prices) and government constraints upon his activities. Even if no such policy emerges in the course of the next decade because of the inability of the interest groups to compromise their sometimes dramatic differences, the concept of such a policy and its potential dimensions must be explored and debated by those groups. Agriculture cannot turn its back and walk away from the discussion, not if it wants to be certain that its priorities remain on the agenda as part of that policy. Indeed, agriculture will obtain renewed—and even majoritarian—support for its priorities only if it participates without ideological reservation in the highly political process of formulating such a policy.

The policy will not be forged in one committee mark–up or in one omnibus bill or in one Presidential program of food reform. It will emerge, if at all, in dribs and drabs, usually implicit and occasionally explicit in tens of authorizations and line–item appropriations and promulgations of proposed and final regulations affecting such matters as nutrition education, nutrition research, food inspection, food stamps, pesticide and toxic substance controls, trucking practices, food labeling, food advertising, food additives and fortification, and hosts of others besides price supports, import quotas, and set–aside land. Agriculture has to begin to view this agenda from an overall strategic perspective, recognizing that it cannot win every, or perhaps not many of the pitched battles over individual issues and that, to secure its priorities, it will have to compromise every inch of the way. Ideology must be foresworn. It is absolutely incompatible with success. Agriculture can expect to starve if it persists in constantly denouncing Ralph Nader, Carol Foreman, and every other spokesman for non–production values to obtain instant applause. It must learn to subordinate its instincts to protect its future. It cannot fight everybody all of the time. It must cooperate and build bridges wherever possible.

THE'SYSTEM OF TRADE–OFFS

None of this means surrendering the drive for fair economic returns to stimulate continued production or to be free from unnecessary regulations. Instead it means protecting that drive, those returns, and that freedom by embracing those concerns of the consumer–oriented groups that are compatible with viable production. The loss of a particular pesticide or additive can be devastating to the cost of harvesting a particular crop, but, in the broader perspective of the best interests of productive agriculture in general it is simply not as harmful as a widespread, deeply–inculcated public belief that the public will be poisoned by ingesting certain foodstuffs.[1] Higher minimum wages will affect production costs, but that may have to be suffered if agriculture is to receive its fair return as the laborer obtains his.[2] This should not spell the end of efforts to join forces with labor, so long as the cost–of–living impact is not intense or easily identifiable or any individual price rise does not substantially reduce quantity demanded.

The object ought to be to forge a continuing series of short–range, one–for–one trade–offs with food policy interest groups that would bind them to agriculture in a mutual support system over the legislative long haul. These trade–offs would involve support for meaningful features of production–centered agricultural legislation. In return, agriculture would furnish equivalent support in the form of positive votes (or purposeful absence in order to delete negative votes) for other portions of such legislation directly impacting those interest groups.

The concept and practice of such trade–offs has been developing for 15 years ever since the first food stamp bill was tied in with the passage of the 1964 farm bill. The trade–offs that have emerged during the intervening years have been characterized most often by the participation of less than a majority at best of farm Congressmen, which hampers the ability of the farm bloc effectively to deliver its side of the bargain; a tendency to hold off and wait until the last moment to agree on the bargain itself, based on underlying ideological reluctance, so

---

[1]Sharon Steffens, American Agri–Women: The loss of a pesticide or additive can also eliminate a particular crop or product from the market. For example, if Benlate which is in the rebuttable presumption against registration (RPAR) process of evaluation should be banned from use on peaches, it would have disastrous effects on the peach industry which uses Benlate to control brown rot. The public has heard so much about pesticides, nitrates, additives, residues, etc. that they pay little attention anymore. It is like the little boy who cried wolf once too often. If you followed every warning and caution that is spread it would require major dietary changes which the public is reluctant to make. No segment of agriculture should have to be sacrificed for the good of the whole. Before it reaches that point, compromises should be negotiated to prevent that segment of production from demise.

[2]Sharon Steffens: Regarding higher minimum wages, many labor–intensive fruit and vegetable producers are feeling the impact of steadily–rising wage rates. Higher minimum wages would result in increased mechanization where possible thus eliminating jobs for many seasonal workers and for teenagers who need to learn how to work. The only other alternative, if some fruits and vegetables which can not be mechanized are to be available to the consumer, is to pass the cost on to the consumer. The question is, will producers be able to pass on that cost and will consumers be willing to pay the price.

that the decision to trade–off can occur too late to salvage the situation; and a fluidity of relationship, with each succeeding trade–off treated in isolation from the one before, reflecting both the swiftly changing nature of politics and the underlying political incompatibility on most major issues of the forces involved.

All of these features of the trade–off system have been apparent since 1964. For example, in 1973, when cotton agreed with labor to help defeat a ban on striker eligibility for food stamps in return for labor's help in defeating the imposition of a $20,000 ceiling on payments and the deletion of funding for Cotton, Inc., only 30 cotton supporters went along in voting against the striker ban, which then was successfully attached to the food stamp bill by a very narrow vote margin. Similarly marginal but ultimately more effective vote deliveries occurred in 1969 and 1970 in connection with payment limitations and black lung and OSHA legislation. Food stamps were more solidly supported by the South in the 1977 farm bill, which helped peanuts survive and corn and wheat secure higher loan and support price levels with urban consumer votes.

In 1974 when the sugar bill came to the Floor, the leaders of the House Agriculture Committee and sugar lobbyists refused to deal with labor about wages and conditions in cane cutting until it was too late. The adoption of three pro–labor amendments on the Floor pursuant to the first open rule (no limitation on amendments) in the sugar program's 40–year history was not timely enough to turn the negative tide, and the entire bill was rejected by 34 votes. The same foot–dragging delayed the 1973 farm bill on the House Floor so that it took two weeks to pass instead of two days and almost caused cotton and labor both to lose their objectives.

The *ad hoc* nature of the trade–offs appears inevitable as each participating group conducts its own pragmatic cost–benefit balance on an issue–by–issue basis to determine whether or not any given bargain is worth it to the group. The volatility of politics and the certainty that economic and political factors and forces will change with each succeeding Congress, if not year, renders any permanent bargain both unlikely and probably inadvisable. Nor could either cluster of interests agree to support the values embraced by the other on any sustained basis given their ideology. Farmers enamoured by the work ethic may stomach a vote for food stamps from time to time, but not forever. Consumers can go along with selected increases in government subsidies for commodity prices, but not each and every one.

The trade–off mechanism is, therefore, a difficult and subtle instrument to administer. It demands much of both parties to the bargain. It is only by recognition of its limitations and the legitimate, even if opposed, interests of all participants that it can be successfully utilized. Each successful trade–off does, however, breed the goodwill essential to consummating the next. The habit of compromising one less significant objective to achieve another more vital one is hard to acquire, but just as hard to kick. Concerted efforts must be made by the agricultural community, first, to keep the lines of communication open with the various components of the urban–labor–consumer axis; second, to forge as many alliances as possible on easy issues, that is, those on which both sides can readily agree (e.g., excessive textile imports are currently disliked both by cotton and the garment workers just as cotton and labor opposed mandatory wage and price controls in 1971); and, third, to negotiate hard and long to achieve satisfactory swaps on matters of the utmost importance. There may never come a time when cotton could support labor law reform or labor agree to the removal of limitations on the factory levels of cotton dust, but the groups can come together on most farm legislation if they seriously seek to.

Trade–offs have saved agriculture's programs in the past. They could furnish even more affirmative aid to agriculture if handled in a more carefully planned and consistent manner in the future.

SELF–IMPOSED LIMITATIONS

Not only must farmers be prepared to swallow legislation they would prefer to oppose in order to accomplish higher priority ends, they must also be willing to modify the extent of their reach if legislation is not to exceed their grasp. How much is too much can only be judged from the reaction of the consumer–labor alliance. Dairy and wheat are equally vulnerable here, even though they would seem to be at opposite ends of the economic spectrum, since the farmer's share of the market cost of butter is 65 percent, but of bread only 10 percent. But the consumer–labor phalanx (and the two are usually closely allied in this context) which views a large increase in the price of milk as anathema, cannot afford to make fine distinctions in the political arena when the bakers conjure up the nightmare of a dollar loaf of bread.

Dairy has, in the past, been able to operate from its own base without making substantial alliances either with other commodity programs or across the lines with consumers. That can be partially attributed to the use of campaign funding resources. But even dairy cannot afford consistently to proceed without regard to other social and economic forces. It fell victim to inaccurate but highly consumer–sensitive price forecasts in 1975 and to budget constraints in 1976. Dairy will have to join the ranks hereafter.

Agriculture could best proceed to reach out to cement its ties with the consumer–labor–environmental voting bloc in the area of regulation by adopting the initiative by way of self–regulation and self–policing instead of waiting to react negatively to every outside proposal. Toy and many other consumer product manufacturers that have dealt with the Consumer Product Safety Commission have managed to modify their goods before the Commission acted to ban them, and, in the process, either defusing or reducing that ban. Agriculture invariably says "hell, no!" to pesticide regulation, for example, and digs in its heels without exploring reasonable alternative approaches. As a consequence, it is enjoined and prohibited in a harsher fashion than is necessary.

All of this is not to suggest that agriculture must put its tail between its legs and limp home. There will still be opportunity for vigorous advocacy on behalf of productive agriculture in the price–supply arena as well as vis–à–vis environmental–consumer–labor regulation. But, however vigorous the advocacy, it cannot afford perpetually to alienate the forces it criticizes. Exaggerated claims of economic injury and extravagant projections of harm to society if X or Y regulation is promulgated and enforced should be abandoned in favor of more careful and less inflammatory calculations of costs and benefits that might suggest modification and restriction rather than abolition of the proposed rules. The boy who cried "wolf" did it twice too often. Precious public confidence in the reliability of business complaints about the impact of government intrusion erodes rapidly. Vigorous advocacy and puffing need not be synonymous.

The historic role for agriculture in connection with each succeeding wave of regulation was to be exempt, whether it was transportation, the minimum wage, unemployment compensation, or wage and price controls. Today, agriculture is generally viewed as part and parcel of the general economy. Total exemptions from the restrictions imposed on this outside world are difficult to secure. Agriculture must understand that it can no longer anticipate what was in effect a production subsidy in the guise of an exemption, although it can advocate partial exemption or reduced regulatory burden if it demonstrates that administrative and production (hence, consumer) cost will outweigh public (consumer) benefit. To seek less may be to obtain more.

THE CONSUMER–URBAN RELATIONSHIP

Even while expanding the links of trade–offs on individual pieces of legislation that bind agriculture and the farmer to the urban and consumer–oriented members of Congress, the agricultural sector of the American economy should conduct a campaign of education (especially through the media) to persuade the urban–consumer public and, hence, their representatives in Congress that the underlying interests of all groups ultimately coincide. While it is true that increases in the prices obtained for raw commodities will eventually be assessed against the consumer, the pocketbook concerns of both groups are not invariably opposed. When farmers thrive it is not solely at the expense of consumers. Every farmer is a consumer. Every dollar obtained through the export of farm commodities helps reduce the present imbalance of payments and thus strengthens the consumer's dollar. This job of persuading the public to disbelieve its automatic responses will be slow in yielding political benefits, but it must be undertaken.

Agriculture in the Executive Branch

AGRICULTURE AND ITS DEPARTMENT

The central issue to be resolved vis–à–vis agriculture's influence within the executive branch is how best to treat the Department of Agriculture—as an advocate primarily for the needs of producers or as a representative of all of the interests involved with and concerned about food and nutrition policy. Many farmers and farm groups feel strongly that the Department should continue to function exclusively as their voice, as they believe that, until recently, it always has. They remember the days when the Department instinctively fought the Surgeon General on the health dangers of smoking tobacco or automatically sided with the chemical industry against the environmentalists on the uses and abuses of pesticides. They do not like or want a Department that has second thoughts about tobacco or pesticides, that does not automatically adopt the producers' position, right or wrong. They contend that if organized labor has its representative in the Cabinet in the form of the Secretary of Labor and industry has the Secretary of Commerce, then farmers are entitled to theirs.

The problem, of course, is that political reality does not comport with these impressions of Secretarial advocacy roles. Organized labor simply does not recognize the Secretary of Labor as its man in the Cabinet. They know that the Secretary must take into account a variety of other influences and interests in preparing his policy choices. They no longer expect him to do their job for them. The same holds true for manufacturers and businessmen. Why must farmers be the last to realize what all other political observers have long acknowledged: that the members of the Cabinet do not (and should not) represent narrow, parochial interests or particular viewpoints and instead consider themselves bound to articulate a broader public interest in matters within their domain.

Producers do exert considerable influence within the Department and its semi-autonomous agencies that often defy control by the Secretary and his assistants. Rather than claiming the Secretary himself, they should have some high-level official within the Department whom they can feel confident is their voice and who can work to resolve differences among them. They are entitled to feel that they have a friend in high places. Some, despairing of reliance upon the Agricultural Stabilization and Conservation Service, have proposed the creation of a nationally-elected advisory committee to function on behalf of producers within the Department. While we are troubled by the efficacy of such a proposal as well as by its administrative details, not to mention the harm that might befall were ideological interests to take advantage of their ability to organize for the election and reinject dogma rather than pragmatism into departmental policy-making, we sympathize with the concerns that prompt such a proposal to surface.

Perhaps the position of Under Secretary of Agriculture for Commodity Programs ought to be created. In any event, the Department should be reorganized to assure that, somewhere in the highest reaches of the chain of command, producer interests will be significantly recognized and given access. If consumers can speak and expect Carol Foreman to listen, producers are entitled to at least as much. The farmer needs to feel that he can flex his political muscles within the Department so long as departmental policy is not absolutely and automatically predicated upon that flex because otherwise the real political thrust of the Department in its persuasive capacity as representative of the public interest in food and nutrition will be diminished.

THE DEPARTMENT OF AGRICULTURE AND THE GOVERNMENT

The Department has undeniably had trouble being effective on behalf of producers when dealing with the White House and other departments on subsidy and regulatory policy. During the course of the tenure of Secretary Butz, USDA was, at best, treated as a stepsister in the household of the Cabinet, downgraded and ignored by more potent departments, like State and Treasury, and rarely consulted at the White House where crucial policy options were analyzed and selected with scant or belated input from USDA. Export controls were imposed on soybeans for a short period of time in 1973 by the White House over the USDA's protests. The Secretary was scarcely involved in the 1974 cancellation of Russian export contracts and played a not very influential role in the 1975 debate about the grain sales embargoes to Russia and Poland. The State Department and not Agriculture was in charge of the 1975 United States–Russian grain negotiations. All of these are indicative of a substantial decline in the USDA's power vis–à–vis other governmental agencies.

The influence of the Department has increased since Secretary Bergland aptly informed the Senate Committee on Agriculture, Nutrition, and Forestry in 1977, when testifying on loan rates and target prices, that "What I am doing today is not what I would recommend if I were a private citizen." The Council of Economic Advisers and the Office of Management and Budget did influence the costs and scope of the Administration's 1977 farm program, and the Secretary was afforded virtually no room to deal with the AAM in the winter of 1978. His position on removing the beef import quota did not triumph in the following summer. But the Secretary did push the White House inch by inch to modify its stand in 1977 and successfully maintained the pressure to raise the budget limits on agricultural spending bit by bit. In 1978, although the Secretary was hardly a supporter of the AAM, he did help secure ultimate White House acquiescence in some price adjustments and credit legislation that had not been planned. He may, however, never be as strong in the immediate future as the Chairman of the Council of Economic Advisers or the Director of the Office of Management and Budget, nor can he expect to be so long as budgetary constraints and inflation are the paramount considerations at the level of the White House.

The most important step the USDA could take to assure that it is not brushed aside as a pseudo–lobbyist for a minority point of view is consciously and publicly to broaden the nature of the USDA to encompass issues relating to food and nutrition. The more public interests it serves, the more effective it will be. Of course, the food and nutrition goals may clash with production goals at times and the Department will have to settle the issues. But if the Department were to seek both sets of goals internally, there would be less of a need to escalate the matter to the White House and many inter–departmental conflicts might be disposed of without intervention at the highest level of policy–making. A Department that viewed its food and nutrition activities as important as its agricultural ones would be a more convincing advocate for agriculture. A Department of Food can do more for farm families than a Department that is concerned only with farming.

The expressed concern of many agricultural groups that the loss of control over child nutrition programs to the proposed Department of Education would be the start of the dismantling of the USDA is a manifestation that seeking multiple ends is vital to its future. Whether or not the Department changes its name, it has to change its approach. It can no longer afford to bemoan the fact, as it did in 1975 and 1976, that two–thirds of its budget was swallowed in food assistance programs. It must be proud of that, proud because it is precisely such programs that give it a substantially enlarged constituency and, ultimately, if properly exploited, power. Those farmers who fear broadening the USDA to encompass non–producer–oriented concerns must reconcile themselves to the fact the Secretary of Agriculture can be a vigorous and effective participant in the decision–making process related to agricultural policy only if he is viewed as taking into account more aspects of food and nutrition policy than the self–interest of the farmer.

The incumbent Secretary has taken major strides toward expanding the political base of the Department, toward making it an effective bridge builder to all of the economic and social forces dealing with food. He has given the Department more credibility at the level of the White House than it has had in many years. It would be foolish to destroy that credibility and tear down those bridges. That would be a substantial disservice to producers, not a step forward in their behalf.

Indeed, the real problem the USDA faces is in convincing the rest of the government that it is no longer what it once was, that is, the promoter of producer fortunes. Officials in other departments, in the Office of Management and Budget, and elsewhere, have to break the habit of assuming that the Department has ignored the needs of consumers in drafting its program. In time, the Department, if it continues its current course, will be able to dispel the negative impression and convince others that it has been transformed into an office for consumers as much as for producers. Reversing course and restricting the Department's constituency is calculated only to render the Department impotent both in Congress and at the White House.

Conclusion

In conclusion, we do not guarantee that the proposals we are advancing will produce a major transformation in the role and power of agriculture in the decision–making process in the White House, in the Department of Agriculture, in other agencies and departments, or in the House or Senate. But we are certain that continuation of some present approaches such as the retreat to ideology, isolation, or confrontation will inevitably fail to restore farmers even a modicum of the political influence they once wielded in the Nation's Capitol.

References

Barton, W. V. 1975. "Coalition Building in the U.S. House of Representatives: Agricultural Legislation in 1973." in *Case Studies on Public Policy.* Edited by J. Anderson. New York: Praeger.

Bonnen, J. T. 1977. "Observations on the Changing Nature of National Agricultural Policy Decision Processes: 1946–1976." Mich. Agr. Exp. Sta. J. Article No. 8180.

Browne, W. P. and C. W. Wiggins. 1978. "Interest Group Strength and Organizational Characteristics: The General Farm Organizations and the 1977 Farm Bill." in *The New Politics of Food.* Edited by D. F. Hadwiger and W. P. Browne. Lexington: Lexington Books.

Foreman, C. T. 1978. "Consumers and Food Policy in North America." *Amer. J. Agr. Econ.* 60: 778–81.

Grommet, A. 1974. "Enactment of the Agriculture and Consumer Protection Act of 1973: A Case Study in Agricultural Policy Formation in an Urban–Industrial Society." Paper presented at the Amer. Agr. Econ. Assoc. meeting, College Station, Texas.

Hajda, J. 1978. "Inside–Access Model for Representation of New Groups in Agricultural Policy Making." in *The New Politics of Food.* Edited by D. F. Hadwiger and W. P. Browne. Lexington: Lexington Books.

Hardin, C. M. 1978. "Agricultural Price Policy: The Political Role of Bureaucracy." *Policy Studies J.* 7: 463–72.

Heinz, J. P. 1962. "The Political Impasse in Farm Support Legislation." *Yale Law J.* 71: 952–78.

Paarlberg, D. 1975. "The Farm Policy Agenda." Address at the Nat'l. Public Policy Conference, Clymer, N. Y., September.

Peters, J. G. 1978. "The 1977 Farm Bill: Coalitions in Congress." in *The New Politics of Food.* Edited by D. F. Hadwiger and W. P. Browne. Lexington: Lexington Books.

Porter, L. 1978. "Congress and Agricultural Policy." *Policy Studies J.* 7: 472–79.

Stucker, T. A., J. B. Penn and R. D. Knutson. 1977. "Agricultural–Food Policy–Making: Process and Participants." in *Agricultural–Food Policy Review.* USDA–ERS, AFRP1.

List of Task Force Members

AGRICULTURE'S ROLE IN GOVERNMENT DECISIONS

John Kramer (Chairman)
Associate Dean
Georgetown University Law Center
Washington, D.C.

Lawrence Bitner
American Agriculture Movement
Walsh, Colorado

Macon Edwards
National Cotton Council
Washington, D.C.

Peter Emerson
Congressional Budget Office
Washington, D.C.

J. S. Francis, Jr.
Valley Industries
Peoria, Arizona

Robert Frederick
National Grange
Washington, D.C.

Charles French
Food & Nutrition Study
President's Reorganization Project
Washington, D.C.

Allen Grommet
House Budget Committee
Washington, D.C.

Don Paarlberg
Dept. of Agricultural Economics
Purdue University
Lafayette, Indiana

Sharon Steffens
American Agri–Women
Grand Rapids, Michigan

Jim Sundquist
Brookings Institution
Washington, D.C.

Gregg Suhler
American Agriculture Movement
Springfield, Colorado

Luther T. Wallace
University of California
Berkeley, California

DISCUSSION

The formal discussants at this session were Lynn Daft, White House Domestic Policy Staff, and Fowler West, Staff Director, Committee on Agriculture, U.S. House of Representatives.

Daft indicated substantial agreement with the Task Force report. Coalitions are a fact of life in Washington. To make them effective requires a broad political base, a willingness to put pragmatism ahead of ideology and a substantial element of intelligence. He suggested that consumer representation in agricultural decisions and in USDA was not a short–term issue, but a long–term fact of life to which institutions like USDA must adapt if they are to survive.

Daft expressed concern that the report may not have given enough attention to the changing structure of agriculture. Without noting specifics, he felt that such substantial changes may be occurring that policy changes are needed.

Daft did not feel that it was the farmers' job to educate consumers. He indicated that universities, experiment stations and the extension service have a key role to play. The lack of credibility of both farmers and government in consumer education was considered a major problem. However, he strongly disagreed with the report's assertion that the Secretary of Agriculture and other USDA officials are rarely listened to in policy decisions, even though increased participation by the Department of State, Council of Economic Advisers, and the Office of Management and Budget is a fact of life.

Daft concluded by indicating that there are five ways of influencing the course of political events in the United States: (1) force or threat of force, (2) ideals and ideology, for example, the family farm as an ideal, (3) economic and political power, (4) economic incentives, and (5) reason based on facts and evidence. He noted that while at one time agriculture could rely on raw political power, those days are past or at least passing. Agriculture will have to gravitate toward the use of reason. This will require more open communication by leaders which have credibility, a reliable base of information that people can agree upon and a sense of trust between people. Thus the answer is not just the formation of a coalition but the need to bring reason, trust and intelligence into the decision process.

West also was in basic agreement with the Task Force report. He noted that farmers need to be friends of labor, consumers and other groups which can have a key influence on many decisions. Pragmatically speaking, we must be willing to get together and make sacrifices. We simply cannot have everything that everyone wants. Sacrifice and compromise are the keys.

West noted that attitude is important. It was the politeness and genuine concern of farmers that got something done when the AAM came to Washington in 1978. It was not the blocking of streets, breaking into the Secretary's office, or the statements that farmers who do not cooperate will be shot off their tractors. That only made people angry. Such counterproductive strategies also will not accomplish anything in the future.

It is doubtful that 100 percent of parity is a politically realistic goal. It also is known from past experience that if loans rates are raised above world prices, stocks will accumulate and production will increase. This has been observed in both wheat and cotton. If someone is not in favor of 100 percent of parity it does not necessarily mean he is anti–farmer. It may mean he simply understands economic history, farm programs and their consequences.

COMMENTS AND QUESTIONS FROM THE FLOOR

Several participants expressed the belief that it is possible to design a food and agriculture policy that producer, consumer, agribusiness and government interests can all be satisfied with. However, one of the problems with designing such an overall food and agricultural policy is that proposals tend to come in pieces when particular problems arise. Overcoming this requires that agricultural interests sit back each time one of these problems comes up and see how alternative solutions fit into the big picture. General support was noted for the broad coalition concept. No one spoke against it.

Increased dialogue between producers, USDA and the White House is needed. However, this cannot be done in a single meeting with the President or in a highly visible White House conference. It requires working conferences where relatively small groups sit down to discuss basic facts, relationships, policy alternatives, and their consequences.

Tighter agricultural research and extension budgets can only worsen the resource and economic problems facing agriculture. These problems can be traced to (1) an inability to identify the relation between research and the resulting benefits, (2) the lack of a strong coalition supporting research and extension, and (3) the fact that society still tends to look at the farm problem as one of abundance.

Researchers and economists have an obligation to be objective — not simply to develop support or evidence that people want to hear or that will support particular positions. A problem does exist in getting data that can be trusted.

RONALD D. KNUTSON*

CHAPTER 6

Summit Review

THE Summit Review Committee was charged with evaluating the work of the five Task Force reports, identifying important gaps in the reports, and developing the overall implications. Our review efforts prior to the Farm Summit are supplemented in this paper by observations on the conference itself.

The Problem Has Changed

The Task Force reports considered many different dimensions of the current problems facing agriculture (Appendix Table 1). Several of the problems were identified in more than one report. A major point that emerges from the discussions in the reports is that agriculture's problems have changed. This is not to imply that all the problems that perplexed agriculture in the 1950's and 1960's have been solved. However, significant new domestic and international dimensions have been added. These new dimensions require that the adequacy and appropriateness of existing policies be reevaluated. First, the major new dimensions of economic problems of agriculture must be identified.

SUPPLY–DEMAND BALANCE

While we agree with the International Trade Task Force that the farm income gains of the early 1970's were in part the result of greater export demand, it seems unlikely that today's farm problems will be solved by continuous rapid expansion of world demand for food and fiber. Yet it would be equally misleading to imply that today's farm problem is still one of substantial excess capacity resulting from the supply of products persistently expanding more rapidly than demand.

*A list of Committee members and their affiliations follows the report.

While we will continue to have periods of excess production forcing farm prices to relatively low levels, years of deficit production as we had in the mid–1970's are likely to recur.

This fact creates greater uncertainty for agriculture than existed in the previous two decades. One thing that has not changed is the relatively inelastic supply of and demand for farm products. This means that relatively small changes in the domestic and international supply–demand balance will continue to have relatively large price impacts.

Uncertainty also has increased for policy–makers in recent years. The use of acreage set–asides combined with the chance of unfavorable weather creates the risk of product prices which are unacceptably high to the public, an inability to fulfill domestic and export demands, as well as a potential inability to honor trade agreements made with important trading partners such as Japan and the Union of Soviet Socialist Republics. For farmers such occurrences run the risk of jeopardizing increasingly important export markets and the reimposition of export embargoes. While current large supplies may tend to divert attention, policy should still be prepared for periodic short–supply situations, while not taking away the price and profit incentives provided by the market system.

INFLATION

Inflation represents a second major dimension of change in the farm problem. Inflation was identified by three of the five Task Forces as a serious problem. Since 1970, the U.S. inflation rate has averaged 6.7 percent as measured by the Consumer Price Index. This compares with 2.3 percent in the 1960's and 2.1 percent in the 1950's.

With an ever larger proportion of farmer's inputs purchased, price increases for purchased inputs have a more immediate effect on farmers today than in the past. Every large investment in farm equipment puts a farmer in an increasingly risky situation. Young farmers in particular find themselves highly leveraged with debt and in a correspondingly high–risk position.

The inflation problem is not limited to purchased inputs. Inflation in land values also has become a critical aspect of economic problems of agriculture. The fact that agricultural land prices have increased relative to cash returns to land places farmers and some credit institutions in an increasingly vulnerable position. This vulnerability arises from the danger that at some point the continuous upward trend in land values might reverse itself. To the extent that commodity programs add false security to rapidly rising land values, these programs are themselves counterproductive.

Even if a reversal of the trend in land prices never materializes, continuous inflation creates a psychology favoring investment in real estate that could upset traditional family farmland ownership patterns in the United States. Compounding this problem of land ownership is the fact that with rising land prices, young farmers find it increasingly difficult to enter agriculture as owner–operators. As indicated by the Resources Task Force, subsidized credit arrangements can result in the survival of inefficient farm operations. Danger accordingly exists that we build a base for larger and more permanent government assistance to agriculture.

STRUCTURE

Issues of structure surfaced as an important problem area. The report on farm prices and incomes identifies the income problem as being concentrated on the middle tier farmers with sales between $20,000 and $100,000. These predominantly family farms are found to be no less efficient in terms of cost per unit of output than their larger–scale counterparts. However, their asset costs per dollar of investment income (return to equity) are twice as high! High asset costs are, once again, particularly important to young farmers. These high costs result, at least in part, from the fact that these moderate–size family farms do not have sufficient net income against which to take advantage of accelerated depreciation, investment tax credits, and other federal income tax provisions. These farms also are found to be in a more vulnerable future competitive position because they have a smaller volume over which to spread the high fixed costs of increasingly strict Occupational Safety and Health Administration (OSHA) and Environmental Protection Agency (EPA) regulations.

The net result of the less competitive position of moderate–size family farms, has been a pronounced decline in their proportion of total agricultural production. One of the statistics presented by the Farm Commodity Price and Income Task Force is the fact that farms not falling in the family farm classification (defined as farms hiring more than half their labor, and nonfamily corporate farms and partnerships) accounted for 30 percent of U.S. agricultural production in 1976. The meaning of this statistic is not clear. It would appear that small and middle size farms are increasingly being offered higher returns from selling their farm operation than they can make from farming. The status of the family farm in industrialized agriculture deserves increased study. Also, it is likely that much of the unrest that currently exists in agriculture is related to these structural issues.

NUTRITION ISSUES

The Nutrition Task Force's report points to the mounting medical evidence showing a causal relationship between diet and heart disease. While asserting that there is still much we do not know about the relationship between health and diet, the report expresses substantial doubt that the evidence will be refuted.

In reality, the problem is much broader than is reflected in the Nutrition Task Force report. For example, the impacts on health of food additives, substitutes, pesticides, herbicides, antibiotics, and highly processed foods are hardly touched upon. Also, questions concerning the role of the government to ensure adequate nutrition standards are largely ignored.

These comments are not made in criticism of the Nutrition Task Force. They are instead designed to point out the complexity of the problems and conflicts in this area. The number of unanswered questions concerning nutrition and the potential for causing serious economic injury to an industry or individual firms creates a high degree of uncertainty. For example, the Delaney amendment and related legislation calling for complete removal of carcinogens from the food supply creates uncertainty. This uncertainty results both from continuously improving technology for detection of carcinogens and Congressional or Administrative action to refrain from strict enforcement.

Thus, barring the government from overtly telling people what to eat, an important effect of nutrition issues on farmers and on consumers is the uncertainty created. It is possible that this uncertainty is one of the reasons hog producers did not initially respond to substantial profit incentives that existed in the mid–1970's. It seems very likely that the nutrition area will increase in importance as an agricultural and food policy issue.

Today's Farm Problem

In the 1950's and 1960's the farm problem was generally perceived as being one of low farm prices and incomes precipitated by chronic excess capacity, resources fixed in agriculture, and immobility of labor out of agriculture. Dimensions of change in the farm problem identified by the Task Force reports raise the question of how the major problems confronting agriculture should be stated today.

The work of the Task Forces sheds considerable light on this question. The Committee presents the following six major problems facing agriculture, not as a final answer but as a basis for discussion.

RISK AND UNCERTAINTY

Risk is one of the major problems confronting agriculture. Risks associated with the biological processes and the weather have always confronted agriculture. What is new is the injection of man–made risks resulting from uncertainties concerning changes in government regulations, inflation, greater dependence on international markets, and the producers' exposure to changes in import policies of foreign governments. In many instances these foreign government decisions are directly influenced by U.S. foreign policy decisions.

At the same time it is important to put the risk and uncertainty situation into perspective. For example, history indicates that price fluctuation was considerably greater prior to the adoption and effective implementation of farm programs in the 1930's. Realistically speaking, farmers do have substantial income protection under the current farm programs. Some have argued that current levels of price and income protection are sufficient to stimulate substantial excess production. Yet, what the government has given farmers in terms of income protection it has taken away in terms of higher costs imposed by regulation in other areas such as environmental protection, occupational safety and health, nutrition, and inflation.

INFLATION

Inflation presents unique problems for farmers. The cost–price squeeze is not new to farmers. However, previously the pressure came from the price side. Today, it is primarily cost inflation. Inflation creates the need for continuously increasing farm prices just to keep even.

As discussed in the Prices and Income Task Force report, inflation creates a "cash flow crisis" that, for many, runs the risk of becoming a survival crisis. As a result, many farmers feel that they did better under the surplus conditions of the 1950's and 1960's than today. It is this Committee's belief that if inflation were brought under control, the current problems facing farmers would be significantly reduced.

PROTECTIONISM

Protectionism stands as a threat to expanding U.S. agricultural dependence on the export market. Despite the fact that significant progress has been made in opening new markets for agricultural products around the world, significant trade barriers still exist. In addition, substantial incentives for protectionist policies at home and abroad still exist.

It is critical that the United States not contribute, either in the agricultural or industrial sectors, to the incentives for protectionism in other countries. The impetus for increased protectionism at home and abroad can be spurred by accelerated inflation, export embargoes, increased unemployment, increased government–imposed cost–increasing regulations, or sabre rattling of the Organization of Petroleum Exporting Countries (OPEC) type in grain pricing policies.

One of the strongest and least costly policy tools available to the U.S. is trade liberalization. Benefits exist across the board—to producers, consumers, taxpayers, and the world as a whole. Yet the costs to specific sectors either at home or abroad of further movements toward a free trade policy cannot be minimized. In agriculture, these costs are particularly important to milk, beef, and sugar producers. At a minimum, it is very important that we not increase our level of protectionism. Making the merits of this case to producers of adversely affected farm commodities, as well as to organized labor and the industrial sector will be particularly important.

PRICES AND INCOMES

The farm price and income problem increasingly appears to be centered on the middle–size farm operations. These farmers have neither the larger off–farm income of some small scale part–time farmers nor the scale of operation over which to spread high fixed costs and take advantage of tax breaks.

Also, agriculture is by no means a homogeneous industry. In many areas of the United States, the Southwest in particular, irrigation creates costs that are higher than the U.S. average costs. Even the large farms in these areas are confronted with an income problem. Thus, despite the conclusions of the Prices and Income Task Force, a substantial number of farmers apparently feel they face an income problem even though they have large operations.

FAMILY FARM SURVIVAL

The issue of family farm survival appears to be more than just rhetoric. The question of what is a family farm is a perplexing part of the issue. The Committee does not feel that the problem can or should be defined away. The fact is that here again the combination of factors—inflation, tax laws, instability and government regulation— have the potential for placing the family farmer at a severe disadvantage. The result is frequently a very practical decision, whether it be voluntary or forced, to get out of farming. The survival of family farms is complicated by the problems new young farmers have entering agriculture.

LEGACY OF PAST FARM PROGRAMS

U.S. agriculture is burdened with a legacy of farm programs designed to solve commodity supply and price problems of an earlier era. Farmers and farm organizations still identify with the high loan rate policies of the 1950's and 1960's despite the fact that such policies would destroy our competitive position in international markets, as they did then! Farmers and farm organizations continue to identify with commodity programs such as wheat, cotton, or dairy despite the fact that decisions with respect to one commodity have to be made in recognition of effects on the other commodities. Currently, nearly all major commodities are covered by a general program—target price–

loan rate umbrella. Farmers identify with the allotment programs of earlier times despite the fact that the probability of returning to this type of mandatory production control policy is nil.

If farmers are to communicate effectively in Washington, they must adjust their proposals to the realities of the post–1972 era. They must accept the fact that the world has changed and the problems facing agriculture have changed. Short–run solutions to long–run problems will not suffice. Farm programs of an earlier era that solved agricultural problems then may actually aggravate the problems today.

The Solutions Must Change

It is always easier to identify problems than solutions. The Committee felt that the Task Forces did a good job of identifying problems. When it came to solutions, however, there was a tendency at several points to fall back on the conventional set of policy alternatives. It seems clear enough that if we agree the problem has changed, a close look also must be taken at whether the conventional policies are applicable to the new problems. Put more directly, if the problems have changed, the solutions also must change.

POLICY CONSIDERATIONS

In looking for solutions, recognition of four points is of critical importance.

1. The domestic and international dependence on the U.S. agricultural economy is increasing. Such a statement has a ring of "agricultural fundamentalism." Yet the reality is that agriculture has become a prime source of export earnings for the United States economy. At the same time, agriculture depends on available export markets. People in countries such as Japan have placed a great deal of confidence in the ability and willingness of U.S. farmers to produce and thus provide a major source of their food supply.

2. Very important limits exist on what government can do in the new situation. The ability of government to take the "right" action is considerably less predictable than it was in the previous two decades when large surpluses existed. Today, the relevant market for grain and fiber is clearly an international market. The United States produces

about 18 percent of total world grains, 29 percent of coarse grain, 14 percent of wheat, and 23 percent of cotton. Regardless of claims to the contrary, the ability of the United States to influence these markets over the intermediate or long term is limited.

3. The increased visibility and importance of food internationally has made it the subject of diplomatic discussions and decisions. In many situations, foreign diplomatic considerations have been a controlling factor in U.S. food and fiber policy decisions. As a result of this new and broader agenda, decisions may not be made in the producers' interest. The risk that they will not be in the producers' interest is one of the consequences producers must be willing to accept with increases in government involvement in agriculture. These risks increase in the "new" agricultural situation.

4. It is necessary to face the fact that inflation is a direct result of decisions made by policymakers acting on behalf of U.S. voters. A political strategy has been pursued to give more than can be afforded. The consequence is inflation. Priorities for spending must be established in each area of the federal budget including agriculture. The government is going to have to tighten its belt if the inflation problem is going to be brought under control.

These four factors led this Committee to the conclusion that in today's situation the federal government is a major source of uncertainty. More importantly, this uncertainty may actually increase as the level of government involvement increases. Those who look to government as a means of reducing risk and uncertainty may be disappointed at the results. Most disturbing is the point made by the Task Force on resource allocation that government policies have tended to deal more with the symptoms of problems than with cures. Policymakers have tended to choose short–run treatments for long–run problems. The result is generally to aggravate the problem, rather than solve it.

POLICY ALTERNATIVES

It would be a mistake for this Committee to prescribe specific solutions to the problems outlined above. That is a choice which has to be made by farmers, the general public, and ultimately the Congress and the President. What we will do is provide a range of policy choices or alternatives. These choices will emphasize where the burden of support for agricultural prices and income falls.

Shift Costs to Domestic Consumers. Most of the proposed solutions for aiding farmers in the past year emphasized raising prices to consumers. Throughout the 1950's and 1960's this was also the primary thrust of farm policy. During this period, domestic prices were supported sufficiently above world prices so U.S. exports were dependent largely on subsidies and food aid programs.

One basic lesson learned was that raising the price level above equilibrium leads to surplus production. The result of these high domestic prices was a need for farm programs to control production. Mandatory production–control programs were unacceptable across commodities. Voluntary land–retirement programs whereby farmers were paid not to produce were the result. These programs were the forerunners of today's acreage set–aside program.

While many farmers feel that they were better off with the programs of the 1950's and 1960's than they are today, reality indicates that these programs are no longer viable long–term solutions to current conditions in agriculture. Policies that reduce exports were acceptable only as long as the United States was running a substantial trade surplus.

Perhaps even more important, in an international market with the potential for a rapidly shifting supply–demand situation, acreage set–aside only adds to the risk of a production shortfall. This in turn creates more instability, the potential for embargoes and/or price controls—even with reserve stocks. At a minimum, it leads to questions on the part of our important export customers as to whether the United States is a dependable source of supply. The result is a counterproductive trend toward self–sufficiency and protectionism.

Of equal significance, acreage set–aside is an increasingly costly policy alternative. Increased land values and higher fixed land costs such as taxes have dramatically increased payments required for farmers to voluntarily remove their land from production. These higher payments run contrary to goals of reduced government spending and efforts to control inflation.

Shift Costs to Foreign Consumers. Policies to shift the burden of price support in agriculture to foreign consumers have from time to time been proposed. Attempts to raise the level of agricultural product prices internationally have been limited to individual commodities such as wheat. Experiences with the International Wheat Agreement have been less than encouraging. Yet the policies and apparent success of OPEC have rekindled interest in efforts to coordinate pricing policies of exporting countries.

One prerequisite to such a change in policy would be the centralization of exports in the hands of a government agency or marketing board. Doing this would represent a major change in U.S. policy by turning our back on a basic free trade philosophy.

Even if this were done, serious questions of feasibility remain. Price coordination among nations has proven difficult, if not impossible, in the past. Of at least equal difficulty is the problem of coordinating production control policies if prices are to be maintained above free market levels. International supply response to higher prices would appear to be even greater than U.S. supply response.

More basic questions of the consistency of policies of shifting costs to foreign consumers and the traditional U.S. position of leadership of attempting to solve global food supply, economic, and political problems exist. Beyond this, explicit endorsement of exploitive food pricing policies by the United States would likely spur the drive for self–sufficiency in food production throughout the world. Of potentially greater adverse consequence would be attempts to establish comparable policies in other commodities throughout the world as countries attempt to equalize their trade balances. The end result would be self–defeating.

Shift Cost to Government. Currently, the burden of price and income support falls primarily on the federal government. This support primarily comes directly to producers in the form of deficiency payments to farmers. However, substantial government costs also are incurred through government payment of storage costs, subsidies on interest charges, and renting government land for grazing at less than its market value. Agriculture obtains indirect benefits from the food stamp, school lunch, and related food aid programs in the form of increased consumption and what many consider to be a more favorable hearing from urban Congressmen on farm legislation.

In fiscal year 1978, the USDA budget totaled $19.5 billion. It is interesting to note that this is 70 percent of the 1978 net farm income of $28.1 billion. Direct government program payments to farmers amounting to $2.6 billion now account for 9 percent of producers' net income. Current government payment levels are the highest ever. In real terms, they are the highest since the late 1960's. Expenditures on farm programs are higher than most had predicted would be possible to obtain from an urban–oriented Congress. But expenditures on consumer programs administered by USDA are 2.5 times larger than farm program payments.

If inflation is to be brought under control, priorities will have to be established on these expenditures. Serious consideration will have to be given, in agriculture as well as in other sectors of the economy, to where these priorities really lie. While agriculture should not pay any more than its share of the costs of reduced government spending, it must be prepared to pay its share! Decisions need to be made on whether priorities lie in consumption–enhancing welfare programs, deficiency payments, land diversion payments, storage payments, or other USDA programs.

Shift Costs to Farmers. Analyses of the impacts of complete removal of all farm programs during the two decades from 1950 to 1970 show sharp declines in both farm prices and incomes. These studies indicate that it would take agriculture up to 15 years to work its way out of the resulting decline in income. Uncertainty associated with greater price variability would increase sharply.

Today, market prices for grains in the United States approximately equal world grain prices. Producer returns from free market policies would thus decline by at least the level of direct government payments to farmers—approximately $2.6 billion currently. Further income reductions would occur as a result of increased imports of dairy products and beef, allowing reserve grain stocks to enter the market as well as removal of acreage set–aside restrictions on production.

Such a change in policy would cause severe hardship. This hardship would be intensified by inflationary pressures on the cost of production. It would be particularly troublesome for the middle–size family farm that is experiencing the brunt of current cost and income pressures.

If policies of shifting the costs of government programs are to be pursued, greater consideration will need to be given to the distributional impact of policy changes. That is, payments will have to be more explicitly directed to those producers who are in the greatest need of government assistance. Current farm programs do not deal with this structural issue. That is, when payments are tied directly to volume produced, large farmers obtain most of the benefits. Current payment limits are by everyone's admission ineffective. Added problems result because payments tied to volume encourage production that in times of surpluses must be removed either by production control or continuous increases in reserves. Numerous recommendations have been made in the Task Force reports for separating government income supplements from the volume of products produced. This Committee agrees with this general direction of policy change.

Demand Expansion. To an important extent, the health of agriculture rests on expanding domestic and foreign markets for U.S. products. Those who espouse that the U.S. pursue a "take it or leave it" policy with respect to markets for farm products are at best suggesting a strategy of short–run gain. The cost in terms of markets for our products in the intermediate and long run could be substantial indeed.

Realistically, most demand expansion will come from international markets. Reliability of supply will play a key role in how much trust foreign customers are willing to place in the United States as a source of supply. Production control policies run counter to building confidence in the United States as a source of supply. Efforts of many USDA and voluntary producer organizations to expand demand can be rapidly nullified by a year of short production or an ill–advised embargo on exports.

Government programs to expand demand including credit and food aid also are crucial to long–term market growth and maintaining a competitive position in export markets. It is critical that these programs be encouraged and allowed to operate in an environment free from other political and foreign policy goals.

Implications for the Decision Process

NATIONAL FOOD POLICY

It has become popular since the mid 1970's to attempt to put agricultural policy in the context of a national food policy. Such a policy would presumably establish an overall policy objective or a set of objectives. Farm programs would be established and presumably centrally coordinated to see that these objectives are simultaneously achieved.

This conference was initiated with the intention to cover the full scope of issues, policies and programs facing agriculture. Note that the same problems were identified by more than one Task Force (Appendix Table 1). Farm programs designed to solve these problems thus have effects in more than one policy area. Correspondingly, farm programs create difficulties in more than one area.

To illustrate this point, inflation was identified by three of the five Task Forces as a serious problem. Policies designed to bring inflation under control thus solve or lessen problems in each of the three areas—international policy, price and income policy, and resource policy. At the same time, if increased government regulation, such as banning an important pesticide, increases costs of production and eventually prices, it creates problems in all three areas.

To establish all of these interrelationships is a major task which the Committee did not undertake. Suffice it to say that substantial benefits would appear to exist using this type of approach to establish priorities, identify policy or program impacts and plan for needed policy or program changes.

It should be recognized that the national food policy approach is no panacea. It does not resolve the serious conflicts that exist among the participants in the policy process—although it does help to identify the nature of these conflicts. Without it, there is a tendency to build policies on top of policies regardless of their compatibility. Equally important, the concept of a national food policy has political appeal. It facilitates the packaging of policies to obtain broad–based political support needed to get policy decisions favorable to agriculture through Congress and the Executive.

ORGANIZATION FOR POLICY DECISIONS

This brings us to the issue of how agriculture should be organized for decision making. Organizing for policy formulation has at least two dimensions: the strategies and the interests to be included. In many respects, one dictates the other.

In 1975, Don Paarlberg set the stage for a discussion of the strategies. He outlined four alternatives: hallucination, capitulation, cooperation, and confrontation. Events since 1975 should have taught us that we can no longer hallucinate that policy decisions are going to be made by farmers in the interest of farmers. Farmers are not of the frame of mind to capitulate—even though it may at times be the best strategy. That leaves two choices—cooperation and confrontation. Paarlberg correctly suggests that both strategies have merit in particular situations. But at the same time, neither strategy should be used exclusively. The problem then becomes one of picking the right strategy at the right time. This notion implies some forum for planning and resolving differences of opinion within agriculture with respect to both the strategy and the choice of alternatives. Such a forum would become a melting pot for resolving organizational differences.

In most issues, the interests will be broader than just agriculture. The result is a need for the development of different alliances within the food and agriculture community. Flexibility must exist to include interests broader than the traditional agricultural establishment such as consumer groups, environmentalists and organized labor. Since decisions affecting agriculture are being made and influenced in many different government agencies, the ability must exist to communicate with all of these critical decision points.

In the process, difficult decisions will need to be made with respect to the role of USDA and the decision making process within the Congress and Executive branch. These same decisions also will need to be faced at the state level. It is entirely possible in the current policy, political and economic environment that it is in the long–run interest of American agriculture to have consumers and other non–producer interests involved in USDA decision processes. The alternative may well be a USDA with little, if any, real decision making authority.

APPENDIX TABLE 1.
Table of Problems and Recommendations by Task Force

Problem Area	Resources	Task Force			
		Prices and Income	International Trade	Government Decisions	Nutrition
Cost inflation	Fiscal restraint, wage-price restraint	Responsible mone-tary fiscal policy	Problem identified but no solution specified		
Price formation	Better information		Improve export information		
Finance	Monitor	Target entry credit, rural development credit; remove pro-gram overlap			
Tax distortions	Index income tax brackets				
Education	Recognize special needs: youth & adults.				
Farm labor	Problem identified but no solution specified				

APPENDIX TABLE 1. (Continued)

		Task Force			
Problem Area	Resources	Prices and Income	International Trade	Government Decisions	Nutrition
Small farms	Special small farm assistance	Retraining, special assistance			
Land prices	Inflation control, stabilize farm prices				
Water rights and pricing	Market system				
Environmental regulation	Cost–benefit decisions, education				
Land use control	Education				
Productivity	Research and education				
Price instability		Reserves	Rationally managed reserves policy		
Labor Immobility		Retraining, education			
Inadequate income		Modest support	Modest support		
Concentration of production on large farms	No restraint	More stringent payment limits			

Production– payment tie	Direct payments not linked to production		
Disaster risk	All risk, all commodity insurance program		
Family farm survival	Limit payments, separate farm program benefits from volume		Tailoring programs to needs of family farms
Trade barriers		Negotiate; set good example	
Reliable world supply of food		Reserves and stability; remove bilateral trade agreements	
Import restraints (U.S.)		Gradually remove restraints on dairy and beef; lower support prices	
Politicized trade arrangements		Remove politics	
Inability of developing countries to buy		Food aid and credit insurance	
Agriculture's isolationism– confrontation attitude			Integrate interests in USDA and form coalitions

APPENDIX TABLE 1. (Continued)

		Task Force			
Problem Area	Resources	Prices and Income	International Trade	Government Decisions	Nutrition
Lack of internal political base				Minimize confrontation, form coalition	
Internal conflicts among groups				Open–end agriculture coalition	
Conflict with non-agricultural groups				Open–end agriculture coalition	
Farm organization dominance by the wealthy landowners				Truly democratic system of control with family farmers in leadership	
Senate excessiveness				Restraint in dealing with Senate	
House minority				Coalitions with consumer labor axis	
Erosion of USDA power				Broaden constituency base	

Relation between diet and health	More research
Lack of nutrition information	Better nutrition education
Lack of agreement on the substance of nutrition education	Development of a forum for conflict resolution
Costs of diet change to the farm sector	Economic assistance to affected farmers
Lack of consumer-oriented grades	Change grades to reflect internal quality
Lack of ability to agree on substance of policy	New forum for conflict resolution

List of Committee Members

SUMMIT REVIEW COMMITTEE

Ronald D. Knutson (Chairman)
Department of Agricultural
  Economics
Texas A&M University
College Station, Texas

Bruce Gardner
Department of Agricultural
  Economics
Texas A&M University
College Station, Texas

R. J. Hildreth
The Farm Foundation
Oak Brook, Illinois

Clifton Meador
Agriculture Council of America
Dumas, Arkansas

M. Allen Paul
Agriculture Council
  of America
Washington, D.C.

Theodore W. Schultz
Department of Economics
University of Chicago
Chicago, Illinois

Frank Whitsitt
Farmland News
Kansas City, Missouri

OVERVIEW

T. W. SCHULTZ*

Economic conditions now and on ahead differ importantly from the conditions of the fifties and sixties. Do not keep looking back. Remember what happened to Lot's wife. Let us not waste our efforts solving the agricultural problems of bygone decades. Instead, look ahead. Our task is to find solutions for the current and the foreseeable future problems of the U.S. economy and of our agriculture.

Believe it or not, there are some economic conditions that are better now than they were two or three decades ago.

1. There is much less slack in agriculture. Off–farm migration, farm population less than half as large as it was in the mid–fifties, farmland more fully utilized, all told little excess capacity remains.

2. There has been a remarkable improvement in the integration of the farm and nonfarm labor markets. It has been a major factor in reducing the per capita income gap between farm and nonfarm people.

3. Closely related to the integration of the labor markets is the large increase in the income of farm families from nonfarm sources, mainly from off–farm work. In 1950, the income of farm families from nonfarm sources was 31 percent of their total income; it is now about 60 percent.

4. Crop exports now provide a market for 100 million acres or 30 percent of all cropland harvested in the U.S. No one would argue that the U.S. dollar is now over–valued as it was during the sixties.

5. The value of the farm assets minus liabilities of U.S. farmers deflated by the consumer price index is now much higher than it was in the fifties and sixties.

My list of economic conditions that are now worse:

1. The U.S. economy is performing badly, primarily because of mistakes in government policy.

2. Investments in plants and equipment are inadequate because of uncertainty with respect to returns.

3. The proliferation of governmental regulation of the private economic sector is reducing labor productivity and the rate of economic growth.

*T. W. Schultz is Professor Emeritus in the Department of Economics of the University of Chicago. The most recent of his many honors is the 1979 Nobel Prize for economics.

4. Interventions by government in agriculture are impairing the economic viability of middle–sized farms.

5. The high rate of inflation is the source of all manner of serious problems facing U.S. consumers and producers including farmers.

In view of these economic conditions, what we should be doing now is trying to find solutions for the disarray in the U.S. economy.

1. We need changes in policy that will reduce the uncertainty that business and agriculture now face.

2. We must search for changes in policy that would reduce the damage to the U.S. economy, including that being done to agriculture, by government regulations.

3. We should bring our efforts to bear in support of international trade. Do not manipulate it, but make it more robust.

4. What also needs to be done is to give middle–sized farms a better deal.

5. In taking on the inflation issue, let it be clear that inflation is made by the government. Don't blame it on labor, business, farmers or on consumers. The sad truth is that our inflation cannot be eliminated by wage and price controls.

6. Lastly, to be ready a few years from now, we should begin to assess and agree on alternative agricultural policy choices when the government starts to reduce federal expenditures. What are the choices in shifting agricultural program costs from taxpayers to con-sumers, or to foreign countries (costs of grain storage for bad crop years), or from taxpayers to farmers, or by reducing the costs of partic-ular farm programs?

LONNIE MORRIS AND JOE SWANSON*

CHAPTER 7

Comments of the American Agriculture Movement

THIS paper provides an overview, from a producer standpoint, of the major areas covered by the Task Forces. The paper does not cover the material in the same order as the Task Forces presented the different problem areas, but instead touches on each area within a general discussion of the problems presently facing agriculture in America. We begin the chapter with a statement concerning our view of international trade and current trade barriers affecting agricultural exports. From here we proceed through the areas covered by the Task Forces, hopefully touching on a majority of the topics discussed.

The International Trade report by Josling states that our main U.S. policy thrust should be to get trade barriers abroad removed. The report also states that this effort may involve compromise in our domestic policy toward imports and other sensitive issues. This seems quite frightening when one considers the position of the United States when dealing with such countries as Japan, West Germany and other countries in the EEC, and the OPEC nations. These countries are very firm about their trade positions, which tend to protect their domestic producers and industries. As our trade deficit continues to increase, it seems that the United States must make firmer trade agreements with these countries. Even though the thrust and concern of the Task Force report leaned toward a more global economic concern, it seems equally important that we realize the domestic repercussions. We cannot help the weak by sapping the strong. The strong must show the weak the means of strengthening themselves.

The idea that protecting a country's industries from imports re-

---

*The authors are members of the American Agriculture Movement. Joe Swanson is a member of the International Trade Task Force.

sults in their becoming inefficient, and their products not being competitive on the international market, has been disproved by OPEC and Japan. As they continue to protect their industries and currency, they also continue to have a trade surplus. Considering Japan and its tremendous lack of raw materials raises the question, "Why is the United States unable to solve its trade deficit problems?" A viable international trade policy cannot be developed until a solid domestic economic base is created.

The U.S. dollar continues to fall on the world market and most of the blame must lie with our continuing foreign trade deficit and inflation. Inflation in the United States has been blamed on wages, prices, and food. We must take a closer look at this domestic problem. We believe that wages, prices, and cost of food are symptoms of the problem and not the problem itself. The government's response is wage and price controls which have failed in the past. We cannot cure the disease by treating the symptoms. We must find the cause of the disease and treat it. Controls are even more disastrous when we consider that they are imposed by a government which, at the same time, continues to go deeper in debt while artificially expanding our money supply. With this attitude, maybe we can better understand the psychology, "Buy now; for it will be higher tomorrow." We are not putting all the blame on government, but it seems certain that increased government spending and expansion of the money supply only adds fuel to the fire. The authorization of more bank reserves and federal securities—not backed by gold or fresh bills but only by faith in the government— cannot support the dollar. What is influencing this type of system?

During the past decade, wages in West Germany increased over 200 percent, but the inflation rate averaged about 4 percent annually. The West German government achieved this by keeping the money supply in the line with the country's true economic wealth. By comparison, wages in the United States increased approximately 100 percent while inflation averaged over 6 percent annually during the same time period.

The American standard of living still appears very high, but the aggregate debt of today's farmers is eight times larger than the total debt for agriculture in 1950. This increasing debt and its interest payments—plus increasing costs of production—make it impossible for the American farmer to sell wheat, corn, cotton, and other products at price levels suggested by Josling and some other members of the Task Force. Josling suggests that if we try to increase commodity prices the United States will lose its markets to other agricultural producing nations. It is from this point that the United States should bargain with those nations we import from. These nations impose duties on farm commodities from the United States. With these duties, they support their domestic producers and also finance export subsidies which underprice U.S. farm commodities on the world market. If we take a firm position with these importing countries—and perhaps suggest the possibility of losing some of the U.S. market—they should be more willing to purchase our commodities at a fair price and possibly lower their trade barriers.

It has been said that expansion of U.S. exports is needed to help balance our imports of oil. The problem is—we speak in terms of gross dollar sales of commodities and not equitable value in comparison with the crude oil we purchase. For example, a few years ago two bushels of wheat would buy one barrel of oil. Today it takes between five and six bushels of wheat to buy a barrel of oil. To add to the problem, recently OPEC increased its oil price by 15 percent. This will directly affect the cost of production for agriculture and will decrease the competitive position of U.S. farmers in the world market.

At the International Trade Task Force meeting in Washington it was suggested that the United States cannot continue to consume energy as it has in the past. A possible solution may be to utilize part of our farmland and rural areas to develop some of the renewable energy sources, such as wind, solar, and biomass conversion. We must search for positive means to sustain our economy, environment, and our standard of living and not take the attitude that lowering the American standard of living is imperative.

Another subject that deserves careful consideration is the domestic regulations U.S. producers must follow. National health, safety, and environmental regulations impose "reverse tariffs" on the U.S. producer because many of the foreign countries do not have to comply with them. Opinion is divided concerning the success of the present commodity inspection system and enforcement of the regulations. High levels of pesticides and drug residues, banned in the U.S., have been found on fresh produce and meat imported from other countries.

The principal objective of the American Agriculture Movement concerning international trade is to export our commodities at a remunerative price which will keep our industry alive and viable. Our concern is that the farm industry today is performing in a country and world where protectionism is the norm. Protectionism also is prevalent in industries that supply goods and services to farmers. To keep the farm segment alive and well, we must consider indexing farm commodity prices in relation to the goods and services the farmer must purchase to operate and sustain a reasonable living. Using a reasonable cost of production, plus a fair wage and return to investment, the sum is close to a parity price. The parity concept is kept current and adjusted monthly. The formula has been established and corrected over the years. It is, at the very least, an indicator of where farm prices are in relation to the rest of the economy.

The International Trade Task Force concluded at one of its meetings that there will be a continual decline in farm numbers. Some members of the Task Force were in favor of the decline. In the 1960's many corporations rushed into farming, i.e., Gates Rubber, Purex, United Brands, and S. S. Pierce. These particular corporations were all disasters at the production level; however, when one considers the tax advantages and capital gains (things the general public may not be aware of), such ventures possibly could be another story. If the companies had been vertically integrated from farm to retail, thus creating somewhat of a monopoly, they could have been a financial success. This type of success causes problems in many industries today, but to measure this success takes a 40 inch yardstick. Corporate farming, along with a liberalized trade policy placing farmers on a world market that is far from free, will generate destructive social repercussions in the rural communities which will impact on the cities.

The very basis of the American social structure stems from strong agricultural roots. Our country's strength has come from its efficiency at providing the U.S. consumer a high quality, well balanced diet. But equally important is the lifestyle enjoyed by those of us who carry on the tradition of the family farm, for it is still the rural community which establishes the pattern upon which our social structure is based. This can best be illustrated by the constant migration from metropolitan areas to suburban or rural areas. Many sociologists believe it is the philosophically unmaterialistic and highly moralistic lifestyle exhibited by rural America that these people are constantly striving to attain through relocation in rural areas. Eliminating this lifestyle by destroying the family farm structure could have devastating effects within our society and most certainly would cause chaos as people strive for a goal which would no longer be attainable.

In order to maintain the family farm structure in rural America, we need to strengthen the broad economic base of all commodities, which in turn will promote the intergenerational transfer of the family farm. It is through this transfer that a true family farm structure can be maintained. There are many other problem areas facing agriculture which can be addressed more effectively from within the community structure of the family farm. One of these problems is energy.

Some scientists dealing with new sources of energy for agriculture believe that hydro–electric power may be the best alternative energy source available. By maintaining the community lifestyle, development and distribution of this or any other future alternative source of energy would be made much easier through area participation and involvement. Based on past experience and recent lack of development of alternative energy sources within the corporate structure of our nation, one can determine that corporate competitiveness does not lend itself to the exploration and development of innovative ideas. This can further be demonstrated by statistical evidence, which indicates the efficiency level of agriculture has increased at a rate almost three times greater than any other industry in America. The bottom line of this discussion could best be stated as: the promotion of movement away from the family farm structure and toward corporate farming involves many broad social and economic implications which should not be overlooked.

This chapter has touched on but a few of the many different areas to be considered. The American Agriculture Movement would like to thank Texas A&M University and the Agriculture Council of America for allowing producers to provide input. We hope that by including the producer in the Farm Summit—along with producers' views in this volume—a precedent has been set. Additionally, each time persons gather in the future to discuss agriculture, we hope the total picture will be considered through involvement of farmers and ranchers. Farmers have a very valuable story to tell, and they now have accepted the challenge to try to preserve a way of life that is so important to our nation.

About the Authors

EMERY N. CASTLE is President of Resources For the Future, Inc. where he has been Vice President and Senior Fellow since 1975. Dr. Castle previously had a distinguished and varied career at Oregon State University, where he had been Dean of the Graduate School as well as faculty member and chairman of the Department of Agricultural Economics. Dr. Castle has written widely in agricultural economics, with some concentration on natural resource issues. In 1972–1973 he was President of the American Agricultural Economics Association, and was selected a Fellow of that organization in 1976. In 1977 he became a Fellow of the American Academy of Arts and Sciences.

TIMOTHY E. JOSLING is a Professor in the Food Research Institute of Stanford University. Before coming to the United States, Dr. Josling had been on the faculty of the London School of Economics and the University of Reading in England. He has written widely on international economic issues, and has been a consultant to the British government and to several international organizations. His work on the interrelationships among national agricultural policies and international markets for farm goods has been especially influential.

RONALD D. KNUTSON is Professor and Extension Economist in Agricultural Policy at Texas A&M University. He has been a faculty member at Texas A&M since 1975. Prior to that time he served as chief economist in the Agricultural Marketing Service of USDA and Administrator of the Farmer Cooperative Service. Before joining USDA Dr. Knutson was on the faculty at Purdue University. Dr. Knutson has written extensively on agricultural policy and marketing and has served on several national commissions and special USDA study groups.

JOHN KRAMER is Associate Dean of the Georgetown University Law Center and Special Counsel to the Committee on Agriculture of the U.S. House of Representatives. He has been a professor there since 1971. Dean Kramer received his law degree from Harvard in 1962. During the past 13 years he has been heavily involved in the drafting and revision of food stamp and child nutrition legislation.

MALDEN C. NESHEIM is Director of the Division of Nutritional Sciences and Professor of Nutrition at Cornell University in Ithaca, New York. He has been on the Cornell faculty since 1959. He is a councillor of The American Institute of Nutrition and a member of The Board of Directors of the National Nutrition Consortium. He has recently served on an Office of Technology Assessment Steering Committee that assessed priorities in nutrition research.

C. PETER TIMMER is Professor of the Economics of Food and Agriculture in the Department of Nutrition of the Harvard School of Public Health. Before joining the Harvard faculty in 1977 he was Babcock Professor of Food Economics in the Division of Nutritional Sciences at Cornell University, and a member of the faculty of the Food Research Institute at Stanford University. Dr. Timmer has had wide experience in food policy questions in both the United States and a number of Southeast Asian countries. He serves as consultant to the National Planning Agency of Indonesia, and recently was a member of a National Academy of Sciences study team in China.

LUTHER TWEETEN is Regents Professor in the Department of Agricultural Economics, Oklahoma State University. He has been a faculty member there since leaving Iowa State University where he received the Ph.D. degree in 1962. Dr. Tweeten has done influential work on many aspects of the economics of agriculture but is perhaps best known for his book *Foundations of Farm Policy* (1970). More recently he co–authored *Micropolitan Development* (1976).

Index